ABOUT THE AUTHOR

Michael Butterworth is an author, editor and publisher. In the sixties, as a regular contributor to *New Worlds,* he was at the forefront of the British New Wave of Science Fiction. In 1976, he went on to found the innovative Manchester publishing house, Savoy Books, in partnership with David Britton. Together they produced almost 100 works of fiction, graphic novels and music recordings by writers and artists as diverse as Michael Moorcock and Fenella Fielding. Britton and Butterworth's own novel, *Lord Horror*, was published in 1989 and banned almost immediately. With support from Geoffrey Robertson QC – who praised it as 'a genuine work of imagination' – the ban was overturned in 1992.

In the 2000s, Michael launched *Corridor8* arts journal. He is the author of four further books and six novelisations, and presently contributes to *Emanations*, the annual American journal edited by Carter Kaplan. A fixture on the Madchester scene, Michael knew New Order from the beginning of their career and was welcomed into the intense studio sessions for *Power, Corruption & Lies* and 'Blue Monday'. For the next three decades, the four notepads comprising his studio diary lay hidden away within the Butterworth household – un-transcribed, unpublished and largely forgotten – until now.

THE BLUE MONDAY DIARIES
IN THE STUDIO WITH NEW ORDER

THE BLUE MONDAY DIARIES

IN THE STUDIO WITH NEW ORDER

MICHAEL BUTTERWORTH

Plexus, London

All rights reserved including the right
of reproduction in whole or in part in any form
First published in 2016 by Plexus Publishing Limited
Copyright © 2016 by Michael Butterworth
Published by Plexus Publishing Limited
The Studio, Hillgate Place
18–20 Balham Hill
London SW12 9ER
www.plexusbooks.com

British Library Cataloguing in Publication Data
A catalogue record for this book is available
from the British Library

ISBN-13: 978-0-85965-546-0

The right of Michael Butterworth to be identified as author of
this work has been asserted by him in accordance with
the Copyright, Designs and Patents Act, 1988

Cover photo by Sheila Rock, Rex Features
Cover and book design by Coco Balderrama
Printed in Great Britain by Bell & Bain Ltd, Glasgow

For Sara

'Blue Monday' 12", Factory Records (FACT73), 1983. Design: Peter Saville and Brett Wickens.

ACKNOWLEDGEMENTS

New Order's management, Rebecca Boulton, who provided sage guidance. The individual members of New Order who read the manuscript; these thanks go especially to Stephen Morris for his useful suggestions throughout and for taking the trouble to answer my numerous questions. 'Blue Monday' and *Power, Corruption & Lies* engineer Michael Johnson for his help and especially for his assistance reconstructing the Brit Row mixing sessions. I was unable to attend these.

Stephen Boyce-Buckley for his sympathetic and detailed reviews of 'Blue Monday' and *Power, Corruption & Lies*, for help with my descriptions of the music. Bob Dickinson's illuminating memoir, interviewing Hooky and P.J. Proby at Suite 16 for *Granada Reports*. Grateful thanks also to David Wilkinson for his contribution, 'Blue Monday': A Fact Sheet (Appendix 1).

My friend and business partner in Savoy Books, David Britton, for his loyal help and support. My agent Geneviève Carden for her patience and resolve in seeing this book published. Stephen Manford for his encouragement in the initial stages of writing this book and for reading it afterwards; his sage advice and suggestions. John Coulthart for reading the manuscript, and for his erudite and expert advice. My editors at Plexus, Sandra Wake and Laura Coulman, whose guidance has been invaluable.

Lastly and definitely not least, for my wife Sara Inkster who got me writing again and who gave her loving support.

If errors or inaccuracies exist in my book they are my own solely.

I would also like to express my gratitude to Peter Saville, Alice Cowling, Susie Stubbs, Jon Savage, Professor Tim O'Brien, Greg Wilson and the people behind the New Order Gigography and waterrat.com websites. My apologies for anyone I have overlooked.

Books I have referred to include:

The Process: A Novel, Brion Gysin, Doubleday (1969)
Bury My Heart at Wounded Knee: An Indian History of the American West, Dee Brown, Holt, Rinehart & Winston (1970)

An Ideal for Living: A History of Joy Division, Mark Johnson, Proteus Books (1984)

Lord Horror, David Britton, Savoy Books (1989)

The Great White Wonders: A History of Rock Bootlegs, Clinton Heylin, Viking (1994)

Factory: The Story of a Record Label, Mick Middles, Virgin Books (2002); first published as *From Joy Division to New Order: The True Story of Anthony H. Wilson and Factory Records*, Virgin Books (1996)

Bernard Sumner: Confusion: Joy Division, Electronic and New Order Versus the World, David Nolan, Independent Music Press (2007)

Joy Division Piece by Piece: Writing About Joy Division 1977-2007, Paul Morley, Plexus Books (2008)

The Haçienda: How Not to Run a Club, Peter Hook, Simon & Schuster (2009)

Tony Wilson: You're Entitled to an Opinion, David Nolan, John Blake Publishing Ltd (2010)

Shadowplayers: The Rise and Fall of Factory Records, James Nice, Aurum Press Ltd (2011)

Unknown Pleasures: Inside Joy Division, Peter Hook, Simon & Schuster (2012)

Bernard Sumner: Chapter and Verse: New Order, Joy Division and Me, Bernard Sumner, Bantam Press (2014)

Poor but Sexy: Culture Clashes in Europe East and West, Agata Pyzik, Zero Books (2014)

The author and editors would like to thank the following agencies and individuals for supplying pictures: Sheila Rock/REX Shutterstock; Peter Saville and Brett Wickens/Factory Records; Qwest Records; Peter Saville and Brett Wickens/Factory Records; Kevin Cummins/Getty Images; Kevin Cummins/Getty Images; Kevin Cummins/Getty Images; Kevin Cummins/Getty Images; Chameleon/Britton; Philomena Winstanley.

THE PLAYERS

Gillian Gilbert – keyboards, synthesisers and guitars
Peter Hook – bass and vocals
Stephen Morris – drums, electronic drums, keyboards and synthesisers
Bernard Sumner – vocals, guitars, keyboards and synthesisers

Rob Gretton (RIP, 15 January 1953–15 May 1999)
– manager Joy Division/New Order, 1978–99

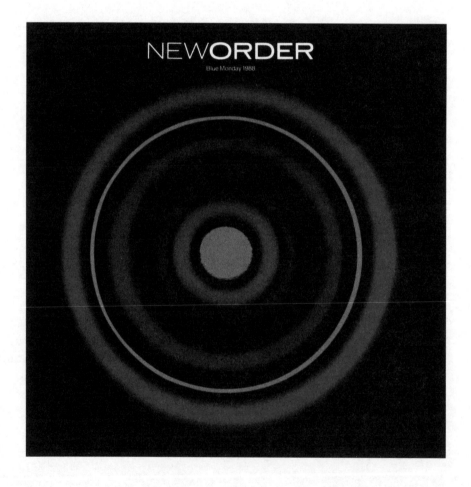

'Blue Monday' 12", Quincy Jones and John Potoker remix, Qwest Records, 1988.

CONTENTS

Power, Corruption & Lies, Factory Records (FACT75), 1983. Design: Peter Saville and Brett Wickens.

FOREWORD

This book is a memoir of hanging out with New Order at Britannia Row studio while they were recording *Power, Corruption & Lies* and 'Blue Monday'. The band was looking for a new musical direction after the tragic death of Ian Curtis, the singer who fronted them while they were still known as Joy Division. Although it was not evident to anyone at the time, the songs recorded at these sessions proved to be their defining moment. What I learned there about 'Blue Monday' – and what I have learned since – form equally strong vectors in my book.

As much as it is these things, it is also a contextual story. It tells, through my personal family connections and through Savoy Books, the publishing house I run in Manchester with my business partner David Britton, how I came to be aware of the nascent Factory Records and early Joy Division; how, by a fortunate fluke, I happened to hear their music playing through my neighbour's floor from the room above me, where a film of their work was being made; how curiosity – the need to learn more – set me on this trail; and how events eventually lead to me becoming a fly on the wall at Britannia Row.

The book is in three main parts. The contextual background is told at the front of the book in my introduction. It is a 'tale of two cities', drawing material from two influential cultural entities that existed side by side in Manchester during the 1970s, '80s and '90s – Factory Records/Joy Division/New Order, with its highly visible ripples spreading across the globe, of which I was an observer; and my company Savoy Books/Records, a much less visible cultural presence in Manchester that Tony Wilson respectfully mentioned in his introductory addresses to delegates for In the City, the international music symposium he founded with his partner Yvette Livesey.

Our paths crossed in two significant ways; first when the then schoolboy Stephen Morris discovered the bookshops run by Savoy and then, more directly, through my personal life. Both encounters were brought about by chance, the kind of happy accident that can occur when you are committed to your interests; when, through those, you suddenly find yourself thrown in the orbits of other adventurers like yourself, your interests grow and take unexpected turns.

My Introduction, therefore, is divided into two halves in order to reflect these dual pathways. The first scene-setting part reveals a hitherto unsung facet of the Manchester music scene – of which New Order were a part. The second tells of my encounter with Joy Division at my home in Altrincham. I have tried to keep the first half, Savoy's story, to a minimum, but the fact is that through our bookshops we played more than a passing part in the stories of early Factory, Joy Division, New Order and therefore the creation of 'Blue Monday'. We were a crucial resource.

My diary (kept in 1982, thirty-three years ago) comes next and occupies the central section of my book. Even so, it is incomplete, because personal circumstances meant that I had to leave the studio before the mixing stage of recording took place.

In the first of my concluding sections, 'Dub It Up!', dedicated to New Order's then manager, the late Rob Gretton, I attempt to reconstruct what I missed at the mixing stage. In the section that follows, 'We Were Like the Guinea Pigs', I tell the story of how 'Blue Monday' was written, the underwhelming reaction at Factory's nightclub the Haçienda when a white-label promotional recording of the track was first dropped there and the problems of its live performance. In the third concluding section, Suite 16, I tell a related story – of how my time with New Order led to Savoy Books starting its own recording wing at Hooky's Suite 16 recording studio, which eventually resulted in David and I recording a version of 'Love Will Tear Us Apart' and three versions of 'Blue Monday'. In the fourth and final part, Science Fiction, I attempt to express what 'Blue Monday' and *Power, Corruption & Lies* mean to me personally, and why I believe they are such special pieces of music.

There are two appendices: Basic Facts about 'Blue Monday' and Overflow, containing information that is secondary or peripheral to the book but that may still be of interest to the reader.

At my request I was invited by all the members of New Order, including Rob, to document the recordings and be with them while the recordings took place – even to stay with them in the flat they rented for the purpose in Kensington. Our meeting to discuss my proposal is covered in Beginnings, the piece that follows after this Foreword. At this meeting, no stipulations were made beyond (at my own insistence) the fact that I would not use a tape recorder or camera. I took only notebooks and a pen.

I set out to record what happened, as it happened. But as much as it is a diary of moment-to-moment 'ordinariness', it is also a regular story of rock'n'roll (and perhaps the two weren't all that different), of which I had the privilege to record only a tiny portion. It is a record of the wilder, more impetuous side of the original members of New Order – their hedonism and penchant for mischief and satire – and, indeed, of myself and the other people who appear within this story.

Re-reading these pages it occurs to me that a discrepancy exists between the people all of us are now and the kind of people we were back then, when we were mostly in our twenties. I have included these more candid aspects as a sociological record and also because without them the book loses its very human element. Very soon, if not even then, we had mortgages to worry about, families to raise. Time passes, concerns change, people change. Once young bloods, some of us now queue up to receive our knight- and damehoods.

'Blue Monday', the leitmotif of this memoir, became a big part of my life. Here is my story of it.

From left to right: Stephen Morris, Peter Hook, Gillian Gilbert and Bernard Sumner, 7 July 1983 at the Paradise Garage, New York. Stateside clubs like this one and Danceteria are what inspired 'Blue Monday' and Factory's own Haçienda, leading to the rise of the 'Madchester' scene.

BEGINNINGS

When I thought of writing about New Order at Britannia Row it was a simple question of okaying it with the band. I knew of their disdain for the usual, unsolicited approaches of journalists. This was my feeling also and from the start I made it clear that no tape recorder would be present. I would bring notepads and pens, and keep a daily minute-to-minute diary. To explain this, I phoned Rob, their manager. We all met one windy day in spring or early summer 1982 over lunch at the Unicorn, a regular's watering hole on Church Street in Manchester city centre, across the road from the busy fruit and vegetables barrows (which are now gone). Although I didn't realise it at the time, and the subject never came up, the band were in the throes of writing 'Blue Monday'. To allay crowd disappointment at their refusal to do encores, they were intending to produce a 'machine' track that could be left playing at the end of performances. But despite 'Blue Monday' being conceived in this functional way, once they started making the song, their perceptions of what it might be changed.

'New Order,' my first diary notes begin:

. . . who have the reputation of treating the capricious media and its agents with impromptu and often violent absurdist displays, have kindly assembled to listen to my intentions regarding them.

'I just want to do a book . . . but not with a tape recorder. An informal book.'

'Yeah, okay. That's okay,' they smile.

Barney complains of a malingering stomach. An ulcer? It is my area, and I try to advise him what to do.

Gillian – the band's newest recruit and Steve's girlfriend – sits tastefully, cross-legged, biting at a Cornish pasty.

Hooky lounges in the comfiest corner, smiling, arm extending towards a glass of Pils.

Steve's disembodied face grins satyr-like at me.

Is that it, then?

Not really. Rob puts me through a dozen questions disguised as casual conversation. Nothing direct. Smiling. Pushes up his glasses to confront me.

I cock up the replies. He is baffled. The band is baffled. I am baffled. Hooky rises to get the next round.

'Is it alright, then?' I ask.

'It's okay with me.'

'Me too.'

'Suppose so.'

'Yeah, guess it'll be alright.'

After lunch, Barney and I have a game of snooker in the 'middle' Yates' on Oldham Street, which still has a sawdust floor. I get soundly beaten, and I think this clinches it.

It was 'a simple question' for, by then, I had known the band for almost three years – though I had not seen them personally since Ian Curtis' death, about two years earlier. On that day in May 1980 the news of his suicide hit me like it did everyone who knew him. My main response was that of shock and disbelief – and perplexity: why would someone want to do that? We were all still young and excitedly making our way in life. What had become so unbearable to Ian that it could have cancelled out this lust for life? Then I felt sadness, for him and his family and friends . . . and the band – what were they going to do? My own sense of loss was strong, despite the fact that I had met Ian perhaps only half-a-dozen times – and this during the last ten months of his life. But 'the kid', as William Burroughs might have called him at Joy Division's Plan K gig in Belgium – 'get lost, kid', the author allegedly responded when Ian asked if there was a spare copy of his new book going – had gotten to me.

Unlike with the passing of J.F. Kennedy or Jimi Hendrix, I cannot remember where I was or what I was doing when I heard the news. Now that I have realised this, it has set me delving into the recesses of memory. Yet, try as I might, I can recall little detail beyond these feelings. Through friends and family who had connections with Factory Records, I came to know about Ian's death before most people . . . and in my mind there is an image of yards of black-and-white newsprint images – *Melody Maker*, *Sounds*, *NME* – all merged into one timeless scream of shock and incredulity. But nothing more.

I did not arrive at the Unicorn with Ian uppermost in my mind. Just over two years had passed and anyway – whatever the band's personal feelings, whatever the practical implications for their music – they had shown a commitment to the future, a determination to keep on working and developing themselves musically . . . to literally *play* themselves out of their predicament. From their first gig after Ian's passing – two months on at Manchester's Beach Club – and Gillian's arrival in September, they had played about seventy gigs throughout Europe and the USA, and released five pieces of vinyl: *Still*, a compilation Joy Division album, *Movement*, their debut studio album as New Order, and three singles. Freshly returned from their second tour of the States, they seemed far from defeated. They looked more like a band who knew they were about to turn a corner.

They had emerged from a long period of musical experimentation to find a new identity, literally learning as they performed. Nothing of use had been wasted. Characteristically refusing to be typecast, they had developed a distinctive electronic rock sound, quite different from that of Joy Division, and had already started performing material – 'Ultraviolence', 'The Village', '5 8 6', 'We All Stand' – that would appear on their forthcoming second studio album. They would soon begin writing specifically for this record, starting with 'Age of Consent'. As they always did when composing, they experimented with new sounds. Some of these were snatched from long hours of rehearsal; others were drawn from the musical maelstrom happening around them. Buoyed by their own collective confidence, they were on the creative ascendency.

By October, in Britannia Row Studios, having crystallised in *Power, Corruption & Lies* and 'Blue Monday' the various desires of each individual member – Bernard, Hooky, Stephen, Gillian, Rob and even Ian, for his spirit was ever-present at the sessions – there was the strong feeling that what had been achieved, especially with 'Blue Monday', would effortlessly plug into the moment and give the new line-up an enduring musical identity.

From left to right: Gillian Gilbert, Stephen Morris, Bernard Sumner and Peter Hook, New York City, July 1983.

INTRODUCTION

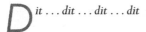*it . . . dit . . . dit . . . dit*

The distinctive synth drumbeat of 'Blue Monday' shudders through the studio at Britannia Row. An ominous bass line peppers over the drum.

Boom . . . boom . . . boom

The singer's monotone voice hovers above the backing. 'How does it feel . . . ?' Not a question, a statement. 'If it wasn't for your misfortune, I'd be a heavenly person today.' Carrying veiled portents of a life lost and gained.

The musicians gather in post-mortem. The future biggest selling single of eighties' Britain had aired, signalling – on their own terms – New Order's coming of age.

In retrospect, the album *Power, Corruption & Lies*, to which 'Blue Monday' was tethered like a huge, gravitational planet and of which it really is a part, strikes me as being a record as significant to the post-punk generation as Pink Floyd's *Dark Side of the Moon* was to the hippies of the sixties – my own generation. '[After these recordings] there was a feeling that New Order were making records that nobody else made,' the Charlatans' Tim Burgess told Simon Hattenstone of the *Guardian* in July 2015. 'It was a new kind of rock'n'roll.'

Speaking with the *NME* in January 2015, New Order vocalist Bernard Sumner concurred that: 'In 1983 there was electronic music, but not much electronic dance music. There were a few people playing music like "Blue Monday" in clubs in New York and London, but it was played on real instruments. Music like "Blue Monday" wasn't being played on the radio or in clubs. There wasn't anything that was as pure and electronic.'

The new music being released by Factory Records (and showcased through its nightclub the Haçienda) provided the perfect soundtrack for a rejuvenated Manchester. It would give the city newfound confidence, bouncing in the future as much as the infamous IRA bombing fifteen years later, when damage to the fabric of the city was the catalyst for widespread redevelopment. The clashes of war, both cultural and political, brought new ways of seeing Manchester.

Ever since World War Two, technological development, such as spaceflight and the growth of the media landscape, had been rapid and ever-accelerating. The future was arriving at the same pace and if you knew how to look for it, it was there for the taking. In the 1970s it was arriving from a past of grime and smoke: science fiction conjuring industrial Manchester as *The Twilight Zone*, the experimental and the outré.

Two dispossessed souls, Ian Curtis and Stephen Morris from the pleasant Cheshire market town of Macclesfield, were readers of the genre, keen imbibers of J.G. Ballard and Phillip K. Dick by way of *Eraserhead* – the film twin-with-Manchester landscape of Philadelphia – contributing to the sound of Joy Division. Both actively sought out bookshops, travelling from their hometown into Central Manchester where they visited the Savoy bookshops run by David Britton and myself, where talk always turned to the English science-fiction author Michael Moorcock and the American novelist William Burroughs.

Ian, the throne-boy of every James Dean-inspired poster, bought books and records off us when he was flush and sold them back to us for cash when he was hard up. During the recording sessions at Britannia Row, when my memory of him was still fresh, I could imagine his presence, virtually seeping through the walls of the studio – a Burroughs-esque flash of psychic energy that would have amused him to know about. He was a questing soul: how to enter and get a handle on the future (while being a heavenly body today) was something that interested him. With Stephen, it was Michael Moorcock who was the primary interest.

As the editor of the revolutionary magazine, *New Worlds*, mouthpiece of the new wave of science fiction in the 1960s and '70s, Michael had made SF relevant once again to mainstream readers. He professed that his ideal readership for the magazine were factory workers and therefore the North of England – where there were plenty of these readers, mostly of the questing kind – was fertile ground. *New Worlds* appeared on every newsstand, with striking sixties' cover designs by Charles Platt.

Industrial decay and badly developed modernist housing estates existed side by side. If you lived in this environment, as I did, and also experienced a vastly different life in the South, as I also did, then the North really did seem like an alternative future land, and was legitimate subject matter for upcoming science-fiction authors. The possibilities that *New Worlds* opened up did not go unnoticed by Ian and Stephen, and the magazine helped inspire Joy Division, as much as it would later inspire 'Blue Monday'.

Even before Factory Records, there was a strong countercultural presence in the

North. However, its power was waning. In the old days, when 'yesterday' was norm, before the 1960s became a byword for every kind of liberation, southern pundits and commentators were venturing there, drawn by a new genre of realistic cinema: films that realistically portrayed those cocky, aspirational, young working-class men and women thirsting with profound post-war desires.

The new wave of cinema at the end of the 1950s found the North's sullen landscapes of brick, smoke and crater far removed from the nation's metropolis. Reaching for phrases to describe it, 'industrial steampunk via science fiction' fits better than most. The narrow cobbled streets crowded with children playing hoops, mothers with scarves and hair-curlers, perpetually belching chimneys overlooking serried ranks of terraced housing, the dark looming ship-like mills holding geometric dominion, the dangerous no man's land of brick-and-bottle-strewn crofts separating its communities and, above all, the communal coat of poverty worn with a kind of prideful resistance – all of this reinforced the image of an alternative Earth floating at the very edges of civilisation. Another planet.

Visitors noticed with fascination the past being cast off before their eyes. Its streets might be narrow, but on closer inspection any young men of working age had a purposeful swagger in their Burton's made-to-measure garb. The women were brassily independent. Freed by secondary education, young people were moving up and out of the social class that they'd been born into. The factories were working at full pelt. Industry was booming and wages had tripled since 1950. Bulldozers and wrecking crews were moving like large purposeful insects amongst the murk. The old North was being physically erased.

After the decades-long collapse of the cotton industry in the northern parts of Britain, the audacious experimental culture seen to be pouring from there was also helping to reverse the social disparity between the two halves of the country. The North became like a never-ending conjuror's hat spewing out creations. After the films – *A Taste of Honey*, *Billy Liar*, *A Kind of Loving*, *Saturday Night and Sunday Morning*, *Room at the Top*, *This Sporting Life* – came *Coronation Street*, or 'Corrie', a UK soap opera created by Granada Television. Then followed Liverpool mop-tops, the Beatles, breeding the Swinging Sixties – in London at any rate. Successive waves of art and culture followed, each one spreading further than the preceding one, before going international. Mods and rockers were followed by splinter-genres – hippies, punks, goths, new romantics and dance.

Over three decades, the North changed, and the nation's interest waned. But the feeling that this was still alien territory never quite vanished. Its big cities – Manchester, Liverpool, Leeds, Newcastle, Hull, Sheffield, further north Glasgow and further west Belfast – still harboured dark and dangerous centres of decay that proved resistant to all improvement; economic booms never lasted long enough to completely transform these stubborn regions. Joy Division, the Fall and the Smiths were among the last musical forces to be shaped by that Old North. The Happy Mondays, who came after them, reflected a ubiquitous quiet modern urbanity. Joy Division eventually escaped by becoming New Order, having the best and the worst of both worlds.

But when innovatory machine-like rhythms suddenly started up once more ('North of Watford,' as the saying used to go), as they had during the Industrial Revolution, heads were caused to turn that way again.

Joy Division, Old Manchester; New Order, New Manchester

Documentarians of the band, usually seduced by satanic mills, the city's doom-laden veneer and the moody black-and-white photography of Kevin Cummins, reflecting a true *Taste of Honey* version of Manchester, stop at Joy Division. Rather than distinctly separate bands with separate core audiences, for me Joy Division and New Order are Janus-headed aspects of each other. The side I will be documenting in this book is its sunnier aspect, the side that, for pragmatic reasons, happens to have called itself New Order – a name claimed by Rob Gretton to have been inspired by a feature he was reading on Cambodia. (An unexpected and – to most Western ears – obscure derivation of the name, mischievously at odds with the widely accepted meaning of New Order: the political 'New Order' of Nazi Germany. The band have embraced the glamour of Nazi myth at key moments, for instance, the name Joy Division; the image of a Hitler Youth drummer boy on the first Joy Division single, 'An Ideal For Living'; and the choice of their second name – not too much, but just enough – and have then sometimes been evasive or disingenuous about it.)

For me, New Order are the Mancs who finally cut loose from their own and their city's past; who, with other bands, discovered black swagger and cool in New York. As part of Factory Records they grew up in a parallel world to my own and I happened to be in the right place at the right time to record a part of what they brought back with them. But to tell this story, I need to first make a detour.

There is a side to the Madchester music explosion that isn't recorded in the annals of the city's musical history, except in the underground press and covertly in books like Clinton Heylin's *The Great White Wonders: A History of Rock Bootlegs*. The company that conceived and disseminated this alternative culture began in 1975, a few years before the founding of Factory. The publishing house Savoy Books consisted of David Britton and myself (both, incidentally, snapped in our Deansgate office by Joy Division photographer Kevin Cummins for the *New Manchester Review* in 1979 – the original photograph, I have learned, no longer exists). The early 'edges' of these two companies, Savoy and Factory, overlapped and cross-influenced one another.

In a city that was still trying to emerge from its industrial past, its buildings blackened from soot, coping with wartime decline and the recent purging of its nightlife by police, the company's retail outlets were oases of alternative youth culture for bands including Joy Division and later New Order. Inhabited by young rockers, leather-clad punks and would-be Baudelaires from the science-fiction wasteland, and positioned on the run-down edges of the city centre, these shops – Bookchain, Orbit Books, House on the Borderland – formed a kind of occult triangle about Manchester's respectable, mercantile heartland; it was an area staked out as Savoyland, an alternative and until now undocumented Manchester.

Growing up as children and teenagers in the late 1950s and '60s, the formative experiences of David and I were seminal rock'n'roll, the literary experimentalism of the Beats, the music of Captain Beefheart and Frank Zappa, and the UK underground magazines *Oz* and *Ink*. By the seventies, instead of conforming, as many of our peers were doing, we blithely carried on.

Our attitude was expressed in the books we published, but it carried through into our retail businesses, where our young shop managers – each a specialist in their own areas of comics, music or literature – reigned supreme over their cultural fiefdoms. At Bookchain, they outdid one another by compiling tapes of newly-released punk and post-punk music, cranking the volume up on the shops' sound systems so that the music was not just audible inside the shop but also yards away outside in the street, advertising the iconoclastic presence of Savoy Books. Over there may be Factory Records, but over here something different was happening.

New tapes were compiled regularly, recorded onto 90-minute cassettes. The eclectic mix of electronic earworms listed below – from erstwhile Bookchain co-manager Thomas Sheridan – constitutes a typical playlist of the time:

Joy Division: 'Love Will Tear Us Apart'
Joy Division: 'She's Lost Control'
Adam & the Ants: 'Kick!'
The Cramps: 'Drug Train'
Blue Öyster Cult: 'Don't Fear the Reaper'
Alternative TV: 'Action Time Vision'
Stiff Little Fingers: 'Alternative Ulster'
Sex Pistols: 'Holidays in the Sun'
Clash: 'Jail Guitar Doors'
The Distractions: 'Time Goes By So Slow'
Department S: 'Is Vic There?'
Siouxsie and the Banshees: 'Helter Skelter'
The Residents: 'Duck Stab'
Iggy Pop: 'Dum Dum Boys'

The Fall: 'Rowche Rumble'
David Bowie: 'Rebel Rebel'
Buzzcocks: 'Lipstick'
Magazine: 'Shot by Both Sides'
New York Dolls: 'Jet Boy'
Captain Beefheart: 'Moonlight on Vermont'
Roxy Music: 'Both Ends Burning'
The Table: 'Do the Standing Still'
Blondie: 'Rip Her to Shreds'
Cabaret Voltaire: 'Do the Mussolini (Headkick)'
A Certain Ratio: 'Do the Du'
Radiators from Space: 'Television Screen'
Patrick Fitzgerald: 'Safety Pin Stuck in my Heart'
John Cooper Clarke: 'Gimmix'

The shops, started by David, were Meccas for the rebels of the city's street life and held a particular allure for the Electric Circus/Ranch/Rafters/Factory/Beach crowd in the sparse era before the chain stores, emboldened by pirates like us, came to monopolise the markets. An integral part of Manchester's music and literature scenes, the shops sold bootleg records in the days when such a venture was dangerous. The bootlegs were principally of Bowie and Roxy Music (the backbone of rebellious youth culture), quickly followed by the New York Dolls, the Sex Pistols and any vinyl bearing a candid photograph of Debbie Harry on its hastily printed sleeve.

Other (legal) merchandise included the latest vinyl from independent companies like Pinnacle and Rough Trade, American import and underground comics, DAW science fiction imports, drug manuals, tattoo books, skin magazines, biker literature, deviant horror, occult books and magazines, and books featuring James Dean, Kiss, Marlon Brando, Marilyn Monroe and others. It was the place where you could always reliably get hold of a copy of William Burroughs' *Junky*, Hunter S. Thompson's *Fear and Loathing in Las Vegas*, H.R. Giger's *Necronomicon* or (Manchester's own) Anthony Burgess's *A Clockwork Orange*.

The company's flagship store, Bookchain, occupied the ground floor and basement of a decaying terrace of four-storey Victorian buildings on Peter Street, where a café bar now perches atop the shop's crumbling cellar foundations. Nearing completion of the new bar, builders scrawled a finger-message in the whitewashed windows – 'Get your mags here!' – over the spot where the shop's soot-blackened front once stood. They knew.

One block up from Bookchain, on the same side of the street, was the Free Trade

Hall, a venue for everyone from Bowie to Beefheart and the site of two of rock's great 'moments'. On that very stage in 1966, Bob Dylan played electric guitar in his act for the first time, to shouts of 'Judas!' from the audience. As is well known, a decade later, at the invitation of Buzzcocks' Howard Devoto and Pete Shelley, the Sex Pistols played an inflammatory set in an upstairs room known as the Lesser Free Trade Hall. On this night, the Pistols' raucous nihilistic performance – combined with the business shamanism of their flamboyant manager Malcolm McLaren – was enough to ignite fires in half the future music stars of Manchester. Peter Hook, Bernard Sumner and Ian Curtis all happened to be in the audience that night. They saw the writing on the wall and, like others, they were galvanised into action.

Between the shop and the Free Trade Hall was Bauer and Millett's specialist car showroom, where I remember New Order being interviewed by Richard Boon, ex-Buzzcocks manager and New Hormones label owner, for a Channel 4 documentary about the band. The date was 23 July 1983, seven months after the Britannia Row recording sessions and whilst I was still keeping a diary. Near the parked Granada vans, Bernard, drunk and tanned after their US tour and wearing an 'I-Beam' T-shirt, whistled to attract my attention. The main action had taken place at the Haçienda a few days earlier, he explained. These shots were being taken just for 'colour'. Through the large plate glass windows of the showroom I could make out bundles of cable snaking out amongst the expensive cars. The stage lights on tall stalk-like stands cast down their pale beams. Richard and Stephen were sprawled leisurely in the front compartment of a shiny black Cadillac, being filmed. Stephen was in the driving seat, looking bemused.

The first future member of Joy Division to discover our bookshops was Stephen on days when he was wagging school. He found us (though not me personally) at the House on the Borderland, Savoy's first shop, opened in 1972. Named after William Hope Hodgson's novel of fantastical horror, it was positioned in Port Street, at the top of the 'triangle' in what is today's Northern Quarter, next door to what is now the Port Street Beer House. Fittingly, its home was the run-down warren of backstreets near to Piccadilly train station. Gaudy posters, fly-pasted around the city, guided wary and not-so-wary citizens to our door.

David remembers a 'hesitant, nervous teenager about fifteen years of age, buddingly eccentric, with an inner intelligence and depth belied by outer appearances; he engendered a keen sense that he was looking for something else in life.' After the King's School (an independent in Macclesfield) eventually expelled him for smoking dope, Stephen's visits became more frequent. Nervy and wiry, he was occasionally accompanied by school friend Adam, who was quiet and reserved. But Adam could also be articulate and knowledgeable, so that in years to come

David misremembered him for Ian, until we realised that Ian did not meet Stephen until three or four years later, even though they went to the same school.

'You're right. I hadn't met Ian at that time,' Stephen confirmed when I asked him for clarification (via email correspondence). 'Adam was a great fan of Moorcock, although he preferred Moorcock's character Elric to his other character Jerry Cornelius, a constant source of disagreement between us at the time.'

He and Adam also gravitated towards more outré literary titles by William Burroughs, *New Worlds* and the weirder fringe magazines of the period – Heathcote Williams' *The Fanatic* and David Britton's *Crucified Toad* – foreshadowing the later friendship between Stephen and Ian who took to each other instantly. Ian and Stephen were to meet for the first time after an Electric Circus gig, and then again when Stephen responded to an ad for a drummer, put up by Ian in Jones' Music Store, Macclesfield. Following this, he joined Warsaw, the nascent incarnation of Joy Division.

Stephen and his friend Adam helped out with minding the shop and running errands. The latter usually entailed getting in supplies of 'hot jam squares' and cups of tea from the sandwich shop near the Crown and Anchor public house on Hilton Street, but 'less serious' work could also be involved, purchasing cumbersome quantities of stock from local wholesalers such as Abel Heywood, World Distributors, or Thorpe & Porter – the latter presiding over a cadaverous mill on Pollard Street in nearby Ancoats. No one could drive a car, so extra hands were always needed to manhandle boxes and sacks back to the shop.

Ian found his way to us much later, at Bookchain, where shop managers Thomas Sheridan and John Mottershead were usually in charge. Thomas recalls the one occasion he met Ian that is still clear in his memory. It was the first time. 'It must have been 1979, because I was playing Bowie's *Lodger* on the shop's hi-fi system. He was wearing one of those long macs that were de rigueur. He always seemed to be wearing one, in fact. I can't remember whether he bought anything, but he had a good look around the shop and then came up and asked me what the music was, so I told him. My impressions were that he was shorter than I expected, quiet and polite. I wished that I had spoken to him more than I did, but I felt a bit foolish doing so.'

He recalls that I arrived at the shop very shortly afterward. Ian then left with me. 'You both went round to the Savoy office on Deansgate, I think to discuss William Burroughs. I know Ian was a big fan.'

Ian and I had only recently met one another. He had invited me to a Joy Division gig and I was now repaying him with a return invite. It was to show him the books we were working on that I knew he would be interested in. I showed him a signed copy of William Burroughs' book collaboration with Brion Gysin, *The Third Mind*, that I had just brought back with me from America, where I had met with Burroughs for the first and only time. Apart from that I can remember very little of the meeting with Ian, except that his visit was in the wake of a police raid on Bookchain – no longer an uncommon occurrence for us.

Trouble began with the rise to power of James Anderton, 'God's Cop', who took over the Chief Constable of Greater Manchester Police Force slot in 1976, just after we had started publishing. As the shops financed our publishing, the relationship between the two arms of our business – retail and publishing – was crucial. Thus being attacked in this way was a serious problem.

The Chief arrived with a mission. He claimed to have been visited by God, who told him personally to 'clean up' the city. (In his campaign, Margaret Thatcher supported him.) The appeal of our shops to youth and the outré meant that we quickly became one of his prime targets. Between 1976 and 1999, the Greater Manchester Police raided us about a hundred times.

His other main targets were family newsagents, who were simply trying to make a living. Even respected department store Debenhams was 'done over'. The laugh was that there was nothing really to 'clean up'. Hardcore porn was not being sold at any of those shops. Nor did we sell it. It would get you jailed. We just wanted to publish books.

Police officers – men and women – helped themselves to our stock, making off with adult magazines, underground comics, horror magazines, occult literature, drug manuals, gay contact magazines, biker mags, books on body piercing, tattoo magazines. Once I can remember seeing a policeman climb into the shop window at Bookchain to seize a display copy of a Conan book. With its Frank Frazetta cover art, depicting a muscular bronzed barbarian wearing a Viking helmet, they believed it to be gay porn. Sometimes, the police just stripped the shops' entire contents. And each time we had to restock.

Among the consignments of all this seized material, copies of Savoy titles began turning up, alerting police to our publishing offices and it wasn't long before the raids spread to Savoy Books. Over time, thousands more books were seized from there as well.

'Is it the duty of the police to protect society or to attack it?' I write in my publishing diary for that year. 'The result [of the repression in Manchester] is a serious erosion of the freedom of the individual.'

For over twenty years, a virtual state of war existed between the Manchester police and us, colouring everything we did. Our artists in this war – Kris Guidio, who defined the Cramps' distinctive look in strips in Lindsay Hutton's *The Next Big Thing* fanzine, and John Coulthart who adapted H.P. Lovecraft's *The Haunter of the Dark* – found themselves at the forefront of the fight back. Our *Meng & Ecker* comics lampooned the police overtly, while the *Lord Horror* miniseries made more subtle attacks on them. We undoubtedly stoked the conflict, but to keep going as serious publishers, the attention of the national media somehow had to be drawn towards what was happening in Manchester. Under James Anderton a culture of collusion existed between the city's judiciary and the police that would otherwise have carried on unnoticed.

As both sides stepped up hostilities, the pressure of the raids meant that in 1982 Savoy Books Ltd was forced into liquidation and David sentenced to twenty-eight days in Strangeways Prison. (This was the first of two jail terms. In 1993 David served another four months for writing *Lord Horror*, published in 1989. The book was the first novel to be banned in Britain since Hubert Selby Jr's *Last Exit to Brooklyn* in 1967. His imprisonment became a *cause célèbre*, and resulted in our one 'win' over the police. In the full glare of the national media the ban was overturned in the Crown Court. The police raided us again, the very next day.)

After our bankruptcy we retreated to the nascent Northern Quarter, where Savoy first began. We moved to rooms above Starplace, a new bookshop we had opened on Oldham Street, where we also let out rehearsal space to Manchester bands. Hidden away there for a couple of years, we kept Savoy going by 'packaging' music and comedy books for other publishers. This entailed conceiving ideas for books, trying to sell them to publishers and then, when we sold them, researching and developing them, and handing the publisher the finished artwork. This avoided the high-cost risk of printing and publishing them ourselves. It meant that we developed channels with music publishers that we wouldn't otherwise have done and it was in the hothouse of these temporary offices – with David and I assembling (under pseudonyms) books for other companies to produce – that the idea first came to me to try to sell a book about New Order. It was where I was based when I met with Rob and New Order at the Unicorn – a ten-minute walk away – and where I was stationed during the recording of *Power Corruption & Lies*. It is also where I kept my diary.

It was our brand of defiant 'art for art's sake' publishing in the face of police harassment that impressed New Order and it was thanks to Savoy's evident concern for artists – Bernard was at pains to tell me at Britannia Row – that they allowed me to write about them.

Surprisingly, except for the indistinct meetings with Ian, I did not meet any of the members of Joy Division or New Order at our bookshops. Although Stephen and I both frequented House on the Borderland, for some reason we were never there at the same time. And after Savoy started up, publishing business at the offices on Deansgate, round the corner from Bookchain, meant that I largely remained there.

My 'port of entry' happened in quite a different way, through a second parallel course of events in my personal life: the filming of Malcolm Whitehead's *Joy Division: A Film*. By a quirk of fate, Malcolm's film happened to be made at my mother's house in Altrincham, south Manchester, in the room directly above mine. Charles Salem's short twelve-minute film, *No City Fun*, featuring music from *Unknown Pleasures*, was made fractionally earlier. Pairing footage of Manchester shot from the top of a double-decker bus with a Joy Division soundtrack, Salem's short was bleak and atmospheric enough; but Malcolm's film, I thought – although not much longer at seventeen minutes – was the first serious Joy Division film to be made. He made it in 1979, at the house in Altrincham where I passed my early adult years; where, for most of those years, he was our lodger.

My mother, Catherine, was an important catalyst in all this for, without her, the film might not exist and I may never have come to know Joy Division. While we were growing up she let out rooms. It was not just to help pay the bills. Congenitally star-struck, she also thought she might get to know professional thespian types, or TV people from Granada Studios in Manchester, where she mostly placed her adverts. Because of her dreams of stardom, 10 Charter Road became a place of refuge for struggling writers, artists and socialist agitators like Malcolm.

At the time, slightly over a quarter of Factory Records personnel were also working at nearby Manchester Airport as baggage handlers – Rob Gretton, Donald Johnson of A Certain Ratio and Malcolm himself. Altrincham is right on the outer edge of the city, close to the airport. Rob lived in nearby Wythenshawe, closer to the city centre, and was already manager of Joy Division and in partnership with Tony Wilson in the fledgling Factory. Donald Johnson's band, also known as ACR and a favourite of Tony's, was on the Factory roster.

The subversive atmosphere generated by these three at Ringway (as the airport was then known), hung about Malcolm when he came home after work, mixing well with the other residents of Charter Road. His main interest was film and he would later become Factory's film wing, Ikon Video. But for now, while moving flight cases about, he was actively looking for material for his first project.

One night, I was woken by very loud, very paranoid music coming from his room – and it didn't take me long to work out that he had found his film. He had shot an early Joy Division gig on Super 8 at the Bowdon Vale Youth Club, just down the road. What I was hearing was Malcolm beginning the laborious process of hand-editing the rushes on very primitive equipment.

In the spring of 1979, Joy Division played two gigs at Bowdon Vale, about a mile from where I lived. The subject of Malcolm's film was the first concert on 14 March. His film utilised two other pieces of film: footage he'd shot of Joy Division at T. J. Davidson's warehouse rehearsal rooms on Little Peter Street, Manchester, (close to Knott Mill and Deansgate train station), while the band were rehearsing for *Unknown Pleasures* and another short piece of Rob Gretton talking to camera about Warsaw (imagine Malc like late-night New York cable icon Ugly George, machine camera-head, asking impersonal and impertinent questions).

Night after night, after the pubs closed at 11 o'clock, the sounds coming from the bedroom above mine continued as Malcolm struggled to synchronise Joy Division's music with the images he had shot. Snatches of 'She's Lost Control', 'Leaders of Men', possibly 'Transmission' and other songs, then almost completely unknown in the mainstream, played loudly whilst I tried to sleep. Malcolm had no such thing as a pair of headphones, so it all had to be played LOUD. At least, that's what I charitably surmised. I have always been a soft touch.

The project continued throughout the summer. In my notes, I write about a man 'locked up by his friends and relatives' who had moved into the house on 'the very verge of insanity'. The harsh, crazed music 'slid through the floorboards above my bed like buzz-wires, making it impossible to sleep'.

Not that I would admit his film inconvenienced me, of course. But I *was* concerned for my mother's neighbours. I expected irate dwellers of the respectable working-class south Manchester street outside to break down the front door at any moment, having had to put up with one rowdiness too much in this anarchic household. But no such thing happened. Perhaps the adjoining attic bedroom in the terrace was unoccupied. The creation grew, in a space preserved for it by miraculous intervention. My notes continue:

> One day the film was complete. By now the band were better known and the film – not simply a film of the band but a carefully wrought delirium that made sense of both maker and music – was given to the faithful. It was passed from hand to hand around Europe and America, drawing capacity crowds in the independent theatres where it was shown – crowds so big they were thrilled to be allowed to stand outside the packed venues simply listening to the piped soundtrack.

As the film neared completion, various members of the band began dropping by. Sometimes all of them visited, including Rob, to watch the film and make comments. They had first done this at a very early stage in April or early May, to watch the performance rushes. Malcolm invited me upstairs to watch with them, which is how I first got to meet Ian, a week or so before I saw him at the bookshop. 'Policy' meetings sometimes took place afterwards. At summer's end, in Malcolm's small attic studio flat, a special preview took place. Rob had brought along contracts for 'Auto-Suggestion' and 'From Safety to Where . . . ?' for the *Earcom 2: Contradiction* compilation 12" EP. After debating whether to sign them and deciding that they would, a white screen was rolled down one wall, the lights turned out and the film was played.

After the film had run, cautiously pleased with what they had seen, the evening took on a more celebratory air. Ian was very taken with the film, but Rob was bothered by the use of Nazi metaphors, which he thought would be viewed superficially and misinterpreted. He got each of us to air our opinions. They decided that the images were okay, provided their use was ironic – which, of course, they were. Part of a press release I wrote for Mark Reeder, promoter for Factory Records, for use at the Berlin Film Festival, March 1980 – one of the events where the film was shown – states:

Joy Division: A Film, by new British and Manchester-based film maker Malcolm Whitehead captures, analyses and celebrates Joy Division the band, but for its own ends. Whitehead is concerned with the social implications of contemporary urban management and uses montage techniques as well as performing-shots of the band to demonstrate some of the surreal realities of 'Technopolis'. Images of Joy Division are juxtaposed against scenes of Manchester where the outward manifestations of the infant police state fostered by James Anderton, already seem to be in existence. (Anderton's strident, insistent voice asserting a new 'Triumph of the Will' can be heard on the film's soundtrack.) The film scores not only against bureaucracy's fascistic sinister side but the dross and illusory façade of much of modern society, and stands against the use of technology as a means of social control. Two television sets are smashed with a sledgehammer, this symbolic destruction juxtaposed with footage of adverts and images of commuters over a soundtrack of Nazi rallies. With this temper, it also assuredly criticizes 'revolutionary' cells such as the Baader Meinhof Group who, with spectacular violence, attack the superficial trappings of power instead of the root causes of social decay.

After this, to my mother's delight, hardly a day seemed to pass without Factory people dropping by. In her mind, Factory equated with Granada TV, where Tony Wilson worked. Tony did indeed call round several times. So did Alan Erasmus, most of A Certain Ratio and many others. For a while, the front top room of the house became an occasional Factory hangout.

Joy Division played their Bowdon Vale gigs about three months after the first Factory Records release, *A Factory Sample* (FAC 1). *Unknown Pleasures* was released in June 1979 while Malcolm was making his film. The film itself came out at the end of the summer. It premiered in *A Factory Flick* (FAC 9), a group of short films including Charles Salem's film, on 13 September 1979, at London's Scala Cinema.

It is no strange thing about Joy Division/New Order that they came out of late 1970s Manchester, which was to me then a depressed, insular, commercial, unsociable city lacking imagination. The cloud that hung about it seemed to oppress its inhabitants, especially its youth, and it is not surprising that the spirit of the Sex Pistols, in the form of Joy Division, rose with anger and a cold cry of anguish there.

But it is not just the rock'n'roll element of the scene that I was trying to capture in my diary – plenty has been written on this – but its opposite. I wanted to express ordinariness; the normality out of which creation and vision sometimes spring when people feel caged and stifled. I don't intellectualise or rationalise, but simply present to the reader, with the proviso: 'Make of this what you will.'

My notes about the recording of New Order's album are domestic, just what and who I actually saw or became involved with – partly because this approach is more 'true' and people are every bit as real as their work, but also because I wanted to show that our ability to free ourselves through art is all-important. David and I freed ourselves from very different backgrounds – he from working in a factory in north Manchester and I from middle-class conformity in a south Manchester suburb. In what may seem a paradoxical way, New Order first freed themselves from their environment, content to be guided by the angry shamanism of Ian Curtis, then freed themselves from their collective death after Ian's suicide, making their pilgrimage to New York and – with other groups like Cabaret Voltaire, Quando Quando, 52nd Street and A Certain Ratio who also found their way there – synthesising a new sound.

Joy Division had been influenced by Kraftwerk. There was something in this German electronic band that suited 'dour' Manchester, where machines had come to be synonymous with redundancy, the dole and industrial collapse. Yet Kraftwerk's music was celebratory of technology, travel and the future. New Order were intrigued to hear Kraftwerk being given a more overt, sunny interpretation in New York. They saw a way they could progress musically and began experimenting. I began my diary just beyond this moment of change, in the earliest moment of transition between punk and dance.

Back when I met with New Order, there were three Yates's Wine Lodges on Oldham Street (like the fruit and veg barrows once outside the Unicorn, there are now none). I left the 'middle' Yates's – where Bernard had just beaten me at snooker – in a high mood of anticipation, already making plans. If my lodgings were to be with New Order, as we had agreed they would, then I would have two most pressing concerns. The first was to arrange for my children to be looked after. The full amount of my Savoy wages would have to go on childcare, so the second was to work out how to finance myself. The Stockholm Monsters and other bands, who were renting our rehearsal room at our Starplace bookshop, solved the problem. David and I decided that I could use the income from this. Each week, the bands were to post the cash down to me in a brown envelope, which they did. There were other events happening in my life that I had to consider, such as helping friends Michael Moorcock and Linda Steele move house from Yorkshire to London. And there was Savoy itself, all periodically interweaving with the diary.

When we were still attempting to sell the idea of a book on New Order, I wrote a rather serious outline for publishers saying that my account would be structured around a week-long recording session in London in October and a live concert in Athens. Recording took more than a week and I did not make the Athens gig. But I did achieve my other objectives.

In any case, the book did not happen. In the end, the publishers we approached weren't interested, so in frustration I shelved it . . . until very recently when I had time on my hands one day and keyed-in the diary I had kept. I read it through properly for the first time and discovered that it provided – exactly as I had intended – a basis for a book about New Order in the recording studio. To my surprise I also found it provided a partial historical and sociological picture of an analogue recording session. So much time has now gone by, today's recording technology is quite different from how it was then.

During the three weeks I spent locked away with New Order at Britannia Row preparing for this book, many local and world events occurred – in Britain, Channel 4 was switched on for the first time; the Soviet leader Leonid Brezhnev died; the first commercial space shuttle took off. These and other events found their way into my diary through a television that was left switched on for most of the time we were in the studio.

What happened there is covered in this book. Suffice to say, the record I kept came to take on more the character of raw video footage than notes intended to be used for expansion into a conventional book. I have tried to keep it like this, interfering only where necessary. It has been tidied up and missing details added where necessary – some from the memories of those present – but it is largely the original, unedited record. I took no photographs and, true to my intentions, no tape recorder. Retrospective contemporary notes I made, tell me that:

Though it isn't intentional on my part, this book will dispel any gathering mystique about New Order of the kind that tends to deify rock stars. They have always presented themselves as quite the opposite of all that shit. The final mixes of *Power, Corruption & Lies* and 'Blue Monday', which were completed after I unexpectedly had to leave the studio, were substantially the same as the tracks I heard on the tapes in the studio. Hooky said in the diary that the continuing 'softening' policy of Joy Division and New Order's recorded material under Martin Hannett perhaps best served their interests. With electronic synth music, unlike conventional kit rock, that 'softening' is not perhaps needed. The main problem New Order faced with the new music was reproducing it exactly, note for note, on stage. One of the tracks, 'Blue Monday', was left off the album completely, much to the regret of both Steve Morris and I, and has since been planned to be issued as a stand-alone single.

Stephen now thinks he was more concerned about 'Murder' being left off the album, as he expressed in an email to me. Before I close, I will mention just briefly a figurehead who was to become Savoy's very own musical shaman. In our office on Oldham Street at the same time as I started work on my book about New Order, David began gathering material for another book, which was to be about the fallen Texan pop star P.J. Proby. A key presence in the Savoy firmament of heroes and heroines, Proby was both a fascination and a conundrum. Unknown to me at the time he was to have a bearing on my entanglement with New Order. He would lead to Savoy breaking out of the book publishing world to produce a version of 'Love Will Tear Us Apart' and not one but *three* versions of 'Blue Monday', a story I will tell later.

But all this was in the future. On 21 October 1982, I found myself on the intercity train to London, my children delivered into the safekeeping of my sister and Savoy, with its flotilla of gaudy merchant vessels – our bookshops – left to fare as well it could on seas riddled with various verminous agents of commerce and Crown. (We had not long been raided by the BPI for selling bootlegs – 'Operation Moonbeam', documented by Clinton Heylin. Police raids were still at their height, and we were also receiving periodic visits by bailiffs acting for the Inland Revenue and Manchester City Council, as we had fallen into arrears with our bills.)

There was no buffet car or drinks trolley on the train. Nor, when I alighted on the platform of Euston Station, London, were there any British Rail luggage trolleys. After much helpless watching of the milling crowds, unable to move because of my suitcases, I managed to bag a free trolley and – mobility established – push off across Euston's huge train hall, which is like a gleaming ballroom, weaving my trolley skilfully through crowds of what seemed like garbed mannequins moving in disjointed confusion, towards a distant phone booth. From there I made my way down to the station taxi rank and out into the wet London night. I landed in Camden Town, where I stayed overnight with friends. New Order were motoring down, and had to undergo a landlady's interrogation to get into their hired apartment in Kensington, which is where I would be staying.

My Diary of the recording sessions occupied four notebooks: two were dark-green, buff and college-ruled; one was a standard red Silvine and the fourth was emblazoned with a cutesy tabby kitten. My entries were handwritten in biro. I limited myself to pen and paper. Tape-recorders and cameras were banned.

Britannia Row advert, *circa* 1982.

THE DIARY

Friday morning, Britannia Row Studios, 22 October 1982

As I cross the city, watching the ingress and egress of the crowds, I sense London's size and restlessness, its relentless presence. As I move through the city in all its ways and byways, for the first time in days I feel as though I am properly situated inside myself. I feel a sense of place, like a Londoner must. Even though I am a Mancunian through and through, having lived in London and visited and been through it so many times I feel like a true citizen, never a visitor.

Britannia Row is the only 'Britannia Row'. The road so named is in Islington, in the north of London, near the Emirates Stadium, off the Essex Road, close to the junction with Canonbury. It is a long, narrow, entry-like street with an unexpected configuration of council flats on one side and industrial units on the other. As I walk down it away from the roar of the main road, struggling with my suitcase, I suddenly feel vulnerable. The Row is like a kind of borderland where an uneasy truce has been struck. A recent municipal attempt at gentrification has not been able to fully blend the zones, and in the grey of an overcast sky, an air of suspicion and hostility is palpable. Britannia Row Studios, a hi-tech low-rent palace beyond unassuming double-doors, open for business for about seven years, lies in a nondescript three-storey brick-built unit on the left.

I am relieved to enter into a cheerful common room full of light and sound. Steve Morris greets me, still wearing the same grin as he had at the Unicorn pub in Manchester where the band first met me, a half-guilty look as though he has been caught with his hands in the till. He is dressed in a T-shirt, jeans and trainers. His trademark smile has been joined by a look of genuine amiable mystification. As he talks, he absently waves a cigarette. They are having difficulty with their drum machine, he explains – part of a batch of new equipment that includes a Sequential Circuits Prophet 5 polyphonic synthesiser, a Sequential Circuits Poly-Sequencer, an E-mu Systems Emulator and the Oberheim DMX drum machine. Its memory keeps fading. They are trying to fix it. Despite working 'with superglue and sweat' for weeks beforehand, most of the equipment still has teething problems, he confides cheerfully.

'The new rationalises the old,' he adds philosophically, 'replacing numerous little boxes with just a few bigger ones.'

He is playing with an ITT 2020 custom-built-for-Morris word processor. The 2020, an Apple 2E clone, programs the drum machine and converts programmed words into electronic speech. It can electronically generate a Japanese woman's voice or permutate words vocally like a duck and can randomise words (chosen at will from memory) and dream its own dreams on the backing tracks.

The Emulator intrigues and I sense it will command a starring role at this gig – feed any tape into its memory and 'play' back the sound on a keyboard. For this reason it is far in advance of its predecessor, the Mellotron, which was less digitally versatile.

As I look over the 'tinker-toys', as he calls the equipment, Steve intimates to me with a self-satisfied smirk that Cozy Powell once found he could get a great drum sound in this very room. Whitesnake and offshoots and, of late, 'a lot of heavy-metal bands' have been recording here.

Overhearing our chatter, Suzie, the new Britannia Row office girl comes over to introduce herself. Thinking I am on the industry side she begins by impressively informing me that Brit Row is owned by Nick Mason Music Ltd, aka Pink Floyd's Nick Mason and Dave Gilmore, built on the proceeds of *Wish You Were Here*, and is where the Floyd recorded *Animals* and parts of *The Wall*.

'Wow! That's amazing,' I say, politely shaking Suzie's hand. I know the studios are so owned, of course. But it strikes me how oddly appropriate and ironic it is that New Order have continued the link with Britannia Row, one first made when the band recorded *Closer* here with Martin Hannett. Pink Floyd were resurgent after the loss of Syd Barrett (for tax reasons, the remaining part of *The Wall* had to be recorded abroad). I look around the room, thinking of Ian, at the same time trying to imagine where Cozy Powell would have played.

We are in the studio's games room, which has been dubbed the 'Hanging About Room' (HA) by the band. As well as equipment, HA contains a dartboard, two or three video games, coffee facilities and a full-size mahogany snooker table with fantasy carved legs. The walls are raw brick. Tall, dark oatmeal-coloured Sonaplan baffles, used to achieve extra separation in the recording of sound, stand about like slim futuristic speaker cabinets, some vertical, others horizontal. Dave Pils, New Order's black-mopped road manager, who has been with the band since early 1979, is quietly playing snooker by himself.

Barney, Hooky and Gillian, all wearing short sleeves in the heat of the studio, are in the Control Room, which is out of the door across the passageway. I wander inside to announce my arrival, and sit and listen with them. Elsewhere in the studio it is almost stiflingly warm, but in here the temperature is kept lower to protect the equipment and the air has a distinctive coolness about it, like being in dark shade on a hot day.

The tape has a dead-solid funky drumbeat, coiled by a tight-wire rhythm that goes gradually, relentlessly through permutations. Barney tells me in a casual monotone that it is the backing track for a song with the working title, 'Blue Monday'. He is looking relaxed in jeans, loafers and a T-shirt. The casual, business-like manner with which he beat me at snooker in the Manchester Yates's is to the fore. They are modulating the tone of the pre-recorded backing tracks and trying to rid the system of a treble buzz. He alters the modulation and occasionally plays overlays while Gillian intently feeds the tapes into the poly-sequencer – another piece of equipment that is causing problems. Set up in the rehearsal rooms in Salford, they had managed to get it to perform. Here in the studio, it is playing up. She wears a skirt and a light short-sleeved blouse. The quietest and most self-contained of the band, she has a ready smile and laugh, once she gets to know you.

Hooky, the least conformist sartorially, is wearing a T-shirt and jeans, and sporting a pair of heavy-looking brown jackboots. He is sitting near the mixer watching Mike Johnson, the other person in the room, who is of a similar age in his mid-twenties, slim, with wavy-brown hair and dressed in jeans, T-shirt and trainers.

Mike has been at Britannia Row for four years, three-and-a-half of them as an engineer. He assisted on *Closer*, Joy Division's second and final studio album. This session is his first album as a fully-fledged engineer. He maintains a quiet, calm awareness that he occasionally breaks with a wry smile. I am happy not to interrupt what New Order are doing, content to just be in the flow with them, catching things occasionally until I can build up a picture of what is going on, but with Mike I sense it is okay to ask questions. He is a most generous guide, explaining to me that almost all the music has been written beforehand by the band and brought to the studio. Their first task, he tells me, is to get the backbone of each track on to 24-track tape, from which to build the finished masters. He adds that they are now in the process of doing this, working their way through the songs.

Back in HA, I find Hooky, who got bored and left the Control Room before me, playing snooker by himself. He asks how book publishing works. We get to talk percentages. He tells me that Virgin paid 0.5 percent for their track on the Virgin Sampler, *Live at the Electric Circus*. Virgin did much better out of the deal, he thinks, lining up a shot to pot a red. I tell him I am not qualified to comment. The two worlds are quite different, I explain. There are usually fewer creators involved in writing a book, often just one. Everything is simpler. In music there are musicians, singers, producers, mixers – in addition to the cuts for retail and industry, which are common to both fields.

All this time Rob has been on the phone in the office, which leads off from the games room, its door almost closed. A sudden period of quiet from that direction tells me I should go in and announce myself. I put my head round the door. He is seated behind a large desk and rises up to greet me as I walk in. He is dressed in sports shirt, jeans and pumps, less bothered with style than the others. It is the first opportunity I have had to thank him for his support, to say how grateful I am to have been invited. There is a deep fug of dope smoke in the air as we seat ourselves.

Like Steve, he is a constant smoker, of either straights or tobacco-rolled joints. He rolls up a joint, pushes up his glasses and lights up. He sits back, with his hands behind his head, quizzing me casually. As another Manchester 'chief' I am to be put through a rite of initiation, I sense. The dope is strong, as I know it will be. Holding on to the reefer for the right length of time before passing it back, I am soon smashed, barely able to focus on the conversation. In meeting such potentates I am, fortunately, fairly experienced and think I pass with flying colours, though I have doubts about the large rubber plant standing by the window. As we sit for a while in a pleasant haze, conversation exhausted, its leaves seem to writhe and waver, and I can't help wondering how much active THC it has mistakenly photosynthesised – in place of carbon dioxide – this past day or so.

About 2:15pm, while we are all sitting in HA waiting for takeaways to arrive, Tony Wilson arrives in baggy pinstripe and orders a joint, which Steve immediately rolls. Tony nods acknowledgement to me, without a flicker of surprise. Whether he expects to see me here or not, I don't know. We are more used to seeing each other in the bookshop on Peter Street where he often breezes in to show off our selection of bootlegs and underground records to whomever he has in tow, chatting affably to the shop staff by name. Today he is on the Granada Studios payroll, en route to New York. Granada is doing a feature on cable TV, with Melvyn Bragg handling the arts side. Tony is covering Ugly George, the video-broadcaster who roams the streets at night, on the hunt for encounters and interviewees to film.

Tony never stays anywhere for long and after fifteen minutes leaves for his plane in his three-quarter-length grey wool overcoat with wide sleeves – but not before forcefully arguing several points about the practice of innovative stateside record businesses, citing the entrepreneur Chris Blackwell of Island Records, who – in a novel manner – *pays* Atlantic to put out his records.

'Fuck off, Wilson,' Rob intones half-audibly from where he is seated on the floor, back to the wall. 'I'm not paying a single dollar to cunts.'

'Well, fuck off as well, Gretton,' Tony rejoins from the doorway, almost nonplussed. 'Anyway, I can't hang around here all day.'

'Has he fucked off yet?' Rob asks more loudly while Tony is still in earshot.

Barry, our freelance tape-operator for the weekend, brings in takeaway sandwiches from the pouring rain. After eating, I re-enter the Control Room where the incessant backing beat of 'Blue Monday' is still playing, will play all day until 10:00pm or so tonight; to be constantly played, modified, played again, crisped, replayed and replayed until it has been gotten as right as it is possible to get it, and they can move on to the next track.

In the Control Room, time expands, like entering first class on a plane. Rob, who has entered behind me and ensconced himself in one of the comfy chairs, seems to be asleep, but may be listening to the thrum with his eyes closed. From where he is slumped, his eyes keep slowly opening to take in the room. Equally slowly they close again, at intervals of about one to three minutes duration. Every so often he lifts up his shirt to scratch at his belly. He is otherwise like a supine but alert gecko, merged into the background.

Hooky is sitting next to the mixer, reading a book but keeping an alert ear open. Periodically he makes suggestions to Barney, who is back technician-ing with the synth. Barney and Gillian are still trying to get the sound adjusted for the studio. Once the raw, pre-recorded backings have been finished, guitars, vocals and other tracks will be overlaid in the coming weeks, some of them in the live studio that can be seen through the huge soundproofed Control Room window. For the sequenced songs they will record the synthesisers plus various timing pulses on to the 24-track and check that the arrangements are correct, whether the right number of bars are present in each section of the song (intro, verse, chorus) and whether the sections are all present and correct. For the 'live' songs they will record the drums plus guide guitar, guide bass, and perhaps guide keyboards and guide vocals. They will do several takes until they have got one that everyone agrees is good enough to be the master.

No lyrics at all have been written.

I return to the games room, HA, where Steve is rolling another joint. Rob has also returned here and is now lying down on the floor without shoes, reading and picking his nose. Steve and Rob like dope. Barney likes to smoke grass only occasionally, but not with tobacco.

They drift in and out of the Control Room into either HA, the live studio, the office to make calls, or the toilets. Occasionally, one of us will go to get provisions. The constant scene shifting is like being in an Anthony Balch cut-up film, but rather than in a New York street, the action takes place onboard a specially adapted long-haul plane. But the whole thing is better than a plane. There are no safety rules.

Whirring of space invaders, James Robertson Justice on the telly, the word processor screen soundlessly alive with millions of scrambling phosphor dots.

Everyone seems unperturbed but strangely alert, alternating between coping with boredom and switching on particular skills.

'They have obviously studied Martin Hannett very closely and have a very good grasp of how to get the most out of a recording studio,' Mike tells me, smiling wryly.

Despite the relaxed approach, they are focussed and hard-working.

Rob, who has gone out and returned to watch *Danger Mouse*, play videos and roll a joint, tells me that the band are 'supposed to be recording something' later.

6:04pm

The track in the Control Room is sounding more solid. The crashing Cannon drum sounds clear and simple. Barney is experimentally playing synth, the tune they will soon be laying down on 'Blue Monday', 'getting the feel, getting the tune right'.

Barry, the freelance tape engineer — who makes almost continuous rounds of tea for everyone — and Barney want speed. As I know someone, I volunteer to score. My friend on the Holloway Road has some, I discover, after making a quick call. The jolt of leaving the warmth and timelessness of the studio is intense as I reconnect with the city outside.

Later

Mission accomplished.

I decide it is the right moment to take my bags and make my way by Underground to the flat at the back of Harrods in Knightsbridge, Flat 6, 15 Basil Street — the apartment Factory has hired for the duration. It is where I shall be staying for most of the next week or so. There is no room in the car for my luggage, so I am to go on ahead.

I let myself in with a borrowed key, make a cup of tea and sit and wait in the silence of the living room. Although New Order arrived only yesterday evening, from Salford to Harrods — they almost didn't make it, scraping alongside a red double-decker bus in a bizarre near-accident — and have had little time to settle into their £400-a-week apartment, it already looks as though they've been living there for weeks. Arrayed on the lounge shelves are video tapes — *Temptation*, *Caligula*, *New Order*, *Les liaisons dangereuses*, *The 1982 World Cup* — as well as a variety of books and magazines — *Custom Car*, Warhol's *From A to B and Back Again*, *The Body Electric* by Thelma Moss, PhD, Peter Laurie's *Drugs*, *Angela Davis* by Angela Davis, Solzhenitsyn's *August 1914*, *Wheelin' with the King* by Doug Domokos and Len Weed. More videos lie scattered on the floor by the television: Brian Ferry's *Dublin Interview*, a Will Hay comedy *Where's That Fire?*, *Altered States*, *The Demon Seed* and *Spectre*.

With only three bedrooms, and an average-sized bathroom and kitchen, the flat, which occupies the upstairs floor of a modest two-storey house, is on the small size for five adults – even if two of them are an item. Certain band members – Hooky and Barney? Gillian and Steve? – will end up sharing, I imagine. Not part of the equation when the original booking was made, I have been allocated the cheap and cheerful accommodation of the living-room floor, where I gently park my suitcase and sleeping bag.

The band arrives not long behind me after a thirty-minute drive across Central London. Hooky and Gillian disappear to their rooms, while Barney, Rob and Steve fling themselves in chairs. Rob and Steve immediately light up and the television is turned on. When the others return from their rooms we sit and watch for a while, hopping channels, but when nothing interesting can be found Steve puts on a videotape. This doesn't suit the mood either, and after about half-an-hour or so they decide to go for a drink at a local Knightsbridge bar.

Rather than go with them I choose to catch up on my notes. Heedful of the wary regard shown to tape recorders, the only recording implements I have brought with me are four large ruled notebooks and a supply of cheap biros. Two of the books are plain schoolbooks with buff, olive-green covers. There is also a standard red Silvine Notebook and a spiral-bound notebook with a cutesy photograph of a tabby kitten on the front that I will use only if I have to. Throughout the day I have been scribbling down observations, recording things as they happen – except for conversations. For the latter, I've been committing anything interesting to memory and recording it hurriedly afterwards, as close to the moment as possible. Another reason for not going is I'm on a tight budget. Money is being posted to me from Manchester weekly, but I don't want to run low on my first night.

I have decided not to bring a camera – partly the caginess of the band for journalistic misrepresentation has disinclined me, but also the thought that an old-fashioned pen and notebook is probably the best equipment to use, for one person to capture a complex creative process like a recording session.

The band return after about an hour and the same procedure occurs as before. Hooky and Gillian go first to their rooms; Barney, Rob and Steve find comfy chairs; Rob gets Steve to roll up; the television is experimentally turned on, a video is chosen instead. We order takeaways.

At about 1:30am, Minu, a friend of the band, drops by to say hello and casts an immediate presence in the room. She is a booking agent and promoter for cult bands like the Virgin Prunes and Birthday Party. I am introduced to a petite, attractive Indonesian lady from Bali who may be twenty-eight. Like the Emulator, Minu is someone who I sense I will see more of.

As the others disappear to their rooms for the night and Minu leaves, Steve and I are last to stay up and talk together about the inevitability of the world, the cunningness of the mass unconscious in circumventing outright destruction of the human race, the bad traffic signs in Macclesfield (Steve's and Ian's hometown), the potholes in its roads, Ian and James Dean – the scene in the planetarium in *Rebel Without a Cause* where rock teen rebellion is brought into unexpected juxtaposition with the infinite – simultaneously a view of man's possible destiny and a reminder of our fragility on Planet Earth. A moment later the young hoodlums step safely back from this abyss, but in the ensuing knife scene the flashing metal seems to be energised with fragments of this vision; the glints of the blades reminders that the music of youth – rock'n'roll – briefly punches a 'hole' through comforting illusion.

Steve and I are both optimists. Nothing ever fazes him or gets him down – at least not for long. But we are also both realists and pragmatists. We know mankind constantly teeters on the verge of destruction. I tell him my children have just returned from living with their mother at the Marine Corps air station base at Cherry Point, Havelock, in North Carolina. The whole time they were there I was kind of relieved, thinking them safer in the hands of the military than living with me in Manchester, in the event of a nuclear war! He grins and nods knowingly. I can't tell whether he thinks this is loopy me or not.

It is 2:01am – the end of day one. I lie awake in the silence of the flat now that everyone else has gone to bed. I am half-stoned as I have been all day – and since mid-evening speeding a little.

New Order have managed to finish three of the backing tracks: '5 8 6', 'The Village' and 'Ultraviolence'. Still no lyrics.

Saturday, 23 October 1982

8:30am rise. We stagger out of bed one after another and watch Will Hay over breakfast – Barney's choice of film. His sense of mischief (and the absurd) today leads him to show us how to suck tea through a Cadbury's finger by biting off both ends and using the middle as a straw – a schoolboy gag, but when he does it he is like a young Tommy Cooper.

Garry, one of our locksmith managers, told me that an old schoolmate of Barney's at St Clements primary school, Lower Broughton, called Peter Miles, remembers how Barney used to say to him, 'Remember me when I'm famous in a band'. They were aged around eleven. It was his catchphrase. Barney said it to Pete not once but *every* day and it became indelibly imprinted on Pete's memory. Pete was mates with both Barney and Garry. Garry lived above Barney in New Bank Towers, Greengate, office to make phone calls or the bogs. ~~it's roll up~~ The whole thing is better than a ~~plane~~ ride because there are actually things to do.

Whirring of Space Invaders, James Robertson Justice on telly, ~~today~~ word processor screen soundlessly ~~list~~ flickering its million of phosphor dots, scrambling ~~about~~

Rob, who has gone out ~~again~~ & are back again to watch Danger Mouse, play video & roll another joint, tell we that the band are supposed to be recording something later on.

Barry & Bernie want some speed. The working title of the track the backing ~~is~~ trying to ~~lay down~~ modify today is "Blue Monday".

Back in the Control Room the track is sounding more solid, with more overlays added, crashing cannon drum

---

A page from the first notebook, written in Britannia Row's Games Room (or the Hanging About Room, as New Order christened it), early in the session. Part of the backing track of 'Blue Monday' is playing in the Control Room. The track has been recorded on to 24-track tape and is being built up to make the finished master.

at No. 21, on the second floor. Barney lived at No. 1 on the ground floor with his mother, an invalid.

Rob is the last to rise. He gets his act together very slowly, cajoled at times rather strenuously by the others, Barney in particularly. 'Rob, get up, Rob!' Barney enjoys this ritual and repeats the mantra venomously at studied intervals, until the morning progresses and Rob gradually sharpens up and begins to fight back.

We drive off in Barney's cream Mercedes 200 through Knightsbridge, round Hyde Park (which Barney thinks is Buckingham Palace) and up the Edgware Road. Hooky, driving with plenty of acceleration and brake, gets us to Britannia Row on the other side of town in a record twenty-five minutes. Barney, looking slightly sickened in the front seat and now ribbed by Rob from the back, advises caution, gives up and retaliates by playing Ravel's *Bolero* over the car's speakers at full volume.

10:30am

The booked and paid-for studio time is 10:00am to 10:00pm. As we climb out of the car, half an hour late, Barney is ribbed once too often by Rob, provoking a kung fu battle while Mike, who has also arrived late, is admitting us. The fight ends with Barney caught in a headlock between Rob's knees and giving one of his howling whoops, perhaps a war-cry to start a new twelve hours of layering sound. Although studio time expands and seems limitless, already a day (£400) has passed, like the minute hand of a great clock moving by a notch.

Rob immediately goes to the Fire Bird video table. Hooky sets up the snooker (which he and Rob then play) and Mike makes tea. The rest of us sit down and talk quietly. Barney is the most horizontal, lying full length on one of the comfortable low divans, dabbing some of the whiz to get him over the 'rigour of the night'.

As we try to relax into the day, Mike and Barry begin to work about us, wiring up the speakers. Soon, they bring the unexpected rest period to an end. The completed backing track of '5 8 6' is suddenly piped through from the Control Room, making us all shrink from the noise. Steve explains, with his satyr-like grin, that if the bass sound is fed into the domestic area like this then it can be checked in a more acoustically realistic club-like environment.

11:46am

But for me, unexpectedly, a different day beckons. I have to leave for Ingleton where I am to help Michael Moorcock, the novelist, and his new partner Linda Steele move from their sanctuary in Yorkshire down to London.

Immersed in the sensory experience of the studio and preoccupied with making friends of New Order, I have completely forgotten I have to go to the small holiday town in Yorkshire where Mike and Linda live, 260 miles to the north. The reminder phone call from the Savoy office in Manchester is a hit out of the blue. I am torn by my outside commitment and the compulsion to stay put with what I'm doing; but Mike and Linda have to take precedence, I decide. I have said that I will help them.

The band's interest is piqued by this sudden development. Steve and Hooky are fans of Mike's novels – Steve in particular. Barney's tastes in literature veer toward realism, but to help with the coming ordeal of writing lyrics he is keen to find appropriate books from which he can lift phrases. As Mike is widely read in both fantasy and realism there will be books there aplenty, I tell him, and promise I will look for something. I find myself reluctantly leaving the bubble-like refuge of the studio and returning to Euston train station.

Mike and Linda's home is Tower House, a large Victorian edifice combining three adjoining buildings. Mike and Linda live in the middle house, which bears in its roof the slender square stone tower that gives the building its name. Dave and I have been there on many occasions, as friends and to see what we can come back with, once searching through mouldering manuscripts to rescue Mike's first novel, *The Golden Barge*, from putrefaction and to give it its first publication. Most recently, we gathered there in June, after Dave's release from jail. Michael told him to 'come straight to Ingleton for a "transition" period' before becoming embroiled in the businesses again.

Situated just outside Ingleton, the Gothic-style demesne is close by Gaping Gill, an entrance into the underworld popular with cavers. Tourists are sometimes lowered into the darkness in a wooden cradle by ropes. Because of its appearance and the proximity of the nearby gill, Tower House is a dead ringer for the edifice in *The House on the Borderland*, William Hope Hodgson's novel, telling of an abode perched above a hellish vent in the earth. The dweller who lives there is overrun by fiends and transported through space and time into the remote future of the universe. The tower in Mike and Linda's house is a book-lined eyrie in the roof, recalling the tower in another fantastic novel, David Lindsay's *A Voyage to Arcturus*. Up this tower, Maskull ascended to begin his interstellar voyage to the planet Tormance. Bought during Londoner Mike's first marriage, lived in during his second and now relinquished after meeting Linda on a recent visit to Hollywood in pursuit of a film, Tower House is set over a fault line in his tumultuous private life. All hands are needed to make the escape back to the capital.

On Sunday, as the furniture-laden vans set off to the new flat in Fulham and we prepare to follow in Mike and Linda's car, I decide to pay one last visit to the tower eyrie, its mildewed bookshelves now empty of books. Reminded of the minaret at

Strangeways Prison and as I look out at the windswept blackened treetops I wonder whether I am facing prison too? As the co-publisher of the books my own case has still to come up. Looking down at the prison warden and fire-fighters running about on the lawn because remand prisoners were setting their mattresses alight, Dave and his three mates in their locked cell feared they would be burned alive. He knew in that moment that he mustn't waste any more time. If he got out, he must write his novel. [*Lord Horror*, David Britton, Savoy Books (1989). His experience in Strangeways was the main spur that started him writing.]

Lingering with these thoughts, I notice a dropped hardback book on the floor by my feet. It is *Kipps* by H.G. Wells; a cheap Everyman edition that I know won't be missed – one of Wells' few social novels. Fortuitous, I think, pocketing it for Barney.

Monday, 25 October 1982

8:00pm

The studio instantly re-envelops on my return, a hermetic cocoon of light and warmth in the darkness. I am greeted as though I have just returned with the sandwiches – with cursory nods or no greeting at all – as though I have never been away, as though no time has elapsed since listening to the completed backing track of '5 8 6'. The only clue that more time than this has passed is the book in my hand, which I sheepishly give to Barney. Absently, he takes it from me, his attention elsewhere.

An experiment is underway and discordant noise like plate glass in mid-explosion fills the air in the room. Everyone is casually intent on what is happening. Steve and Rob are very stoned on a mix of home-grown and imported grass; Barney is coming down off speed.

In an attempt to relieve monotony, rather than wait until all the backings have been completed, overdubbing has started on five of the tracks and 'white noise' – a random, multi-frequency sound generated by Steve on the synth – is being tried on 'Ultraviolence'. It issues from the three speakers positioned on the floor of HA – two 400-watt JBL speakers and an 800-watt cabinet – a solid, invisible matrix of sound filling the room.

It is being fed back to the Control Room by freestanding mics, to Mike, where it is being monitored. The acoustics in the larger room give the sound a deep, crisp resonance, ready to be dubbed onto a backing track.

New Order producing themselves are more like a team of NASA space scientists. Despite occasional appearances to the contrary, everyone is fully engaged, all the time. Mike tells me that when he worked on *Closer* as assistant engineer, the relationship was a bit different. Martin tended, to a large degree, to engineer the record himself and was often fiddling with effects for hours without saying what he was searching for (he probably didn't know). The result was that everyone felt a bit excluded from the process. With New Order producing, all of the engineering is being done by Mike, or on Mike's behalf, so he knows what they are trying to achieve.

There is not much sign of 'music production' in the conventional sense – of one person modifying and layering sound, working to a preconceived idea while members of the band hang about waiting to take part at different moments. The lack of a formal structure to the recording session indicates an impressive degree of spontaneous innovation and is redolent of the band's polycephalous dynamics on stage, where each performer is given equal room for expression. The members arrive at the studio with a pre-agreed plan and work out the detail as they go along, open to experimentation and happy accidents.

I ask Mike if there is a member of the band he mainly deals with and he confirms there isn't. Major decisions get taken democratically. Though they have different roles and specialisms, each takes the lead at different times; they are also virtually interchangeable.

Barney and I talk about the effects of listening over and over again to tape. Familiar, as a publisher, with the necessity of doing this I tell him I have to re-read the manuscripts up to a dozen times per book, word for word, at different stages of production, to make sure the text is exactly how we – and the authors – want it. I tell him I know how hard it is to keep focus, how easy to lose objectivity. Barney gets completely absorbed in listening. During the course of a twelve-hour day, he claims, what wears him down is not so much paying attention to detail as the volume of sound, which is continuously there. A bit like eyestrain caused by reading then, I tell him.

Hooky tells me he finds time goes quickly now they are producing themselves. With Martin, who produced the band up until the release of *Movement*, there were long periods in the studio when the band could not be directly involved. They would go to the cinema to kill time until they were needed. With a shared aim, they work more closely together, leaving on-going situations in the hands of each other as they tire, wandering in and out of the Control Room to rest. The increased responsibility is also more wearying. He produces Stockholm Monsters, Beech Red, The Royal Family, sometimes Vini Reilly, and others, but because he can delegate he finds all this less tiring than co-producing New Order. I ask him whether he prefers their pre-Hannett music and he replies all ambassadorial that he has come to like things the way they are: a polished studio sound – as 'super-polished as Genesis,' he jokes – contrasted with a rough live sound at concerts.

He is ever-present in the Control Room, and on a minute-by-minute basis effectively seems to be the producer; yet Bernard is the main arranger of the band's music and probably the originator of most of the tunes. And he comes up with the songs and hooks. His style is quite different, and a lot of time is spent lying around when he isn't required. When he is needed, he is right there in the moment.

Gillian spends a lot of time prepping for her overdubs and a tour New Order are embarking on immediately after the album is recorded. She is very methodical and patient, and happy to work quietly on her own in a corner until the time comes to record another keyboard part.

Steve, when he is not drumming, is always tinkering with some piece of equipment or other. If something is playing up he is always prepared to have another go. With the new equipment there is plenty of opportunity for that! He and Barney come up with ideas, linking equipment together to get new sounds. In the Control Room, he taps out a riff on a Simmons electronic drum machine, overlaying it on 'Blue Monday'. A short synth bass sound has also appeared – 'Whoooeeeeoooeeeoooooo . . .' – overlaid by Gillian whilst I have been away.

Rob is present the whole time. He doesn't contribute to the music apart from group discussions when they are trying to finish a lyric, but he has an equal say in what's going on.

Back in the games room, Gillian, who does not have much to contribute at the moment, is reading. Drums are the last to be overlaid, she says. It's still difficult to assess what each member is contributing – they are so laid-back. So much of what they do seems passive.

Rob jokes that before joining New Order, Gillian played guitar 'in a Macclesfield version of the Runaways'. He's alluding to the Inadequates. She flashes, 'Oh, *yeah?*' and sticks two fingers up at him.

'Blue Monday' is sounding richer. It is still very funk – electronic funk – but funk in a heavy, tribal sense, with an intricate percussive sound and a high Mellotron note made by the Emulator in an echo of doomy *Unknown Pleasures*-era Joy Division, though Rob clarifies that no Mellotron was used on this record. The band had only a simple synth to get those sounds; by the time of *Closer* they had better equipment.

We get back to the flat at around 12:30 at night. No one seems inclined to go out. Hooky and Gillian retire to their rooms almost immediately, leaving Rob, Barney, Steve and I smoking and watching a video of *Some like it Hot*. Barney is very high on a mixture of Mogadons, grass and booze. From his position on the sofa he swears he sees, through the open door, a figure who he thinks is Hooky, cross the hallway. No one else sees this apparition and after investigation it is put down to 'memory shadow'.

No working titles, as yet, for the other tracks . . .

Tuesday, 26 October 1982

3:30pm

'I could suck the raw guts out of a cat,' Barney says when I arrive at the studios, my morning spent trolling over to a friend's optometry practice in Mill Hill to borrow money.

New Order started on the 'good' grass earlier today. Steve jokes wryly that they have therefore gotten on top of the music faster. They have indeed started work on a new track, with the very loose working title of 'KW1', but Barney doesn't seem to know what it will be. When I arrive they are still working on 'Blue Monday'. Working together with Gillian, Barney is playing on their ARP Quadra – a four-in-one synthesiser incorporating a bass synth, a strong synth and two others – overlaying a passage of flighty cathedral-like strings from Kraftwerk's 'Radioactivity'.

The Control Room is full of people and recording is intermittent. Opinions and suggestions fill the intervals. Nearly always their discussions entail one person offering a suggestion and other members either agreeing or offering counter-suggestions. Their approach is calm, unhurried and always constructive. I have not yet heard a serious disagreement.

They decide to alter the tune and Hooky disappears to get his guitar, returning with a Shergold six-string bass. Before playing, they 'vocalise' the tune they want, one making harmonic synth sounds while another whistles the bass line. They find this almost impossible to do because they cannot get past the whistling part without cracking up. Gillian and Hooky eventually manage to complete it, and Hooky begins playing. It has an Ennio Morricone Western feeling to it. His bass is deep and humorous, laid over the disco rhythm of the backing. When he cocks it up, he laughs, carries on playing and then re-does the whole tune. When he's finished, Gillian is left on her own to re-lay the synth 'strings', Barney also having gone. When *she* cocks up she looks briefly annoyed and purses her lips.

On the television in the games room, by-election campaigning is taking place in a key Labour constituency and various MPs are making appeals to their constituents. The Tory wants to improve the neighbourhood by attracting commercial investment. The Labour candidate is a young, pregnant woman who pledges not to give up office once her child is born. There are too few young mothers in Parliament representing the interest of families, she says. The Social Democrat (SDP) candidate maintains that the newly formed party, split off from Labour and pitched to the Right, has become a credible and realistic alternative. Since the collapse of socialist power, Labour has drifted too far to the left, neglecting voters' interests and causing staunch party voters to become uneasy. Martin Webster, the National Front helmsman –

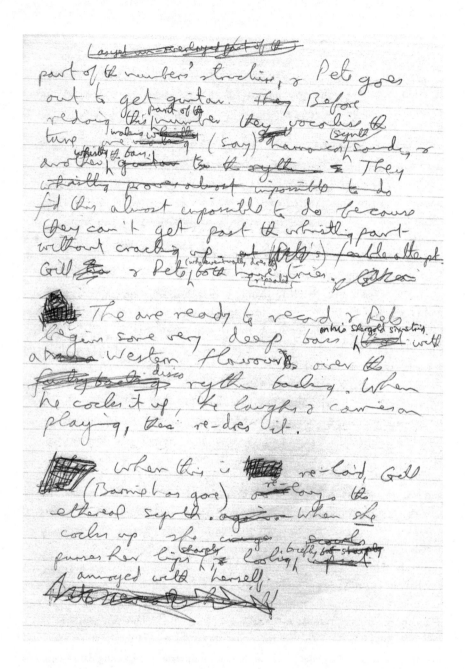

From the first notebook. My fifth day with the band. They have decided to alter the tune for 'KW1' ('Your Silent Face') and are attempting to vocalise it so that Hooky can lay down bass. They are cracking up with laughter, but eventually manage it. After the new bass has been put down, Gillian has to re-do the synth.

in the news frequently these days – maintains there is strong local interest in his policies. He confidently predicts people will vote for him. It is peak-time viewing and after the news, *Angels* comes on, a kind of '*Crossroads*-in-hospital' soap opera set in a Midlands infirmary.

Steve declares they are getting on top of the recording and that he is now looking forward to their Australian tour, a prospect that daunted him a few days ago.

Rob hikes up Gillian's skirt with his big toe, on the pretext of comparing her skirt (which is one-and-a-half inches above knee level) with one worn by one of the girls in the Britannia Row offices, which ends at crotch level.

In the Control Room, Mike is listening to Barney play melodica, an instrument with a mouthpiece and keyboard, in HA, like the reggae artist Augustus Pablo – perhaps for the tune they started work on earlier. If so, the tune now has a new name – 'Your Silent Face' – which everyone seems happier with. He makes suggestions over the speakers until Barney has got the high, mournful harmonica-like sound exactly how they want it.

In the evening, Michel Duval, Annik Honoré's partner in the Belgian independent label, Les Disques du Crépuscule (Factory Benelux), arrives with two Joy Division *Closer* bootleg tapes, *Closer 1* and *Closer 2*. A company in Thailand has released them. He brings news that Island Records have signed A Certain Ratio and 52nd Street. Perhaps these are the bands that Tony Wilson says Chris Blackwell is paying Atlantic to distribute?

In the Control Room, Barney and Hooky are listening to the last Emulator-generated note of the almost completed 'Blue Monday', with its Morricone 'Leave Me Alone' bass line, discussing whether it needs to oscillate or whether it needs to stay as it is – down. They go for down.

In the games room, we watch Bauhaus, for whom there is a certain admiration. Rob and I enthuse about the Cramps.

Hooky drives us home, with Barney complaining he is feeling unwell because he has had too much coffee, though we all know that he's also had a large amount of grass, resin and cocaine. Showing no sympathy, Hooky accelerates, slamming the car from side to side to make him throw up.

Debating whether to go straight to Heaven, the nightclub at Charing Cross, they elect to change and freshen up at the flat first.

I decide to remain behind, to write up my notes. When they return, in the early hours, Hooky goes straight to bed as usual, followed soon after by Gillian. The rest of us stay up talking and smoking. Unknown to me because I have been out of the studio so much, lyrics for 'The Village' and '5 8 6' have been written. The possibility of recording vocals is being discussed. They compare different studios with Britannia Row, which they think has a good sound and is an easy, relaxing place to work. Chosen by Martin Hannett, it was as big a jump up the ladder for them as the move from Cargo to Strawberry Studios, where they first found the producer. Hannett started at Strawberry as an engineer. Barney relates how they were like kids being taken to a restaurant for the first time. He still finds Brit Row inspiring, he says, but nowadays more because of Mike – their engineer's musical knowledge, creativity, empathy and patience, his genuine interest in the music and ability to take charge of situations.

As the others drift off to their rooms, Barney and I are left on our own. He will soon be coming under increasing pressure as the singer, because it means he has to take the lead with writing the lyrics. The band and Rob usually help him to finish off a lyric, but he has to do most of the graft himself. He reminds me again to get books for him. Since Ian died and the role of writing has fallen to him, he has to get ideas from wherever he can. Literature is a rich source, he claims. He often chooses phrases at random from books, but he also gets ideas from conversation, from passing thoughts, from suggestions others make to him. Then he fits them to the music. The greatest test is delivering them in live performance.

We talk about Savoy. The difference between Savoy Books and Factory Records, I say, is that Savoy is book-based and Factory is performance-based – the audience for books is far smaller. For an idealistic company like ours is, it is smaller still. But in real commercial terms, both companies are handicapped. Their autotelic operations mean that neither fit the mould.

It's the reason, he claims, that New Order aren't given much press – or any that isn't endlessly repetitive. The media typically wants to see only what 'happens on the surface', not the people involved. 'A person – any person – is worth far more than their job,' he declares. Their reluctance to 'play to an image' means they have to bide their time. It gets mistaken for elitism, he adds. They have to contend with being regarded as snobs.

Because of the police runs-ins Savoy has suffered we talk a great deal about the law, the politics of censorship and how it affects people. Barney was trained by his parents to be a political scientist – at Salford Tech – before he began expressing himself in a way that suited him better. The reason they have allowed me to work so closely with them, he confides, is because we have the reputation of producing books out of personal enthusiasm – and for helping artists. My oppo at Savoy, Dave's imprisonment for twenty-eight days in Strangeways Jail at the hands of James Anderton, the evangelical Manchester police chief, has only served to cement this impression of us. The band is incredulous of the fact that someone can still be imprisoned for publishing novels. Barney is incensed by Anderton's public exhortations to house the poor in work camps, and to bring back corporal punishment and identity cards.

Wednesday, 27 October 1982

Barney isn't needed until about midday and he and I sleep in. On waking, we each take a cool, deep soak in the apartment's spacious bathtub, then travel in by bus and taxi, stopping off at Hyde Park to sit in the autumn sun.

They have decided not to do vocals today, he tells me, but to overlay more bass and drums on '5 8 6' and 'Ultraviolence'. The wrong manual was sent with the Prophet synthesiser, leading them to believe that its memory could accommodate only 2,500 notes (New Order's tunes have an average of 3,000 notes), when in fact it could accommodate 10,000. When they sent off for the correct manual, one wasn't available, so they had to work it out for themselves.

I tell him what I know about the tracks from Mike and he confirms the tracks were laid down very roughly in the rehearsal rooms in Salford. The band arrived at Britannia Row with the arrangements completed except for two, 'Murder' and 'Only the Lonely', for which they have only drums and a few bass riffs. He will write lyrics for the tracks that haven't yet got them, by a group process, and vocals will be overlaid last, he thinks.

When we arrive at the studio a programme is showing about the pre-war depression in Germany during the rise of Adolf Hitler (six million people out of work, compared with our current three million). On his black Shergold Marathon, Hooky is laying down more bass for a section of 'Blue Monday' that sounds like a machine-gun track. He asks Mike to get rid of a 'mellow texture' from his guitar and make it sound more savage . . . then decides, with the encouragement of Barney, to put in a *Fistful of Dollars* riff – Adam Ant through Bow Wow Wow. Hooky's other guitars are a Fender Precision, a Yamaha BB1200 and a black Gibson.

Other working titles for tracks are: 'The Village' and 'Fairy-tale'.

Clinton Walker, the Australian music writer and London organiser of New Order's forthcoming Australian tour, arrives with the band's touring contract. The agreement is with Eddie Zimblis & Co., who have done only one international tour before, with the Fall. It is as big as an author's book publishing contract – the biggest they have received for a tour; normally they get about a page. It specifies ten dates, at £800 per date. New Order have to provide their own sound engineers including a foldback engineer, who manages the onstage speakers so they can hear what they're playing, a lighting engineer and a stage manager – which means Terry Mason, their tour manager school-friend of Barney's and Hooky's, and Dave, who will double-up to cover everything.

Clinton needs a press release, but doesn't feel like writing one, and Rob startles me by allocating me the job. I spend the rest of the evening mostly preoccupied with writing this.

After several attempts, careful to tone down sensation and concentrate on the facts, my first draft is still too racy, and I pare it down even more. While I am working I have the vague notion that Barney's voice (pre-recorded in Salford) is playing in the Control Room, and being put under the microscope.

Leave England – Sun/Mon, November 21/22
Melbourne, Palais Theatre – Thurs, November 25
Melbourne, Seaview Ballroom – Sat, November 27
Sydney, Capitol Theatre – Mon, November 29
Auckland, Mainstreet Cabaret – Fri/Sat, December 3/4
Wellington University – Mon, December 6
Christchurch (New Zealand), Hillsborough Hotel – Wed, December 8
Sydney, Selinos Hotel – Fri, December 10
Sydney, Maryvale Hotel – Sat, December 11
Perth, Melbourne Hotel – Wed, December 15

I escape from the typewriter for half an hour and catch Hooky on his own in the HA, stretched out on the couch. I tell him his bass has a sense of humour that has more to do with rock'n'roll than new wave. He agrees that some could see it that way, though he is quick to point out that it is not the rock'n'roll of Shakin' Stevens that interests him. He is the only member of New Order to play with a sense of humour, I insist. He admits that he deliberately plays with his tongue in his cheek to counter the over-seriousness of the others. He adds that he is doing more with the six-string Shergold these days, finding four strings more limiting.

Later, Rob, who likes to jolt people out of whatever it is they are doing and force them to take notice of *him* – he especially enjoys doing it to them if they are new – comes up on Mike suddenly and squeezes the backs of his thighs.

'You alright, Mike?'
'You alright, Terry?'
'You alright, Steve?'
'You alright, Hooky?'
'You alright, Bernie?'
'You alright, Gillian?'
'You alright, Mike?'

Thursday, 28 October 1982

Hooky wakes us with Michael Jackson's *Off the Wall*. A stuffed rat, no one is saying from where, 'moves' about inside the apartment to worry Barney. Once, someone left the toy inside his open suitcase, the contents ruffled to give the impression that it had burrowed its way in. Another time, it was found drinking out of his bedside glass of water. This morning it has been left in the hallway, lying on its side as though dead. Barney reacts to this with a wry 'I'll get you back when I find out who you are' smile.

As we drive to the studio he suggests cutting 'Blue Monday' as a single for release before Christmas, but the others are unsure. They think this about nearly every track they complete, Steve warns.

Hooky is driving Barney's Merc again. I discover the reason is because Barney hasn't passed his test yet. He's got this huge fucking car, though! As I scribble notes on the back seat next to Rob and Gillian, Barney tells me from the front that after their Australian tour they may do two US dates, 30 December and New Year's Eve, at New York's Danceteria nightclub. Rob adds that they may record with New York producer Arthur Baker either a re-mix from the album or, more hopefully, if the teething problems with their equipment have been ironed-out, a piece of new material. Baker works with Afrika Bambaataa who, as a DJ in the seventies, mixed Philly soul with tracks like Kraftwerk's 'Trans-Europe Express'. New Order recorded a song called 'Confusion' at his New York studio in February, and may leave him to do the final mixing. As Rockers Revenge, he has now just cut a version of the Eddy Grant number 'Walking on Sunshine'. They saw him as a contender to produce their album until they decided to do it for themselves.

Barney announces that he is to guest with 52nd Street, the jazz, funk and R&B band, this Friday at the North London Polytechnic. Brought to Factory Records by Rob, 52nd Street, who are beginning to experiment with electronic music, have just released their first single 'Look into My Eyes'.

It is Steve's twenty-fifth birthday and a sponge cake with twenty-five candles made by Gillian last night is produced at the studio. Barney warns Steve: 'If you don't blow out all the candles in one go, we're going to put your face in it.' Steve directs one long breath at the cake, easily putting them out. As the cake is being shared they arrange to see *Tron* on Saturday. I make hot drinks for everyone, before picking up the threads of my press release in the calm of the office.

I have to bring all my experience as an advertising copywriter into play. Not a great deal, as I didn't last in the industry above a year. Writing functional copy to order, marshalling facts and communicating them to the target readership, then making these dull facts appear interesting – finding the right angle, making the copy chatty while pleasing your subjects and missing out nothing crucial – is the most difficult of arts to do well.

The English author M. John Harrison typed his novel *A Storm of Wings* in Bookchain, our shop on Peter Street, while customers milled around. American writer Harlan Ellison went one stage further, typing short stories in bookshop windows (one complete story per day). But these were feats the writers brought on themselves. With my commissioners looking over my shoulder, I'm right back in the open-plan office at my copywriting job at Dale House where designers chattered to each other, playing Santana on a ghetto blaster. Artists — and musicians — are creatures who more easily work socially together like that. But writers find it hard. At least this one does. Fortunately I was able to train myself to blot out the well-intentioned clamour. At Britannia Row, even more fortunately, there is Rob's office to go to, and it is empty, and I steal a few hours while I can.

4:00pm

I am invited by friends Liz and Richard to visit Stuart Goddard's (Mr Adam Ant's) house-to-be, a converted barn. Adam is moving into the property for use as a 'top secret' hideaway — somewhere he can rest-up while he's gigging — and the neighbours who still live in it have asked my friends to dinner before the sale is complete and he moves in.

Liz and I are both big Adam Ant fans. I am also at work on a proposal based on Goddard's stage character for a possible Savoy book. Knowing this, she and Richard have arranged for me to join the dinner table.

I decide to break off work on the press release and make my way to Little Berkhampstead. Ant and manager Don Murfet are both buying houses in the Hertfordshire village, taking a house each.

I set off with conflicting feelings, but as soon as I approach the two pairs of electronic wrought-iron gates that have been installed on the driveway to the new residence — great atmospheric detail for my book proposal — I know my hunch to drop everything and come here has been right.

Friday, 29 October 1982

The press release is finished, to the apparent satisfaction of everyone except Gillian, who doesn't like the use of the word 'dance' to describe some of the album's music. But Rob likes it, and as no one else objects, it is left in.

New Order Australian Tour/New Zealand Tour, November 1982

The British band formerly known as Joy Division, whose music has become virtually synonymous with the sound of Factory Records, the independent record company that first launched them, are making their first tour of Australia and New Zealand this autumn. Their short ten-date visit follows the tour earlier

Pete drives + on way intimates
that he's only going to see ABC
(with the rest of N.O.) after
word) to relax only

We go through heavy traffic up
Holloway Rd, Bernie clearing his lungs
desperately every so often & hawking
out of the car window.

North London Poly — we drive to the
stage entrance. Bernie runs out to find
his friend (keyboards) in 52nd
Street to help carry in the
gear.

Swamp Children
Prince Farai (headliners)
52nd Street.

I'm coming down, but very slightly
while Bernie sets up with 52nd
Street who are already sound-checking.
They play some very tight number with
two heavy members (keyboards fellow &
bass guitarist).

Hooky drives Bernard and me to the North London Poly, where Bernard is making a guest appearance with 52nd Street to try out some of the new equipment on-stage before New Order's Australian tour. I am acting as roadie. Prince Far I is headlining with Swamp Children in support. After dropping us off, Hooky and the others drive to Hitchin to see the Sheffield band ABC.

this year by Manchester band the Fall and, although they are among the last of the Factory and British North West independent bands to come to these shores, they are the most well-known internationally.

The band were formed in Manchester, England, early in 1977, after hearing the Sex Pistols performing, but they struck out in a musical direction of their own (their contemporaries being Adam and the Ants, the Damned, and Siouxsie and the Banshees). They were known first as Joy Division and, between the periods 1977 and 1980 (and the tragic death of their first singer, Ian Curtis), and 1980 and the present day, they have created two distinctive musical styles.

The influences they brought together as Joy Division are varied, and come from rock music and literature – Captain Beefheart, European machine rock (Kraftwerk, Chrome, Can, et cetera), the Velvet Underground, Jim Morrison and American novelist William Burroughs. These influences they worked into a raw, expressionistic, distinctly personal and anguished sound that resonated far outside their hometowns. In 1979, on the Factory label, they released their first album, *Unknown Pleasures*, which went to the top of the UK independent charts, followed in 1980 by a single, 'Love Will Tear Us Apart'/'These Days', which reached number eleven in the National Top 20, and by a second winning album, *Closer*.

Since 1980, as New Order, and the recruitment of new member Gillian Gilbert, part of the group's music has moved even further from rock toward an electronic black-influenced New York sound. Some current studio work is characterised by a dead-solid beat and contemporary dance elements. The intent of earlier material has not been lost but brought forward and intensified into a broader musical context. It is cooler and more knowing than disco music. It points to a new sound and their coming stage performance will strongly reflect this development.

The band's line-up since 1980 – it is unlikely to change again – has been Bernard Albrecht (vocals and guitar), Peter Hook (bass) and Stephen Morris (percussion), who with Ian Curtis were founding members, and Gillian Gilbert (keyboards and guitar).

Movement, their first album, which showed the band's new direction, was released in 1981. In the same year they cut three singles – 'Ceremony'/'In a Lonely Place', 'Everything's Gone Green'/'Procession' and 'Temptation'/'Hurt' (which reached No. 29 in the British charts earlier this year). Until the formation of the band's new Australian label, Gap, their records have been available in Australia only as imports. Joy Division's 'Love Will Tear Us Apart' and 'Atmosphere'/'She's Lost Control' both entered the national charts in Australia and New Zealand in 1980/81 ('Love Will Tear Us Apart' reaching No. 1 in New Zealand).

New Order's chart status is deceptively modest. Their restraint is characteristic of their cult image and is a deliberation on the part of both the band and Factory

Records to avoid distorting their musical intentions. Looks are deceptive, though, as in fact their singles sell 110–150,000 discs – more than an average UK Top Ten Hit. The relationship with Factory – who play down the marketing side by allocating descriptive brand numbers to their productions, viz. FAC 1, FAC 2, FAC 3 – has been a long and solid one, and the interests of band and label are mutually reinforcing. To keep their aims intact, Factory have remained an independent label, at the moment the only successful recording company in the UK outside London.

New Order have recently finished work on their new album, scheduled for release in the UK in the spring. An outtake single from the album is due to be released this Christmas. After touring Australia and New Zealand they will make their third appearance in America for two New Year dates at New York's Danceteria and begin fresh recording work.

Late afternoon, and I am relaxing back into my usual state of alert repose, cultivated to cope with Britannia Row, when Clinton calls to say that the release is no longer required. He wants an article instead, saying roughly the same thing, for Oz rock music paper *RAM*.

4:40pm

Steve is laying down real drums on 'Ultraviolence' in HA (the working title for this was, appropriately, 'Who Killed My Father?'). Several of the tracks are to have in-fills. His kit has been erected between the couches and the snooker table – the sound being fed back into the Control Room. As on previous occasions, the volume is enormous and everyone else has been driven out except me. He hits the drums determinedly with his arms, not his body. His torso is held almost stationary, while a savage nervous energy pours out of him through his sticks onto the skins. It is Steve with his 'drumming head', and as I am watching the head of Worzel Gummidge suddenly appears on the television next to him.

Eventually, even I, a newcomer to studio life, have had enough and escape from the noise into the Control Room, where the drums are being recorded but the noise is a lot less. Here, Mark, the new freelance tape engineer who has replaced Barry, informs me that four backing tracks have been entirely completed: 'Blue Monday', '5 8 6', 'Ultraviolence' and 'The Village'. Five to go, then?

We talk about time. For him, he says it goes very fast in the studio. He loses track of it, and has more or less stopped looking at his watch. It is of no importance 'inside', he says. I agree, adding that, in here, the life processes may paradoxically speed up. It is a very unusual mental atmosphere and fully engaging – a good training ground for an airline pilot or an astronaut. Freed from temporal constraints, mental processes work at maximum intensity, as though we are speeding. But the effort may be wearing out the body faster, reducing life expectancy at a greater rate.

For me, the sense of being cocooned is about to fracture. Out of the blue comes news that on Sunday, I will have to return to Manchester. I must organise a new minder for my children and will have no sure knowledge that I will be free to return, throwing my whole project into doubt.

Recording abruptly stops, while preparations are made for Barney's impending guest spot with 52nd Street. I have suddenly been made roadie for the evening, and muck in, packing the equipment.

This is not a job I am totally unaccustomed to, having been roped in once in a similar way for Hawkwind. But the prospect of roadie-ing for the evening seems totally crazy and I feel sudden disorientation – perhaps not helped by the very strong home-grown grass brought back with me from Hertfordshire. Nearly the whole time I've been in the studio my attention has been switching constantly and the availability (or not) of money – having to make elaborate credit arrangements whilst waiting for packets to arrive through the post – has seemed sometimes close to sabotaging everything. Venturing out into the unknown suddenly seems a change too far . . .

But madness or not, the Quad and the Prophet are packed away in their heavy aluminium-lined cases and humped into the boot, and I am suddenly in the car with Barney – Hooky driving again. On a spur-of-the-moment decision, the others – Hooky too – are to catch an ABC concert, which Hooky tries to tell me, is purely for relaxation.

Steve will do more drumming and then, later in the evening, re-joined by Hooky and accompanied by Rob – who is already quite incapable of proper coordination – set out to Hitchin, taking with them the video camera to record the show.

We drive through heavy traffic up Holloway Road, Barney hawking out of the car window, desperately trying to clear some catarrh from his throat. We arrive at the Poly, where the gig is taking place – Prince Far I is headlining, with the Swamp Children also on the bill – and drive down a ramp to the stage entrance. Hooky and I wait whilst Barney runs out to find his friend John Dennison, keyboard player from 52nd Street, to give us a hand with the gear.

I decide to just go with whatever is happening. The physical activity soon helps earth me, and leaving the containment of the studio suddenly seems less of a threat than I thought. I'm coming down very slightly too, as Barney sets up with the band who are already conducting sound checks. As I begin taking things in around me, they start playing some tight warm-up numbers. The main reason Barney is here is to get the chance to use some of the new gear on-stage, prior to the Australian tour. Proving his scepticism, the Quadra packs up and he has to make do with just the Prophet. Another reason is to go on what he calls a 'holiday', away from the studio.

While Barney readies himself on-stage I bump into Minu, who has come to watch. While we are waiting she takes me to a pub across the road, where I learn more about her. She is stateless because of a military coup on her Indonesian home island of Bali (by odd coincidence, this reminds me of 'Basil', the street name of the band's Kensington apartment), rather like a Portuguese-Goan student my mother once took in. The situation actually works well for what she does. Like Adam's 'Jordan', she tells me, she nurtures obscure but talented bands, helps get them gigs and travels with them. She has turned her statelessness into a virtue, organising counterfeit visas for her bands and owning three faked passports for herself. She enjoys being able to put down roots everywhere rather than in one place. Without domestic responsibility, she can do as she pleases, and imagines nothing nicer at the end of a hard day than the snug luxury of a hotel room.

Her path often crosses with New Order's, and at a gig a few weeks ago in Athens, she tells me, Barney wore Alpine shorts on stage. It wasn't Bavaria, it wasn't cold and no one could speculate as to why. For no reason that Barney could later think of he threw his melodica into the crowd at the end of the act, and injured a member of the audience. I tell her I sometimes get the recurring impulse at events to smash my glass on the floor. It is so overpowering I sometimes have to leave the room until the feeling passes.

We find our way back to the Poly. The Swamp Children, who I first heard on the Disques du Crépuscule sampler *Fruit of the Original Sin*, come across as bland. The image is Hawaiian 1930s Jazz/Latin smart club. Their singer, Ann Quigley, has a rock voice reminiscent of early Grace Slick, which seems out of place with the music.

52nd Street are like a headlining band. Solid bass and keyboard, powerful 'Motown' singers, a driving sound from ACR's percussionist who is a white drummer, friend and pupil of Donald Johnson's. Barney does four numbers with them, scarcely knowing what he's supposed to be playing, for his colleagues haven't been able to tell him and he's still out of his head. Driving home afterwards he concludes he needs to practice with them more. But what Minu and I hear from the floor sounds good enough, a long burst of infrasound from the Prophet partway, hitting the chest just right.

Prince Far I's band come on. They tune-up, amps crackling with random sounds, so dead-cool I don't realise they've broken into a number, which is very heavy, very loud dub, as the club's sound engineer turns up the volume. Then Far I himself appears, an immediate presence cajoling the audience with a Rastafarian rap as he prowls up and down the front of the stage. But for some unfathomable reason, he isn't inclined to give the audience or the management what they want. After a quarter of an hour of a deliciously dangerous musical experience, he quits the stage.

Behind the scenes, it quickly develops into a fiasco.

While I wait for Barney, I retreat upstairs, following Minu to the changing room where she has spotted a friend. I find myself in a nondescript college classroom – all metal, white-painted concrete and glass – with members of the Swamp Children, 52nd Street and their friends. Their dress styles are simple, bland and functional – shirts, trousers and jackets that look like they've been bought from C&A, regulation short back-and-sides haircuts on the men. The women's clothes are more adventurous, but still restrained. We might be in a police cadet training college cafeteria or Army NAAFI – off-duty, of course – thirty years ago.

On the way out with our gear I have to wait by Far I, who is getting wound up with a representative of the Poly management. Rightly, he is being refused payment for such a short set. After a bout of wrangling and threats, the Prince and his group storm off. He exudes gangster. I don't know whether he is one, but if he is then the management guy has got some bottle. But I'm thinking to myself that *I* wouldn't like to be the one to tell Prince Far I he wasn't getting paid!

Minu returns with us. Back at the Kensington flat, Rob and the others arrive from their ABC concert. The 'others' include New Order's lighting manager, Andy, whom they plan to take with them to Australia. Rob is still completely out of it. Ditto Andy. Between them they have polished off more than a bottle of vodka, had general rounds of drinks and done the usual quantities of dope. Rob can't recall anything about ABC except that they wore suits on-stage. The film he intended to make had to be left to Hooky and Steve to do. He starts clambering on top of Andy, trying to mock-fuck him. Andy, almost left for dead on the stairs has had to be dragged into the flat and is propped heavily unconscious in a seat.

Barney puts on the flipside of Ravel's *Bolero* (which is serene and quiet by contrast to the A-Side) and I can see why he likes that kind of soothing kitsch. After the incessant clamour of the studio – the drums, as well as the people – and the partying, he needs something to physically calm him down.

Still intent on provoking a reaction and having found Andy too gone, Rob throws himself on Gill, who recoils in disgust. He then tries the same thing on Minu, who expertly deflects his attentions. Finally, he launches himself at Barney. This is the last thing Barney is expecting and he responds angrily, pushing Rob's heavy, almost supine form off him on to the floor.

Rob rolls onto his back. Not yet spent, he calls for tea and toast. He likes to get other people to do things for him and at Basil Street usually homes in on Gillian, prevailing on her to put on a brew or make toast. In a flared-up mood, Gillian retaliates this evening by toasting some stale pitta breads that have been lying around for several days and have green mould growing inside them. She smothers them in hot butter and brings them in from the kitchen. The room goes quiet as he scoffs them and we all watch with mingled incredulity, amusement and disgust. It is a lesson in human nature.

Andy's violable form reminds me uncomfortably of a medical examination I once had – being knocked out on the operating table for an internal bladder inspection, with a micro-camera on the end of a wire. I remember coming to afterwards wondering what had really happened during those missing moments of my life.

Continuing our talk about quietude, I tell Barney that speed, paradoxically, has a calming effect on me. Same here, he says, confiding that he usually only does it to help him through his work. Me too, I say.

Saturday, 30 October 1982

. . . is the last day I can hang on for an awaited package of Savoy cash, but when we arrive at Britannia Row I make the discovery that, because its main office is closed over the weekend, the mailbox is locked. I have to wait until Monday.

1:00pm
I pay a visit to my friend on the Holloway Road to get some blueys for Barney. No blueys. Get yellow sulphate tablets instead and drop four on the way back.

2:30pm
A new idea for 'Ultraviolence' has occurred to Barney and he is in HA laying guitar over the Beefheartian drums and bass put down by Steve yesterday – sawing and sliding at his black Gibson Les Paul – making the track sound very lusty, savage, triumphant and redolent of Captain Beefheart's album, *Shiny Beast (Bat Chain Puller)*. Breaking off, he tells me he likes Beefheart's *Bat Chain Puller* better than *Doc at the Radar Station*. *Doc*, he says, contains many tracks that should have come out on *Bat Chain* but which didn't for contractual reasons, and drummer John 'Drumbo' French, who played on Beefheart's third and defining album, *Trout Mask Replica*, wasn't credited on the album. He goes back into HA to do more guitar and feedback, which gets fed back and overlaid.

According to Rob, Sharon out of *Coronation Street* mentioned Joy Division in an episode several weeks ago. This band *are Coronation Street*, I think. You wouldn't be surprised to come across them drinking in the Rover's Return while performing a charity gig for Rita Fairclough, the Street's long-standing fictional character.

Mike plays back 'Ultraviolence'. Barney notices a short burst of high, ascending feedback notes – 'yuhuup yuhuup yuhuup' – and asks Mike to loop it.

Horse racing is on the TV. On a copy of the *Daily Mail* I read that automaker John DeLorean has been released on $10-million bail after spending eleven days in jail on charges that he financed a $24-million cocaine deal.

Dave, the band's road manager, who is in and out of the studio on an almost daily basis, drops by, today wearing a 'Roland: We Design the Future . . . for the Musician' T-shirt.

The looped feedback sound – which is like a berserk alarm siren (but not too fast) – is down. I call it 'Barney's Loop' because it also reminds me of one of his stage whoops. Now complete, a short while later it is overlaid on 'Ultraviolence'.

Gillian (who has gone shopping) returns with shampoo from the Body Shop and a bra-corset, which has a creamy, pale design of flowers and leaves overlaid with fine black lace and edged in black. She dresses differently each day, yesterday a black leather skirt and top, today a simple, straight red wool dress with a wide black belt, black pointy stiletto-heeled ankle boots and black fishnet stockings.

Very speedy on these yellow sulphate tablets and resin-and-grass joints that are going round, I venture out to the post office to send what money I have left to my sister who has run short and is looking after our army of kids. What is a quarter mile at most seems an infinitely long walk through busy streets, with everything catching my eye. On the way back, walking past colourful fruit-and-veg and flower stalls I am strongly drawn by a display of brilliant yellow chrysanthemums. On the spur of the moment, I decide to buy one for Gillian. She doesn't do drugs and, thinking that these motionless yellow flower heads will in some way compensate her, I buy the largest I can see and take it back with me.

But on arrival at the studio Rob and Steve spot the flower, and it is decided instead to pretend to Hooky (who is in the Control Room) that the flower has been delivered from an admirer, so I take it to him where he is working. The flower has been unwrapped and placed gracefully in a tall, ornate silver teapot as a stand-in for a vase. I gravely present it to him, declaring that three girlfriends of Suzie's have dropped by and brought it for him. Hooky is the least susceptible of all of us to trickery, but because he doesn't know me as well as the others, he almost swallows this. Then, both of us colouring up and laughing, he accepts the flower . . . perhaps it was always meant to be for him.

A cluster of equipment – drums, mics, et cetera – has slowly grown around one of the JBL speaker cabinets in HA. Amidst the clutter, Dave has set to work improving a bass rack he built for Hooky. The rack is a kind of trolley-cum-cabinet containing trays for the amps, analogues and pedals used on-stage. He is making a new top tray. When he first came into the recording studio with the band three albums ago, he used to sit and listen to them whenever they were playing, but now he gets bored and maintains their equipment. If anything too complex goes wrong, he gets out the people at Strawberry North to put it right – the best, he declares quietly.

Dave confides to me that Hooky hasn't yet got the bass sound he's looking for. The old, less sophisticated equipment had a more raucous sound, but lacked the versatility of the new stuff.

Work in the Control Room abruptly stops as Hooky announces that all the synths are out – even though they've been tuned. This precipitates a rare moment in HA, other than meal times, or arrival or departure times, when all the band and recording staff find themselves together in one room.

They discuss what to do, but soon take out a tape of themselves to watch (filmed at the Toronto gig earlier in the summer) and take the piss out of their performance instead. Then back to the sport – football and rugby – for a strangely subdued Rob, who suddenly startles everyone by offering to make tea – a very rare occurrence – perhaps to atone for his behaviour of last night. Everyone hurriedly takes him up on the offer.

5:10pm

Still very speedy.

Irish supporters of the rights of Protestant political prisoners to be segregated from IRA prisoners, daub graffiti over a football stadium. Because of the local elections, physical violence is growing again in Northern Ireland.

I am living on a diet of chips, peas, white bread, tea, coffee, chocolate bars.

7:56pm

Retreat to the office to work on the article Clinton has arranged for the Oz music paper, *RAM*, for delivery in the morning. Rob joins me, escaping the noise of drums in HA, which in here sound distant and muted. We sit in the relative quiet, me occasionally tapping the keys of the Brit Row golf-ball typewriter, and talk leisurely about Savoy and Factory. He thinks the companies are similar – with the exception, he jokes, that Factory makes money. I reply that if Savoy were working with music instead of words, then we'd make more money than Factory! Savoy is upfront and polemical, Factory pursue a non-image. They have made the sound of the moment, so they can get away with that. Savoy is a late-seventies and eighties crystallisation of the fifties and sixties and has to try to sell something that by rights oughtn't to be there. We decide we both sell something that by rights shouldn't be there.

I tell him we keep wondering whether to make music, but get put off by the idea of dealing with performers. As a publisher it's a relatively quiet life. Writers send in manuscripts – you never get to see them in person. But the way we see it, all our authors and artists are 'rock'n'roll' anyway. They have the same rebellious larger-than-life spirit. Michael Moorcock is rock'n'roll, so is Harlan Ellison, Jack Trevor

Story, Henry Treece, M. John Harrison, William Burroughs, Ken Reid, James Cawthorn, Samuel Delany. To us they are as rock'n'roll as Little Richard, Jerry Lee Lewis, Chuck Berry, the Cramps, or Devo, or DAF, or Esquerita and the Voola.

Hooky and I taxi back to Basil Street, while the others see Disney's *Tron*. Leaving our Tardis-like studio, we enter London again, slipping into a warm dangerous pool, protected by the darkened space inside the cab.

Hooky: 'Lester Bangs had his material well grasped, wrote interestingly and penetratingly in an easy, flowing style, and was true to himself.'

Hooky has a child, somewhere.

The name Stiff Kittens was erroneously tagged to the band at their first gig, he tells me. Their road manager, who doubled as a drummer, booked the band at the Electric Circus, supporting Buzzcocks, whose manager Richard Boon was promoting the night. They didn't have a name and told Boon they would get one within twenty-four hours. But Boon was unable to wait and when they arrived the following day, publicity had already been printed. Looking at the posters they noticed that a band called Stiff Kittens had been billed, and thought they had been replaced. In fact Boon had invented a name for them. Stiff Kittens was a non-starter. They had arrived as promised with their own name, and went on as Warsaw. They planned to keep the name, but later a London agent told them that if they wanted to play in London they couldn't use Warsaw. Punters might turn up for their gig thinking they were coming to see Warsaw Pakt. So they set about changing their name, narrowing down a list of possibles to just two and choosing from those.

Sunday, 31 October 1982

New Order Australian / New Zealand Tour [Copy for *RAM*]

New Order are tilted at various receptive angles, their music expanding exponentially since shedding the Joy Division skin. Before starting their first tour of Australia and New Zealand in Melbourne on 25 November, they are in London in the studios of Messrs Mason and Gilmore (the Floyd's Britannia Row Studios) recording the new nine- or ten-track album provisionally titled *Power, Corruption & Lies*, for release in the spring. A possible outtake single from the album is planned for Christmas.

The sound on some tracks is a metamorphosis of contemporary disco – as much a grab from Steve Morris's new customised word processor, designed to program drum machine and Japanese voice electronics onto backing tapes, than a desire to dance. In extreme contrast, another track is a lusty, savage, triumphant Beefheartian 'Run Paint Run' dedication.

This is their first self-production, a decision taken to get more directly involved with the music.

Much of the equipment is new – the Prophet 5 synthesiser, the Sequential Circuits poly-sequencer and the Emu Systems Emulator – and will eliminate many of the smaller, less efficient electronic units they have used until now. They have spent time breaking in the equipment prior to the tour, when it will be used live for the first time. 'Ultraviolence', 'Blue Monday' and 'The Village' are some of the working titles so far completed.

New Order are from Manchester, England, came out of (in fact are synonymous with) Factory Records, the company that still maintains total independency, marketing its productions through global replicas of itself, first as Joy Division (when they got praised by the British and American press) then, in 1980 (after the death of their singer, Ian Curtis) as New Order. They rose in 1977, inspired, like many, by the Sex Pistols, and did not become punks (Adam and the Ants, and Siouxsie and the Banshees, came out in a similar way at roughly the same time). First influences were the dole queue – probably hardly contemplated in Australia, but dragging at the barnacled hulls of the old countries – European machine rock (Kraftwerk, Chrome, Can), Captain Beefheart, the Velvet Underground, Jim Morrison, American novelist William Burroughs, and time and place. Their first sound was raw, expressionistic, personal, anguished. (American rock critic and writer Robert Palmer dedicated his book *Jerry Lee Lewis* to Ian Curtis). Their first album, *Unknown Pleasures* (Factory, 1979), went to the top of the UK Independent Charts. A single – amidst a prolific outburst of singles and limited releases, re-releases/mixes that then found their way – called 'Love Will Tear Us Apart'/'These Days' (1980), reached number eleven in the UK National Top 20. The same song dented the Oz and New Zealand national charts later in the year (reaching No. 1 in New Zealand). Ditto 'Atmosphere'/'She's Lost Control', a high chart entry over here. An equally successful second album, *Closer*, appeared in summer, 1980.

As New Order, the band released *Movement* in 1981. Musically uncertain, it both looked back and showed a more melodic sound open to new influence that has developed into the black, New York-inspired sound of New Order today. In the same year came three singles – 'Ceremony'/'In a Lonely Place', 'Everything's Gone Green'/'Procession', and 'Temptation'/'Hurt'. Some recent history is the formation of Gap, the band's new Australian record company, and Eddie Zimblis & Co., who promote this tour (Zimblis's first band, touring earlier this year, were Manchester band the Fall). After their tour, New Order make their third visit to America to do two New Year dates at New York's Danceteria, and do more recording.

After delivery of the above to Clinton, I phone home, discovering to my dismay that my kids, aged ten and twelve, have been packed on a bus to a coach station in Manchester two hundred miles away, where I am supposed to be meeting them. They have no house key, no money, no food and no comprehension that I won't be there.

The timelessness of the studio, the infectious casualness of New Order and the drugs, have played another a trick – only far worse than the last one. It is the first time that I have *ever* forgotten them.

Panic-stricken, I make several long-distance calls, managing to make a temporary arrangement.

3:00pm

Everything in here is intensely felt, as though we are in a bubble adrift in a vast city. How many other strange, musical craft like us are out there, I wonder, each trying to create a new music, a new reality?

In the vacuum, where image is lost almost as soon as it is made, where everything seems not to happen, but does, where the ringing brain listens to the show that only noise will take away.

Mark Johnson, not the tape engineer but the author of a forthcoming book about Joy Division, has arrived, and I try to avoid him, to dodge being questioned. But my reticence is picked up on by the band who have been reminding me of this 'imminent' encounter for several days beforehand. Mark has dropped by on several occasions to garner material. A delight is taken in letting him know – at first with small hints dropped here and there – why I am here. Two alleged writers together at the same time! New Order move in for the kill.

Mark wants them to allow him to include a flexi-disc of Joy Division tunes in his book and I sense trouble. From the off-go his rather presuming manner has antagonised them. He has been questioning them for months, and now he and I have been introduced to each other it is obvious that he is considered to be a pain in the neck.

They deal with him humorously. He is doing the book for Proteus Books, which coincidentally is Michael Brecher's company for whom David and I packaged David Bowie and Led Zeppelin books last year. I look at his manuscript, a highly detailed, conscientious work containing almost every known fact about Joy Division's performances, more or less in its finished state. It is what every band who make a name for themselves have bestowed upon them, whether they like it or not. It goes with the territory. If Mark could just climb down off them for a moment, stop treating them like idols and relax with them somewhere, the going might be a lot easier for him. But it is not in his nature and by now too much water has gone under the bridge. He gets nowhere with his flexi-disc idea and is none the wiser as to why.

Before he leaves he reads a copy of my original press release and kindly corrects my use of Barney's surname. It is not Albrecht, but Sumner. Barney read the release, but either didn't notice or wasn't bothered.

My head has been hurting all day, and the *RAM* article has taken it out of me. I edited it from a much longer piece, which had been more experimental. After reading it, Clinton is very polite.

I should be at home with my kids, back in Manchester, where others have to pay for my indulgencies. From the beginning (and it will continue to be until the end) this project has been carved out of time that I do not own. It is an impossibility I have made real, a dream I have managed to find no convincing reason for.

Still speeding on those yellow tablets (no sleep last night – Barney, Minu and I up talking till the dawn, till she had to leave).

9:30pm

Malcolm Whitehead (Ikon Video, Factory's video wing) is supposed to be arriving today after filming at Heaven, to show the band what he's got, but so far hasn't shown.

They are still having problems with the synths, but Steve tells me he thinks they've now solved the mystery. They just have to get it physically fixed.

Hooky and I leave to get food – a choice of pizzas, or chicken and chips. He is dressed in his regulation tight jeans and black biker's boots – a slightly agitated energy coming off him. They are suspicious of Mark's motives, he tells me, airing their misgivings. The book has its merits, but they worry about being taken advantage of and being made out to be something they are not, for ends that conflict with their personal views.

When we return, Clive James is on Channel 4, introducing televisions from Japan that talk to their owners with sexy electronic little-girl voices. Everyone is watching, spell-bound.

The band finish early and as we wait for Malcolm in the games room an impromptu strategy meeting takes place. It is the first time I've seen New Order so concertedly planning since the meeting in my flat to view Malc's completed film. Rob and Hooky think Barney should start putting down the two vocals that he's got lyrics for instead of waiting until all the tracks are completed. Rough lyrics exist for '5 8 6', 'We All Stand' and 'Ultraviolence'. The latter two are thought to be a bit sketchy, as Barney has been making up the words as he goes along. So the two tracks will be either one of these plus '5 8 6'. The tally still stands at five completed tracks – in ten days.

When it becomes clear that Malc isn't going to show, we set off to Heaven, London's first mainstream gay club, opened not long ago in a huge space under the arches in Villiers Street in Charing Cross.

It is a special Halloween night and a costume competition is being held. The club is filled with Virgin Prunes fans, showing Minu's hand. Factory Ikon films are supposed to be being shown in the bar upstairs, but no one manages to catch them.

It is like the metaphorical world of Michael Moorcock's *Dancers at the End of Time* novels – highly stylish, the immortal inhabitants of an era where 'entropy is king and the universe has begun collapsing upon itself' confidently drawing on the wardrobes of history. The tenor of the 1980s actually makes it seem like the end of history. Downstairs the music is new wave, heavily disco. As I watch these angels and pantheists I think their dynamic is indifference. Rock'n'roll, direct, hostile, exhibitionistic, confrontational, has been transmuted. Fear of the world ending has been suspended, at least for tonight. It is a place of escape, rather than a cauldron of rebellion as it would have been in the sixties and might still have been in the seventies had not the competition for jobs started to get harder and people become frightened of being put out of work. The one intrusion of genuine danger happens in the palpitating menace of the Prunes' music, which throbs from an empty stage when we arrive. We have missed them.

After her work there has finished Minu travels back with us again to hang out. Stateless and homeless, it is what she does.

Back at the flat, Rob gets her to wait on him. She copies Gillian in what is now in danger of becoming predictable, putting something horrible in his food, which he eats, apparently happily, while we settle down to watch home movies.

The band are being interviewed by a blissfully un-savvy Irish radio DJ who is coming on with promo patter, delivering one too many 'shocks'-to-the-floor – metaphorically speaking. The DJ senses something and attempts to change from standard hype, but too late: New Order have taken over his air space and have talked him into playing two tracks off an Iggy Pop live bootleg they've brought along, 'just in case'. One of the tracks is a recording of Iggy's audience who are hooting, jeering and whistling while he attempts to play them a . . . *slow* number.

Asked by the DJ whether they will ever leave Factory for a bigger label, Hooky, who has brought out a camera and has started filming them being filmed, says there would be no point unless they decided to control every aspect of their product. Who does their covers, the DJ asks Barney. Factory do, he replies. The covers have to be exactly right, he adds.

When the DJ asks Hooky why he likes the track they have chosen to play, he replies with feeling: 'Because it captures a moment'. Like this home movie is doing, he could have added. It is a unique moment and is followed by some outdoor footage taken by Steve of skylines, tree-branch matrixes (at one point a match flares suddenly in front of branches) – apparently random scenes, shot in Wales.

Barney makes a point of telling me that the name Albrecht, which he used in the band's earliest days, is his mother's name. But it stuck, and was never updated by the press.

Monday, 1 November 1982

In the car, for the last two mornings New Order have taken to playing a taped conversation with Mark Johnson, music journo Dave McCullough and Joy Division photographer Paul Slattery, in which Mark attempts to defend the band against McCullough's angry attack in *Sounds*. McCullough had gone to interview the band after Ian Curtis's death and been frozen out.

In the street outside Britannia Row, a parked Renault with its side-window smashed and contents ransacked belies the new arboreal street landscaping with its attempts to improve the rather drab semi-industrial, semi-council-estate environs, proving the sense of menace I felt on my arrival. The car door has swung open and perhaps the attack occurred only moments before we arrived. Further down the street, a second tell-tale pile of glass litters the pavement, the traces of another hapless victim. As it's my turn to get the takeaway toasted sandwich breakfasts, I pass the Renault again on my way out, where a window-screen repair van is now parked, and the woman owner and the fitter are examining the damage.

Barney crashes out on the sofa, eats and then gets a carton of fresh orange and a bottle of Pernod from the office fridge to 'clear his throat', before doing some speed. Later, he says, he plans to do some acid.

The band still seem very unhurried. As I prepare to leave for my train, Barney casually asks me to bring books back with me – '*interesting* ones,' he says, with a knowing look. At my frown, he sheepishly explains, 'So I can get ideas for my lyrics'.

'I know,' I reply, reminding him about the Wells book, which seems to have disappeared.

Hooky drives me to Euston. On the way, we pick up a local kid who has befriended the band. New Order left the studio early last night, the kid volunteers. Hooky says they are taking it easy before the twenty-three- or twenty-six-hour flight to Australia. Asked who presses their records, Hooky replies that they use a London pressing plant. There are none in the North and only a few in Scotland. After we drop the kid off, Hooky tells me that when he first parked his Mercedes in the street the boy had warned him that the local smash-and-grab kids had their eyes on it and he should park it elsewhere.

On the train back, I am tired. The weather has been fine during the week and is still not cold. By the time the train docks at Piccadilly, it is raining and I take the train to my mother's house in Altrincham, where my children will soon be brought to me.

I have to wait a week before the live-in baby sitter I have arranged will arrive. Bitterly frustrated I am plunged back into the affairs of Savoy, when I really want to be back in London. On my first night home I have a dream that I am being judged for a sex crime I cannot remember doing. I have never, in real life, committed any

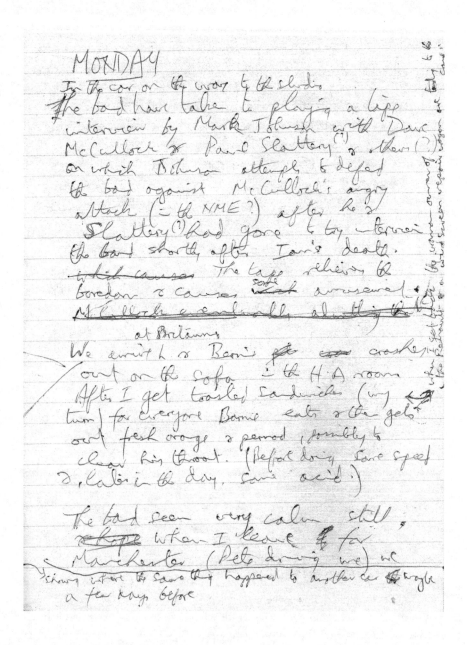

From the second notebook. We are in Bernard's Mercedes on our way to the studio from the Kensington flat, with Hooky driving. To pass the time, we listen to a tape of Mark Johnson's interview with music journalist Dave McCullough and Joy Division photographer Paul Slattery. Mark, who is in the throes of writing *An Ideal for Living*, a book about Joy Division, attempts to defend the band against an attack by McCullough. Hooky later drives me to Euston to catch a train.

such crime but in the dream my offending organ is the 'object manifest' of my identity, of the vital force of who I am, and my punishment is to have it removed. Breaking in a panic through the press of people in the courtroom I make my escape, but not far from the court I take a wrong turn, down a dead-end and am trapped. My pursuers push into the narrow thoroughfare behind me. Putting up no struggle, I am re-arrested. When I awake I decide the dream is an allegory of what has happened to me. I have been thwarted by the real world in my cultural pursuit. It is not a new revelation. I have always known that to bring anything new into the world – anything that goes against the grain of the nine-till-five mill – is the hardest thing you can do.

Malc still lodges on the top floor where he made the Joy Division film and where my mother excitedly met Tony Wilson. Apparently he filmed at Heaven after all. He has just returned from London, he tells me, but 'for several reasons' he's feeling shadowy. So we probably just didn't *see* him, then! But I'm not convinced. He is in a weird mood and if he was feeling 'shadowy' then we didn't see him for the simple reason that he wasn't there.

As he reads my notes, sitting in his room, he breaks off with sudden good humour: 'Why, the bastards! The *Caligula* tape [in the Basil Street flat] is mine! Barney stole it from me before they went away! The little *rat*!'

Mark Johnson has written and his long, neatly typed letter lies on Malc's table. Having drawn a blank with his flexi-disc insert idea he has taken up a suggestion of Rob's to use interview material instead. With Rob's 'help', he can get round the problem of direct official involvement with the band and wants Malc to enhance the sound-quality of a tape he has provided. He has enclosed a sheaf of carefully typed transcripts to act as guides, together with an offer of £100.

Toying with the offer, Malc has decided he will accept it, but on the proviso that he is allowed to mix the tape. But, ever contrary (sometimes to the point of Manc bloody-mindedness) he decides the interviews will be edited as a cut-up. Even if by some remote chance this condition pleases Mark, I think to myself that it won't in a million years get past his editor at Proteus Books. So for Mark, once again it is a no-no.

Malc's strange humour and level of agitation makes me detect something bleak. He eventually tells me he has decided to quit Factory and go it alone. I am the first to know, he confides. But this is nothing new. It is actually a re-run of his intention precisely a year ago to quit Factory, which he eventually decided against doing. At the time, a year ago, I couldn't see why he wanted to leave. This time I can see there are fewer reasons why he should stay. Archiving the bands appearing at the Haçienda and before then at the PSV club in Hulme, where Tony Wilson and Alan Erasmus started putting on Factory nights, is no longer a challenge to him. The other way of looking at it, I think, is that he is retiring at the beginning of a successful career. All has not been well at Ikon for some time, with some of the other directors becoming disillusioned by Malc's increasingly erratic style.

'Factory is a factory,' I pronounce, playing Devil's advocate. 'You go along with it until something better comes along. Not jump now.'

But his mind is made up. He has the contacts and experience that he didn't have a year ago. He'll have more time to devote to managing As Deviants Stagger (one of the bands using our Starplace rehearsal room) and to *Peterloo*, the full-length feature film he plans to make about the nineteenth-century Manchester massacre. He braces himself to ring Rob (one third of Factory).

Saturday, 6 November 1982

Malc and Rob are like weary lovers, who go back to their time as airport baggage handlers. Malc tells him that he wants to leave and why; what else he wants to do and why it's nothing personal. Rob listens at the other end of the line – I can't tell whether sadly or resignedly – and asks him if he's sure and whether there's anything he can do. Finally, Rob wishes him luck, promising he can still number New Order among his clients. In response to a possibility that raises itself he comments that the band have a favourable, water-tight contract with Factory so there would be no gain at the present to setting up their own label.

Mike Scott, from As Deviants Stagger, and Michelle, formerly with Hooky in Doppler Effect, arrive. Mike pays me his band's rent for rehearsal space above Starplace, our Oldham Street bookshop. Since being back in Manchester I have overheard envious talk about New Order's Emu Systems Emulator, and there is now more of this. Malc says that Barney is always trying to find sounds to put through it and suggests to me the sound of breaking or clanging bottles.

The harsh sound of breaking glass was the sound I wanted to extend, electronically, seventeen years ago, to make a backing track for *Stick*, a film about a satiric character of the same name, of microscopic size, the opposite of the two giants, Gargantua and Pantagruel, that Rabelais set loose on the world. The film would have had an 'insect-eye' of screens massed together, each a picture of Stick's face . . . backed (as I now re-imagine it) by the Emulator sound of breaking glass.

For Hawkwind's autumn tour, presently underway, I am told their lighting man has arranged a backdrop of television screens, each flickering with silver-and-white images, often multiple, sometimes split – silver faces, nuclear spirals, mathematical patterns, stars.

'No, you're not leaving Factory.'

'Yes, I am.'

'No, you're not.'

'Yes, I am.'

'No, you're not.'

'Yes, I am.'

Ginger – Howard Jones, Haçienda manager – and Malc at the Haçienda. The depth of blind refusal on Ginger's part to accept that he is leaving seems to touch a nerve, for when we travel back from the Haç later in our taxi, Malc seems less certain about his decision. Dermot, his Factory cameraman and roadie, who has only recently entrusted himself to Malc's tutorage, has been going around slightly dazed at the news, wondering about his future – too inexperienced to be hired in Malc's stead, redundant if Malc leaves.

Sounds for the Emulator: expanding/contracting metal; creaking rigging (for a restful, old-time feeling); a noisy bar; frog-bat cries as they swoop on their prey.

Monday, 8 November 1982

Wait in for my child minder to arrive, then get myself back on the train, anxiously waiting to hear what I have missed.

6:20pm

London, Euston main line. Northern Line. Four stops to Old Street. British Rail. One stop to Essex Road. Already I feel the tension in me as I approach the studios – a worry that is to do with the silly anxieties everyone experiences when joining or leaving friends. I doubt my ability to make the right greeting, or say the right goodbye, to each one of them in turn. The problem, I know, is an imaginary one, for the band will accept me just as they accepted me before. But it takes a tremendous resolve, for this negative energy is about as deep and unknown in me as the winter dark that has now pressed up against the buildings – a damned darkness, like a snarling dog, which drugs will only temporarily whip back.

Wind-blown streets, damp stones and there it is – Barney's Merc looking like any other car in the narrow street full of parked cars and maple leaves scurrying in the mild air. As though on cue, Barney emerges from the studio door and my shyness instantly leaves me. He is on an errand to get fish and chips for the band and crew, and catches me leaning against a brick gatepost doing my Byron bit. I add my own meal to the order.

Inside, there is still the atmosphere of warm timelessness, where Steve greets me affably, Hooky is horizontal on the couch, Rob is playing space invaders and Carl Sagan (or 'Kermit', as Steve nicknames him) is on the telly. Space sounds warp the internal galaxies. Spiral time of evolution, which can be *felt*.

Nothing has changed here since I left, after all my worries.

I ask how it's gone. It hasn't, Hooky says cheerfully. Inwardly, I find myself feeling relieved. Perhaps I haven't missed as much as I thought.

Barney arrives back with the chips just as *Coronation Street* comes on.

'You can see our 'ouse from here!' Hooky suddenly shouts, as the opening scenes roll. The rooftops of Salford look like the warrens of *Watership Down*.

Barney slyly draws my attention to Rob's forehead and one of his hands where two angry-looking blisters have formed, one in each place. Petros Moustakas, promoter of their recent Greek gig, who took them out to dinner a few nights ago, caused the first of these. In the drunken aftermath he introduced them to a bizarre betting game. Laying a fiver on the back of Rob's hand he asked to be allowed to stub his cigarette out on it. If the glowing end burnt through the note, Rob would win the fiver. He would get burnt, but he would win. Rob agreed. Petros stubbed out his cigarette; only what happened – Rob didn't know his physics – was that he got burnt and the fiver didn't, and he lost the money. The heat from the cigarette gets transmitted through the note straight to the skin.

Excited by the sight of flesh being burnt on a willing partner, Barney had not been able to resist taking another cigarette, leaning forward and, before Rob could do anything, stubbing it out on his forehead. No trick at all in that one.

As loveable Scouse rogue Eddie Yates comes on screen, Barney comments that Geoffrey Hughes, who plays Eddie, once offered to manage them when they were Warsaw. They turned him down because, he adds, with a meaningful look at Rob, he was too bright.

While I have been away the backings have all been done. Four or five songs have been completely finished. So a lot has been achieved. They are undertaking final dubbing and vocals.

In the Control Room, Gillian is laying guitar – a brown semi-acoustic Gibson – on a new track, a ballad, provisionally titled 'We All Stand'. The ballad is different from any previous New Order song I have heard. Barney's guide vocal – 'It's a red sky tonight . . .' – put down a week before, is slow, lazy and melodic over a creeping, slinking drum-backing that always seems to be overbalancing, throwing forward the listener, who is walking to the 'end of the road'. Gillian's guitar is haunting, slowly contracting and stretching like elastic, or else moving menacingly like a boa. She is playing fluidly, her personality unexpectedly mercurial for one so self-contained. She is happier, more involved in her work than when I last saw her. Mike and Mark (the tape engineer), who are working with her, look as though they have never left their positions since I last saw them.

Barney drops me an acid dot and debates whether to join me or not. The dot looks like a microscopic diagram, a piece of printed circuitry. I ask Steve, who is also having some, how strong it is and he says he'll tell me in an hour's time. I figure that if *they* are, I might as well go in at the deep end on my first night back.

Rob comes in and hands me a joint, expressing alarm. I ask him why. He replies because he's seen what happens to me on speed. There's no correlation between the two drugs, I tell him. But he's right. Drugs do seem to have an amplified effect on me.

I ask Gillian whether they've decided to stay on a final week, and she says 'not yet'. Mark – who is leaving on Thursday to work with Elvis Costello back at Jam – comments that they'll need the extra time and Gillian exclaims, looking worried, that it will mean they'll not be able to go home before leaving for Australia.

I pay a visit to the toilets before the acid starts and meet Barney on his way back from them carrying a tall cool-looking glass of water. That's for me! I remember Rob's concern.

In HA, when I return, Hooky is playing a light brown EKO twelve-string acoustic, which I recall seeing propped up against the sofa. He has had a style change, wearing white moccasins in place of his boots and is sporting a four-colour *The Wild One* T-shirt, which he bought for Rob. (Unsurprisingly, Rob didn't take to it.) They went on a mad spending spree on Saturday night, when he and Steve bought themselves a leather jacket each – a brand-new black one and a brown second-hand one. He breaks off and begins playing 'Love Will Tear Us Apart', which on this instrument makes it sound Japanese. They may do a bit of acoustic later, he explains.

The band assemble in the Control Room to give 'We All Stand' a critical first listen, mainly to decide how fast it should be played. Mike plays it through – fast, then slow. Gillian thinks it should be slow, the others fast. A compromise is reached. Whilst this is going on I detect a crisis of some kind building up in Rob, and I realise they're running out of dope again. He leaves to phone Ozzy.

Barney decides he is ready to lay down finished vocals on 'We All Stand' and leaves for the live room where he dons headphones. From the Control Room, we watch him through the soundproof glass as Mike plays him the track and he begins to sing. Through his cans he can hear the track, which has a guide vocal he laid down last week. But only the microphone picks up his voice. Just its raw tentativeness can be heard in the room where we are listening.

'Fucking hell!' he suddenly breaks off. 'It still sounds too slow!'

It is speeded up slightly.

In HA, Hooky is back on acoustic and confirms to me that since the days of

Joy Division – only two and a half years ago I realise with a jump, when Ian used to arrive with the lyrics – they all have a hand in writing the lyrics. It has become an additional job. The music has to be overdubbed more, in sections and patches, whereas as Joy Division they used to do songs in just one take.

Another reason they split from Hannett, he says, is because they were taking too long over numbers. They would have to do one vocal line six or seven times, whereas now, possibly, producing themselves, they are not so demanding. But they are looser and let more emotion back in again.

'At the end of the road . . . ' issues from the Control Room, as Mike gets Barney to do another take, while on the television A.J.P.Taylor, the historian who advocates internationalism as the political 'saviour' of mankind, is declaring that we are probably nearing the end of history.

Rob returns from his phone call, beaming. 'Ozzy sends his love,' he says happily.

Hooky tells me that Mark – the journalist – has been round twice since I left. Last week they had joked among themselves about opening the compressor cap on the new bike he'd bought out of the advance royalties for his book; while I was away they had gone ahead and *done* it! Mark had struggled with the bike, pushing it up and down the street to get it to go. Hooky, finally, had to go out and correct it.

The acid is not very strong, lifting and bending colours a bit, and speeding a little. Pleasant, but hardly the stuff we used to get before the police busted the two big cartels in Operation Julie, I announce. But it has done the trick, and I am 'in gear' again after being away. I re-enter the Control Room, where Barney is still getting to the end of the road. The rumbling, purring Iggy Pop drawl that I heard earlier in his voice has gone, replaced by a more 'classical' feel. On the powerful high parts there is a touch of Jim Morrison.

Hooky comes in to listen/produce and suddenly laughs as a stray thought strikes him. Whilst driving from the flat to the studio this morning, during the entire journey *no one* spoke, the result, he reckons, of a prolonged period of sheer knackeredness. Same thing happens on tours, he says. Everyone is 'up' at the beginning and gets more levelled out as the tour progresses.

I feel suddenly cold and can't tell whether it's the acid, the Control Room temperature or a general drop throughout the building.

The copy of *Caligula* they've got is Terry's, not Malc's, Steve tells me. After all that!

On Channel 4 there is a live discussion between Jeremy Isaacs, the Channel's controller, and members of the public, about Cable TV. A member of the audience declares passionately that he believes television won't reach its full potential until programmes, financed out of taxes, truly express communities. 'Get up off your arses and do it – it's down to you!' he rips into the viewers.

Cocteau Twins and Killing Joke come on next. Rob winds up Gillian, telling me in her earshot that she likes Killing Joke. Steve comments that bands like that are not going anywhere – they are the same now as they were then. Rob adds that they are well produced. They are just as regular as metal acts, I say.

Despite missing a big chunk of the session, I don't feel as though I've actually missed anything. Even though I'm living and travelling with them, and being with them every day in the studio, I hardly ever hear them plan anything. They just seem to know what to do and how to do it, when they do it. So in a sense there is nothing to miss.

It is like being inside what it is, a big experiment.

I talk to Mike about my feelings. He thinks I'm not noticing much pre-planning because no planning is going on. The arrangements were mostly done in Salford and what they are doing now – developing the tracks and giving them structure – they are working out as they go along. What I've also been seeing a lot of is them getting the sequencers and drum machines to play together, he thinks, which again is very in-the-moment work, and very hit and miss.

He says he is being kept on his toes by the band always pushing to innovate. Other artists have been making sequenced synthesiser music for a few years but this is perhaps the first time a rock band has used these techniques at the heart of their music. They are trying a lot of things that are new to them – himself, as the engineer, included. Sometimes sessions with other bands get bogged down by band disagreements or someone's inability to perform a particular vocal or solo, but this never happens with New Order. They make the most of their skills and play within their capabilities.

11:00pm

For the first time a sense of 'outside time' begins to intrude. I keep waiting for people to start to pack up and leave, as they have on other nights at this time, but there is no sign of this happening. Perhaps this is the first indication that more work remains than there are days booked. But another part of me says that it is *only* 11:06. It is not late for a studio.

Channel 4 is community/cable-orientated, and intrigues the younger generations. At the same time it is nostalgia for thirty-, forty-, fifty-year-olds (and older), who want to feel young. By comparison with the programme content, which is refreshingly subversive, the commercials seem as glib and empty as they really are. Enlightened capitalism. A.J.P. Taylor is a good spokesman, an example of how the media can help *warn*.

I take a closer look at Barney's acid tabs. They are from America, called California Gold, which makes them sound like a brand of dope. They are not printed circuit designs as I thought but various small pictures – magnified snowflakes, electronic symbols and mystical signs. He has given Steve and me only a quarter-tab each. No wonder they seem weak.

A Raymond Williams quote scrolls up the screen at the end of Channel 4's *Eleventh Hour* that says we can only grow away from capitalism and imperialism by the formation of *complex* societies. Spending too much time worrying about *death* – a thought matrix, unwittingly put in me by my disturbed father, with his advocating of health and fitness – I prefer to think, with Burroughs, that we must go the whole hog and aim to be immortal.

We drive back to the flat, Haydn playing over the car sound system, and manage to get lost travelling through Hyde Park. Whilst finding our way the band josh me, telling me it's a good job for me I didn't come back last night when A Certain Ratio stayed. They had fifteen in the lounge where I'm crashing!

We watch the second half of the Will Hay film, *Where's That Fire?*, with Charles Hawtrey. Barney and I have only ever seen the first half, as it's never been allowed to run its full course. He shows me three 'bargain' hardback books he's bought for writing lyrics – *The Greatest Disasters of the 20th Century*, a collection of fiction from pulp magazines called *Science Fiction by the Rivals of H.G. Wells* and *Ludwig van Beethoven* by Joseph Schmidt-Görg and Hans Schmidt. Hooky has managed to get *William Blake: The Seer and His Visions* from somewhere. I have brought along Hunter S. Thompson's *Fear and Loathing in Las Vegas*. Somewhere there is also *Kipps*, I remind Barney. I *know* he will like it!

Hooky turns in, taking the Beethoven with him.

The Will Hay film ends in a spermy mass of foam pouring out of Buckingham Palace. Steve puts on *Demon Seed*. They are planning more vocals. Barney says that it would be good if they could score some more speed for the session tomorrow.

Tuesday, 9 November 1982

It's 9:15.
It's 9:16.
It's 9:17 . . .

As Hooky's 'dictum of touring' has set in, the synthesised voice of Barney's talking alarm clock is now often the only voice to be heard. The quiet spreads to the car, until halfway when Barney asks Gillian if she's finished her string sequences. They have been sent a Mark One manual for the Sequential Circuits Sequencer, instead of a Mark Two, so until the new manual arrives she says she can only do certain notes. The rest will have to go in later.

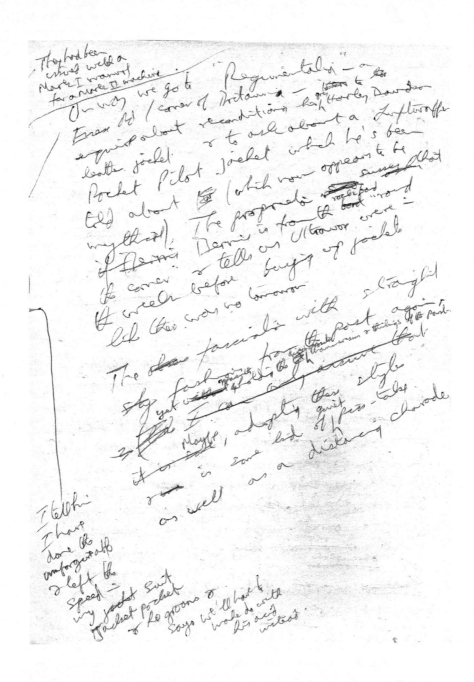

From the second notebook; in the last full week of recording. It's the turn of Bernard and I to get the toasted sandwiches in for breakfast. En route to Jim's Café, we detour to Regimentalia vintage clothing shop in search of a Luftwaffe rocket pilot's jacket that Bernard has heard is on sale. The staff can't recollect seeing such an item, but tell him Ultravox have just been in buying up their stock. He asks about having his grey Harley Davidson jacket reconditioned instead.

Barney and I get in the toasted sandwiches, and visit Regimentalia, Essex Road, on the corner of Britannia Row, where he asks about a Luftwaffe Rocket pilot's jacket he's been told about. No one at the shop can recollect having the jacket, although Ultravox were in there last week buying up jackets. He enquires about having his grey Harley Davidson jacket reconditioned.

Whilst we wait for the order in Jim's Café, Barney admits that he isn't looking forward to Australia – he'd rather have a 'holiday'. He's done another night with 52nd Street, this time at the Lyceum, and enjoyed the diversion.

'We go from one tiny box – the flat – to an even tinier box – the studio – then back into the small box and back into the tiny box,' he says.

'You don't want to go straight from a box into a tube,' I say, thinking of the plane journey. Planes, to me, always feel too much like what they are – a tube with an explosive mixture at one end.

'From a tube into another box – the hotel . . .'

'And into a window – the stage . . .'

'With thousands of people suddenly watching you . . . then back into the tube again . . .'

They will undergo eight flights in total.

I've done the unforgivable and left the speed in my suit pocket at the flat. He groans. We'll have to make do with his acid instead, he says.

They still want to get the new material on-stage, but he can't see how. When the new equipment first arrived it took them a week just to program one piece of it. The mixing will take about a week, leaving two days to do the programming. They could do with a weekend to get distance on the material, which they won't get.

'Then it all starts to sound like rubber,' he says despondently.

They have to feel, not think, whether a thing is right or not before okaying it. I say it is different with me, as a writer, because I have to analyse things, but add that I usually go on feeling first and 'verbalise' afterwards.

I say there are too many films that are effects and production and nothing else. He cites *Space Odyssey* as being weird without feeling, and therefore without reality for him. *Altered States* has effects with feeling, I say. He agrees but says that kind of surrealism/symbolism doesn't appeal to him much. He prefers to find strangeness in ordinary life, and likes artists and writers who portray this. He likes books and films that are about ordinary situations. He doesn't see why there shouldn't be recorded things that are weird in themselves, which are as strange as anything in symbolism or surrealism. I tell him that's what I think the best surrealism and fantasy is. The best exponents describe reality every bit as well as realist writers and artists, but indirectly.

Minu is a distant friend of Annik, Ian's Belgian girlfriend.

Back at Brit Row, Steve tells me dryly that they've had to return the DMX drum machine to the manufacturers and get a replacement, and now that has also packed up. He's trying to input the program for the tour – the new material as well as older songs like 'Temptation' – which got wiped when the first machine went faulty. It's the revolt of the sequencers and drum machines.

Rob is called away to the phone. His car at home, which is parked outside the Apollo in Manchester, has had its windows smashed, but nothing has been taken.

'Great news!' Gillian declares, abruptly coming in from the live studio. 'The sequencer's packed in.'

With a sardonic smile, Steve rises to fix it.

Then a key on the Emulator sticks. After tinkering, it is found to be broken and can't be repaired until the morning. A mood of quiet desperation is building in the final week of recording, with the mixing still to do.

2:00pm

Barney drops me some more acid, and the day starts for the second time.

In the Control Room, Gillian, Steve, Mike and Mark repair the tape of the number with the ironic working title of 'Only the Lonely' (now to be re-titled, 'Ecstasy'), so Gillian can overdub extra interest. She begins playing some low lively bass on the Moog, which is patched into the multitrack by Mark. She is mostly perfectly still and intent, an almost mean look on her features as she concentrates, while her crossed legs tap and her fingers play animatedly. She gets on the beat and chases it, embroidering it with light-hearted tight patterns that remind me of a game of hopscotch. She is loving, caring and I suddenly see quite clearly why Rob wanted her in. If I was that beat, I would be happy to be caught.

Rob is now horizontal, asleep I think. Steve is listening to Kraftwerk.

I keep thinking it is still morning, but when I look at my watch it is almost tea-time. I talk to Steve about sound effects. He says they got the 'broken' bottle sound on *Unknown Pleasures* by recording the sound on tape and putting it through a harmoniser, which works similar to an Emulator except the Emulator comprises sixty harmonisers instead of one. Most electronic machines used in rock music, 'tinker-toys', he says, are mainly derived from military surveillance equipment where sounds are used to make objects visible by profiling them. I ask if he defines physical objects with his music and he replies yes, by remembered experience as well.

Dave delivers new purpose-built cabinets for the Emulator and DMX, and the two pieces of damaged equipment are packed away.

In the games room, Barney and Steve play the backing track for 'Your Silent Face'. Barney has whistled where the vocals should go, and played the whistling on his melodica – a sad little sound in contrast with Hooky's happy bass, underlying the dramatic melodies of the strings. I think of shorelines and crashing surf, sheer granite walls and endless journeying, perhaps for an unrequited love. The music is a moving, living machine expressing each of the individual personalities of New Order.

They listen intently, hoping the music will evoke words. As the track finishes playing, Rob (who has awoken, or might not have been asleep) humorously chides: 'Yo, Bernie! Recovered from the past to the present?'

'From the past to the present' becomes a serious contender.

Another play-through and even more intense concentration on Barney's part. But he concludes that his reading of it is conditioned and coloured by his involvement in some element of its musical structuring. He cannot objectify – and someone else should write the lyrics to this one.

Still lying low, Rob is reading the diary I have written about them (the first notebook, now full). Barney transfers another tape to a portable player and this time listens over headphones, but the sounds of space invaders being fought off by Dave intrude, and he takes it into the isolation of the live studio, leaving Steve with the 'Cowboy' song. Rob, still reading, does his Peter Grant bit and attempts to get someone to roll a joint. Eventually, I am the one to do it. I begin to feel the weight of the studio – tireless, endless, like the song. But I can only feel it because it is coming to an end. Paranoia is creeping in . . .

Snooker with Hooky, against Steve and Dave. Our side wins, quids in . . . thanks Hooky.

Barney, Gillian and Steve take over in the Control Room. In HA, Dave breaks open a carrier bag full of fun books, which he claims aren't his. Hooky and Rob pick up the porn mags and they are looking through them when Gillian comes back in. Hooky and Dave discreetly put theirs away, but Rob hasn't noticed.

'Very childish. Some of us have grown up,' she quips.

We order Polynesian, which Hooky goes to collect.

Back in the Control Room, Gillian is working with Barney on the Prophet 5, getting the sound right on 'Age of Consent', a savage dance track, before Gillian puts down a deep alternating two-note line. It is partly overlaid by Barney's non-verbal vocal sounds from 'Temptation' and has a semi-acoustic Gibson 'banjo' strum. Barney and Mark take out the Prophet and bring in the faulty Emulator.

Bespectacled Nick, Britannia Row's soft-spoken, cost-conscious studio manager (who tries vainly to get everyone to log long-distance calls in a charge book), is showing Bernie Marsden, ex-Whitesnake guitarist, and two friends round the studio. Marsden is in the process of putting together his own band and is being sponsored by Yamaha with new equipment when it comes onto the market. Whitesnake did an album at Britannia Row last year and whilst he talks with Nick, his two friends sit and watch *The Young Ones* with us, before *Arena*'s profile of Joe Orton comes on.

11:22pm

In the Control Room, Gillian, on long shift, is overdubbing Emulator and double-tracking and putting on strings (ARP Quadra), using the faulty Emulator as best as she can. The programs for the Emulator — some pre-recorded standards supplied by Emu Systems, others recorded by the band from their own library — are recorded on thin diskettes that slot into the instrument like a disc into a computer.

Hooky has picked up *Fear and Loathing in Las Vegas* and is a third of the way through. Every time I look at him, he is reading without showing the slightest sign of humour, but rather avidly as one might a thriller or a western (which, on one level, the book is: a freaked-out western-thriller). But I wonder on what level he is reading it; if he is reading it on all its levels, how he is receiving it.

To Barney's comment that he's heard her play better, Gillian completes her marathon overdubbing session.

The day ends at 00:40.

In the intimacy of the Control Room, with its padded seating along the wall, we sit talking for ten minutes about the day. Rob lists the equipment that has broken down. Barney and Steve gather up the girlie mags. We leave through Kings Cross, with the hookers in short skirts waiting, playing in the video parlours, and head towards Euston and Hyde Park. A Ford Capri races us away from a set of lights. Hooky catches up before the next shortly-spaced set, effortlessly overtakes it and sits purring, first at the lights again.

Hooky and Gillian retire. The rest of us sit up, smoke and re-watch *Spectre*.

Having read from my diary earlier, Rob has let it be known that he is now aware that 'foreign' substances have been finding their way into beverages prepared by Barney, Gillian and Hooky. Forgetting, Barney asks Rob for a glass of orange, and when he receives it, remembers, suspects it has been tampered with and schemes revenge.

'Jaded prayer talk. Write that down,' Barney tells me, last thing.

'What for?'

'I don't know yet.'

Wednesday, 10 November 1982

Over breakfast we discuss the Manchester Police and David's imprisonment. Under Chief Constable James Anderton, the coppers have become a force of their own, raiding material from bookshops and newsagents, and then selling it back onto the market. Both Factory and Savoy have been in their crosshairs at one time or another. Hooky says he used to work in the car park at Manchester United football grounds where four policemen were always on duty, working shifts. They regarded their job as 'us against them'. Even the youngest cops regarded the crowds as animals or scum. I tell him that the Savoy bookshops and offices have between them been raided about forty times since Anderton came to power.

Near the Edgware Road, Sale Place W2, we pass Proteus Books, workplace of Mark Johnson, our journalist friend. Mark, I learn, is a bank clerk in the employ of the Proteus's associated company, Bremer Merchant Bank. His gleaming new scooter, purchased from the proceeds of *two* advances for his book – one from Omnibus Press, who cut back on titles, releasing him from his contract, and a second from Proteus – is parked in the bay at the front of the small office block.

Under our 'Savoy Editions' moniker as music book packagers, as well as the Bowie and Led Zeppelin books sold to Proteus, we also sold AC/DC and Ted Nugent books to Omnibus Press. But when we later approached them with a book about New Order, 'Miles', their editor there [one of the founders of sixties' alternative newspaper *International Times*], turned us down – so I am not surprised to hear they relinquished Mark's book. As we grandly sweep past in the big car, reflecting on how the hapless journalist has had to jump through such hoops to satisfy his paymasters and inescapably irritate New Order, I'm privately relieved Omnibus didn't take our book.

Barney and I get the breakfasts from Jim's. *This* time, to our satisfaction, I've remembered the speed.

I ask how they go about composing a song. He tells me that first they jam loosely together, lock away the resulting tape for a few days, then listen to it. 'Usually, what comes out is crap, but maybe five seconds are good. We build on that.'

No one instrument is allowed to predominate. They gradually build up an interlocking composition. Lyrics can come by listening to the music afterwards and seeing what images are evoked. Two or three lines might come at first, more or less unconsciously. After that, the process becomes more conscious. They write the lyrics on different days, not all at once, to avoid them being coloured by one mood or one train of thought only. They have never started with the words first, to see what music is evoked, but he would like to try.

They didn't write the lyrics in Salford, as ideally they would have done, because programming the new equipment had to take priority. They worked at doing that every night until 11:00pm and had never worked so hard before.

Back at Brit Row, the broken equipment has been carried away and Gillian is working out the program sequences for the tour. To find quiet, she has gone in to the live studio and is seated bare-foot on the carpeted floor, encircled by an array of equipment – pens, paper and a pocket tape recorder.

Full of renewed chemical energy, Barney is now back in the Control Room, improvising a medley of Joy Division, rock and Merseybeat tunes on his Gibson Les Paul, for overdubbing on 'Age of Consent'. The music is being patched through into the games room and fed back again for monitoring. Mike and Rob oversee him. At intervals they wander into HA to listen over the speakers there, before returning. He does several re-takes until 'it sounds mean'.

A friend of one of the office staff is moving from room to room like a foreign particle, leaving doors open and affecting the acoustics.

A copy of *A Humument: A Treated Victorian Novel* by Tom Phillips, has appeared on one of the chairs, brought in by John, one of the tape guys. Published in 1980, the book started life as playthings based on William Burroughs' cut-up methods and became 'half a lifetime's work'. Phillips designed 'found' pages from Victorian novelist W.H. Mallock's *A Human Document*, chosen by Phillips at random from the shelves of a second-hand bookshop. Using overlays of paint and other materials he formed patterns suggested by the text, sometimes highlighting certain words, other times creating abstract effects. Phillips first came across Burroughs after reading his interview with Conrad Knickerbocker in the *Paris Review*, a seminal source for Burroughs and for me also.

Everything suddenly looks brighter, sharper.

Rob is preoccupied with the arrival of more equipment cabinets and casually announces that the consignment of drugs ordered yesterday won't arrive until tonight and will be minus the speed. This news is of high importance to Barney and I, and I make a quick phone call.

The sound of Barney's guitar still being patched through is deafening, but bracing – like shards and cascades of metal and crystal. Today wearing a b/w MAXWELL 'Epilaxial Video Cassette' T-shirt, Hooky and road manager Dave, chance making alterations to the bass rack but are unable to hear themselves talking and soon go elsewhere. Everyone else leaves, so that I am now alone. Something even 'louder' than Barney's guitar has come uppermost in my mind.

In a noise Valhalla I have picked up a copy of the William Burroughs/Brion Gysin/Throbbing Gristle edition of *RE-Search* that is lying around. It contains an appreciation of Gysin extracted from *Planet R101* (*RE-Search*, 1982) by Terry Wilson. *Planet R101* is a book I commissioned for Savoy after hearing that Brion's health was declining. His work has not been properly explicated and I wanted to give him a platform. I appointed Terry Wilson to interview Brion and to assemble the book, and worked closely with him, but to my distress, in the wake of the police raids on Savoy, I had to relinquish the rights. What is now speaking to me at a volume louder than Barney's guitar is that the book appears to have been published. But how can I get a copy?

The sands of Present Time are running out from under our feet. And why not? The Great Conundrum: 'What are we here for?' is all that ever held us here in the first place. Fear. The answer to the Riddle of the Ages has actually been out on the streets since the First Step in Space. Who runs may read but few people run fast enough. What are we here for? Does the great metaphysical nut revolve around that? Well, I'll crack it for you, right now. What are we here for? *We are here to go*!

The Process, Brion Gysin, 1969

The Stockholm Monsters have written a note apologising for the delay in rent for the rehearsal space above the Starplace bookshop. They promise the money will arrive later in the week.

I join Gillian in the live studio. It is almost perfectly still and quiet in here, the noise of the guitar muted and very faint, as though heard from a great distance. Dave and Hooky have had the same idea and are working on the rack. Rob has sought refuge in here too. Gillian is still quietly working. You can hear the blood singing in your ears, notice every cough, every click, every footfall, every human rustle, even the writing of biros on paper, despite the volume outside.

The door to the room is heavy and deep, precision-hung with no air gaps. The walls are a raw grey breezeblock, the ceiling low, supported by two huge concrete pillars on either side of a stage area, the lighting sunken, the carpet thick-pile and wall-to-wall. The room is cluttered with drums, mics, guitars-on-stands, cabinets, baffles, chairs, tripods, papers, cables, a black Steinway grand piano, an organ. On the wall are two JBL speakers.

Through the thick twelve-foot-wide window into the Control Room, Mike looks remote. He occasionally reaches down to make adjustments to the desk, looking as though he is moving in a strange, faraway world.

'The reverb in here is terrific!' says Rob.

He has covered himself with Gill's coat and is horizontal. From this vantage point he talks forward to the weekend, bemusedly contemplating what they will have to undergo to get everything finished. His brief vision of this time-strip coming to an end brings another little shudder and we feel glad that, for the moment, we are still safely aboard Liner Britannia, in her sonar studio, protected by the immensity of her bulwarks.

Rob is in good form, testing, cajoling. Instead of going to sleep, as he claims he will do, he calls on first one and then another of us to assist him with cigarettes, cups of tea, joints, a blanket (Gillian's coat).

Dave once played in a punk rock band called SX and gets a ribbing for liking Adam and the Ants.

'The *early* Ants,' Dave stresses apologetically.

'Good on you!' I hear myself say.

Then Mark Johnson arrives, dressed in a dapper brown suit, and gives up his card so that I may send him a copy of my article. We talk about his book and my early meetings with Joy Division. Moving over to Rob, he asks whether the band have finally decided whether to accept his offer of 1 per cent of his royalties to use Joy Division's music on his flexi-disc. He is still not giving up. It is like watching Don Quixote returning again and again to the same windmill. The answer is still a very positive 'no'.

I lie down and stare up at the ceiling. The halogen lights shine like myriad bright jewels from their niches in the soundproofing and I can't resist the momentary feeling that I'm on a tropical beach, submerged in sunlight – only instead of waves breaking softly over the shore there is Barney's much muted guitar.

Rob gets Mark to roll a joint for him.

As we smoke, Mark moves to where Gillian is working and inevitably manages to irritate her, fishing for information. *Mark, for fuck's sake – go away!* Though she doesn't say it out loud, but politely humours him instead.

The now legendary Greek tour promoter, Petros, moves in on us next. He and a friend arrive like the Greek mob. Petros is suited, dark-haired, olive-skinned, magnanimous – a gesticulator. Seeing Rob, and reminded of the £5-note trick, he is soon regaling his friend theatrically with the details.

'It is a humorous Greek custom,' he justifies in conclusion, seating himself on the floor and making himself comfortable.

I think what a motley crew of art-scullions we are – the kind whom Rob must now have to encounter on a daily basis.

It appears that no drugs at all can be got. 'It'll have to be Alan, then.' Rob attempts to cajole Hooky and Dave into collecting it. He looks at me, pissed off. 'The last time I did this for *them* I got my third endorsement for speeding.'

Mike enters to see if Gillian fancies doing a bit of guitar – Barney has to do vocals later, and needs a break. She does and leaves off sequencing.

Petros starts a discussion with Rob about importing a quantity of records into Greece. He proposes a 'marriage', a 'beautiful relationship' between himself and Factory/New Order.

'So long as there is to be no pre-marital fucking.' Rob is serious.

Petros laughs. Of course there is no possibility of pre-marital sex, he exclaims. Greek custom certainly forbids such behaviour. Rob tries to get at why Petros wants to import from Factory when he can import direct from wholesalers. The reason, Petros explains, his voice becoming high and impassioned, is because he *likes* New Order. He wants to see the band prosper. If they strike up a trading deal he will promote their records above all other bands, whereas if he bought from a wholesaler, it would be nothing special. 'I know you don't want money,' he states cajolingly. 'I know you don't want fame. You want to remain anonymous.' Rob relents, asking him to prepare figures.

Something makes me look down at my watch. It is already 7:26. Time *is* speeding up, but really the figures have no meaning and they still just amuse me.

I return to HA, where Steve is reading and Gillian's guitar – a warm and wistful addition to 'Leave Me Alone' – is coming over the large speakers.

Steve and I doze off in skittering speed dreams.

Barney, who has been restlessly moving about the studio like a haunted spectre since finishing and seems far from tired, eventually settles, turning up the volume of the television, which has been silently showing Channel 4, waking us. It is the story of Solidarity, the Polish trade union founded by Lech Walesa. The film is carefully angled against the Red-influenced Polish authorities and soldiers of the Warsaw Pact, and has plenty of jackboot marching shots, tanks with long guns tracking up and down rough terrain, and rousing military music – part of the West's media war against the Soviet Bloc. The military hardware gets Steve's attention, and he becomes alert.

We eat a chip shop dinner brought by Barney, watch *Remembrance*, then he and I decide to return early to the flat for showers. The streets round Harrods are ablaze with Christmas lights. The air is warm, the sky dark and filled with pale clouds illuminated by the city lights. Barney draws my attention to the British flag fluttering surrealistically from Harrods' roof. He is surprised and laughing, but I can't tell whether he's pleased – proud that it's there – or just pleased by the night.

He takes two calls from New York – the first from Michael Shamberg, who runs Factory's New York office. Michael introduced Arthur Baker to them. He announces that Baker is free that week and interested in working with them. The second is from booking agent and music promoter Ruth Polsky, who has a close relationship with Stiff Records and brings bands both ways across the Atlantic. She has got prices for two hotels for New Order's New York gigs – the Parker Meridien on 5th 6/7 Avenue, at $150 per night per double room, and the Sheraton City Squire on 51st 7th Avenue, at $135. Each has a swimming pool – a requirement stipulated by Hooky – that is inclusive in one of the prices, but not in the other.

They usually stay at the Iroquois, Barney tells me afterwards, but it is full of cockroaches. He tells me they've decided they aren't going directly to New York after finishing their tour, but home to England for two weeks. That will make Gillian happy, I think.

He is still very anxious about the new equipment, which he fears may break down on stage. 'It's quite possible,' he admits, before adding: 'If it does it does, and if it doesn't it doesn't.' *Que sera, sera* . . .

The others return. Predictably, Rob asks what we have been getting up to in the showers. I tell him that it might not occur to him, but showers are for keeping clean. Some of us are on a higher level.

We get round to watching *Altered States*, Steve observing that the film is an anthropological mix of Don Juan, werewolf and other elements. I wonder aloud whether Ken Russell, the film's director, borrowed from the English writer and philosopher Colin Wilson, who writes on crime, mysticism and the occult, unintentionally opening a hot subject. Steve retorts that he hopes not. Rob agrees vociferously. Neither approves of what they see as Wilson's didacticism, nor the way – as they see it – in which he simply collects other people's ideas from literature. I'm surprised as it's the first time I've encountered this view of Wilson as *poseur*. If there's one thing that seems to unite the whole of Factory, it's hostility towards pretension and artificiality, evident in their 'couldn't give a fuck' attitude to the music industry. But they've got Colin, a working-class man from Leicester, completely wrong, I tell them. The accusation that *The Outsider* and *Religion and the Rebel* – his two best books, one examining the role of the social outsider and the other providing summaries and interpretations of existentialist thinkers – were simply 'cobbled together' is what the Oxbridge academics and critics level at him. If the books were so easy or obvious to write, why did no one else write them? And why did key establishment critics like Edith Sitwell and Cyril Connolly at first hail *The Outsider*, the debut book by a then twenty-four-year-old Wilson, as a work of genius and then almost instantly retract what they had written? Without providing any convincing reason why Wilson's work was not, after all, bona fide, the literary pack turned against him, and it is still the case. Ironically, it makes Wilson's work credible in a way they could not begin to comprehend.

Barney and I stop up to watch the end of the film and swap strange experiences. He tells me he uses speed for the guitar, not keyboards, because the latter don't involve so much body tension. Perhaps, I joke, requiring no performer, electronically generated music *needs* digital drugs to properly come alive.

Thursday, 11 November 1982

Gillian is first up, at about 8:30am – because, Rob explains lamely when he arises thirty minutes later, she has an alarm clock.

Hooky is next. Steve rolls out of bed at 9:45. Barney 10:20.

He and Hooky are now taking it in turns to drive; today it's Barney's turn. They always sit in the front, with the rest of us on the back seat. Passing Mark's blue scooter in the street outside Proteus, the car is stopped to allow Rob to sticker its seat with a Factory crack-back sticker. He jumps hurriedly back into the car.

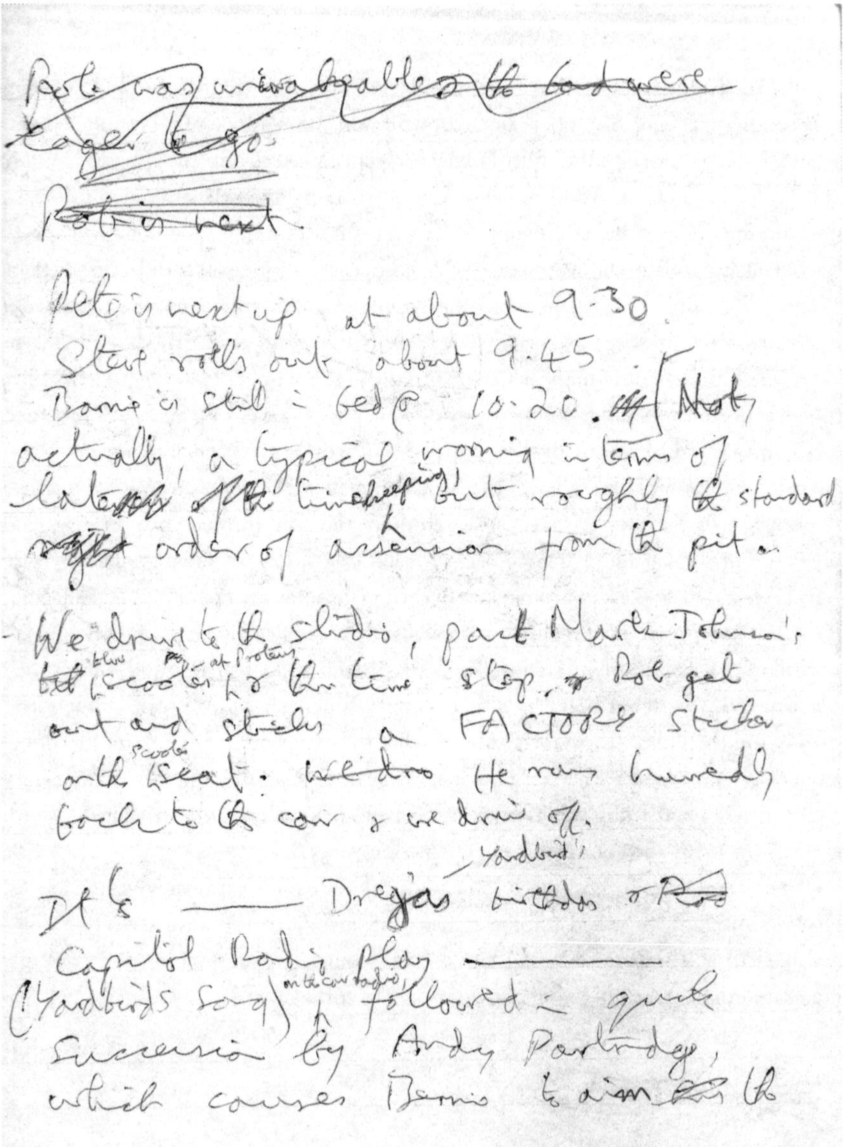

[Handwritten notebook page — partially legible:]

Rob was unavailable & the band were eager to go.

~~Rob is next~~

Pet is next up at about 9·30.
Steve rolls out about 9·45.
Bernie is still in bed @ 10·20. Not, actually, a typical morning in terms of lateness of timekeeping but roughly the standard order of ascension from the pit.

- We drove to the studio, past Mark Johnson's blue scooter (parked at Proteus) by the time stop. & Rob got out and sticks a FACTORY sticker on the scooter's seat. We then He runs hurriedly back to the car & we drive off.

It's —— Dreja's birthday Yardbird's or Rob's
Capital Radio play ——
(Yardbirds song) on the car radio followed in quick succession by Andy Partridge, which causes Bernie to aim the

From the third notebook. The backing tracks are mostly complete, ready for Bernard to begin laying down vocals (the lyrics for which mostly haven't even been written yet). The band are rising at their Kensington flat. Crossing London on the way to the studio we pass Proteus Books, Mark Johnson's publisher. His blue scooter, bought with the advance for his Joy Division book, is parked outside. As a prank, we stop the car so that Hooky can leap out and slap a Factory Records sticker on the scooter's seat, after which Bernard hurriedly drives off. When an Andy Partridge song comes on the radio he aims the car at a pedestrian, causing Gillian to gasp in alarm.

It's Chris Dreja's birthday, and Capitol is playing 'For Your Love', followed by an Andy Partridge song – which causes Barney to aim the car at a pedestrian and accelerate, swerving at the last moment and roaring off down the street. Gillian, the only one of us to flinch, gives a low disbelieving cry as we almost achieve atonement.

I am dropped off at Jim's to get breakfasts, the music papers and an *Electronics & Music Maker* for Barney. When I arrive at the studio, money has arrived from the Stockholms in the form of cash notes from their drummer Shan – a week's rehearsal rent. The good news is tempered by the arrival of a phone message, which I think at first is from Mike Moorcock, who is due to read at both Eton and Cambridge University; we have arranged to have lunch this week in Derry & Toms. But I discover it is a call from Dave, with the unwelcome news that a tax bailiff is about to move in on one of our companies. I will be needed back in Manchester next week. I will miss the mixing.

Barney is called by Mike to start on vocals. Halfway flush, I leave to get cigarettes.

When I return, Barney is at the Prophet Synthesiser in the Control Room, overdubbing more of the scrunchy, jazzy notes on 'Only the Lonely'/'Ecstasy'. Hooky reads out Johnny Waller's put-down review in *Sounds* of ACR's Lyceum gig, then breaks off. Barney's playing is too jazzy and will have to be toned down a bit. Steve agrees and Barney becomes less swanky, the notes clipped, less lingering, more shrill.

I join Rob and Gillian on the carpet of the live studio, to be somewhere quiet and 'pass the dutchie'. Rob is reading the *NME*. Gillian is quietly sorting through papers, working again on the pen-written Australian program.

I take off my jacket and boots and lie on the soft-pile, listening to my heart, its beat amplified by the strong grass. Hooky wanders in and out, still working on his bass rack, as though none of us have moved since yesterday.

2:38pm

Medical Feature, a programme about therapy for alcoholics, is on the telly.

'Only the Lonely' is being reprogrammed. It is more disco than 'Blue Monday', relieved at regular intervals by three bars and three half-bars of a low, dark reverberating wave from the Prophet.

Ginger and Mike ring from the Haçienda. Two of the doormen got beat last night. One of them, Marty, had his nose bitten off. This macabre news causes Barney to crack up and slap his thighs with excitement.

The replacement drum machine – another Oberheim DMX, newly delivered from Chase – has a fault like its predecessor and wipes a disc, losing hours of work. Chase are actually a helpful firm who attend to faults promptly, Barney says. The fault is defective Oberheim software and reprogramming it will delay things for the tour. Rod Argent, suppliers of the elusive sequencer manual are contacted, but no joy.

'It's like pushing a stone up a hill and having it constantly roll back,' Steve mutters, cutting some coke on the glass top of the Fire Bird space invaders game. It has arrived this morning from Manchester.

'Purpose-built,' I comment, nodding to the table.

Barney swaps places with Steve at the table, before starting vocals for 'Age of Consent'. But everyone is startled when he leaps up, letting out a cry of pain, his hand clutching at his left ear. He has been toying with a ballpoint pen – poking it in his ear – and jammed it in too far.

No one seems particularly surprised by this except for Barney, and Steve drifts back to the drum machine to tamper with it. Wearing a *Man from U.N.C.L.E* T-shirt, he hands me a soggy joint, looking slightly more distracted than usual.

I brew up and join Gillian at the billiard table, where the DMX drum machine has been temporarily stationed. She has got the completed program sheets, which look like graph paper, cut up, edited and sellotaped together – a long strip of paper running the length of the table.

Somebody has taken my boots, which I left in the live studio. They are not there when I look for them. I return to HA to get a confession from Rob, but he blames Barney or Hooky.

Barney is now lying prostrate on the couch, still clutching his ear. After a prolonged stint laying down bass, Hooky emerges from the Control Room and asks him if he wants to do vocals yet, but he says he is not psyched-up.

On the silent TV screen, Brezhnev has died and Russia is in mourning. We watch the soldiers in Red Square marching in their jackboots. '[The Soviet Union cannot expect] the imperialists to meet pleas for peace. Peace can only be upheld on the basis of the invincible might of the armed forces,' states Yuri Andropov, the new Russian leader.

Space Shuttle Columbia takes off, marking the shuttle's first operational flight and the first to carry four astronauts.

A note arrives from the main office. The Moorcocks have confirmed my lunchtime appointment tomorrow in the rooftop garden of what used to be Derry & Toms (and then Biba's) high above street-level in the old Barker's department store building on Kensington High Street.

Mark Johnson unexpectedly calls, dressed tonight in fawn corduroys, a greyish-yellow chequered shirt and brown wool tie with clip. He has come to confront Rob about the sticker. Nonchalantly, Rob owns up, and moves to the far end of the room to join Steve and Gillian. Barney and I notice he has left his black plimsolls behind and I quietly put them on.

To trick Barney, when Rob leaves the room I take off the plimsolls, quickly hide them and take myself to the Control Room where Hooky is laying down bass on 'Murder', a track that till now I haven't heard much of. It is another with a Beefheartian flavour, with fast-moving tribal drums and savage bass. I am just getting into this when Rob enters, wanting to know if I've got his shoes. He says he needs them to get the evening takeaways, which sounds to me specious.

'So you got yours taken, too?' I say. 'I wonder who it could be?'

He looks suspiciously down at my feet. 'Barney said you'd got them on.'

I shake my head. 'Look,' I point. Black socks. 'Barney probably mistook them for black shoes.' This seems plausible, because Barney is in fact prostrate and very tired.

'Well, *I'm* not getting the food,' Rob says, and goes out.

Ten minutes later, back in the other room, I comment that Barney is the only one who isn't doing any work who has shoes. If we are to eat tonight, he will have to be the one who goes out. He looks at me incredulously. With a knowing but uncertain look in his eyes he tells me that I had Rob's shoes.

'Well, look,' I say, pointing down again at my socks. 'How could I have done? There is definitely a shoe thief about because mine have gone as well.'

Back in the Control Room, Hooky has broken off to recount to Mike and Mark (tape Mark) that a lot of this kind of bass – in fact anything too 'risqué' – would have been played down, or edited out, by Martin Hannett.

They listen to the completed section of the track, but it isn't quite mean enough yet for Hooky. 'Evil enough, you mean?' Mike asks him, laughing. They complain they are hungry and do a re-take.

Returning to HA, bearing the menu for the Chinese takeaway, I announce that if I can locate my shoes, I'll take the order.

Hooky has now moved to the live studio and is playing with headphones so he can be monitored. I go back to the Control Room to subtly spread dissatisfaction among the ranks at this grave state of affairs. But before I can generate sufficient determination to make my shoes reappear, Barney enters with a compromise: if I take the orders and phone them through, he'll go and collect them. No shoes for me, in other words, but as we are all hungry, we agree to this temporary solution.

When the food arrives and we begin eating, the shoe joke takes a bizarre turn. Barney has the idea of taping fluted white coffee percolator filters to his feet to act as shoe substitutes. He tapes himself up, using a big reel of shiny black sticking tape about 1 1/2" wide. The filters, attached to his feet, look like baby bootees. Then he tapes one on his head.

Rob docilely agrees to be taped next, fluttering his eyelids as he is crowned with a baby bonnet. To hold the 'bonnet' in place, Hooky helps Barney run the tape round the top of Rob's head and under his three-day-stubble chin. In his pink short-sleeved aertex sports shirt, Rob could not better look the part, and everyone is soon cracking up, and money is produced. If he agrees to be filmed ripping off the bonnet taped onto his stubble he'll win a whip-round of £1 a piece. He is game. As the camera belongs to Barney, who will be doing the filming, perhaps this has been in Barney's mind all along, but I don't think even he knows where this chain reaction of ideas will lead to.

Filming starts and Rob commences a long, agonised 'strip', his face soon bright red and eyes watering with the pain. The strip eventually ends and he wins his money. The exertion fires him up and when he has finished, he suddenly charges about the room, opening his flies and trying to attack Barney. Barney brings the camera in close on the cigarette burns, still visible on Rob's hand and face, saying (voiceover), 'This looks arty'.

Mike, suddenly worried about the lateness of the hour, gets everyone except Barney and I to listen to the now completed section of 'Murder'. 'Those guitars will make the Cramps sound boring!' he declares for my benefit.

'Apt comparison, but totally untrue,' I harrumph wryly.

Barney and I are laughing so much we can't do anything except lie down in HA. The film will look great at the Haçienda, he says. We try to think of ways of taking the idea further. Suddenly seeing how I can pay Rob back for taking my shoes, I suggest we could intercut the film with a picture of an arse with balls hanging down. As there are only the two of us and he will be doing the filming, he understands what I mean and a gleam sets in his eye. It can be filmed now, on the tail end of the other film, and have its premiere at the flat later.

'I shall need a bicycle pump, then,' I say, thinking of a bicycle we've both seen and know is in the studio. Acting fast, having no desire to be caught being filmed, I quickly borrow its pump, drop my jeans, give myself several pumps of air . . . and let go to camera.

But when Barney checks the film on the camera's display screen after we finish, the images seem to have broken up. The whole film may be un-viewable, he thinks. As the others could return at any moment, there is no time to do a retake, and we slump into the chairs.

His left ear is still hurting from the pen jab and he is still worrying about it, massaging it carefully. We talk about extra-normal experiences. When they came to record 'Decades', he says, during the sessions for *Closer*, they played it in the room where we are now sitting – HA – to check 'ambience', and found an eerie whistling sound had appeared. It was about 4:00am and the weather was stormy outside. The giant Norwegian oilrig Alexander L. Kielland had just tipped over in the North Sea in the gales, killing riggers trapped inside the on-board cinema. The image of this was still in their minds and the whistling sound spooked them until they found it to be nothing more than amplified tape hiss. By a fluke, it had integrated perfectly with the music.

The tricks don't stop. Soon, the carpeted areas in common passageways and near doorways become sodden where drinks are being sloshed – water, beer, tea, coffee, orange, mineral water – so that Rob and I get our socks and feet wet, leading me to think for the first time that Rob might be an innocent party. Whoever is doing this has a very devious turn of mind.

00:35am

Rob is now making out that it is Barney who has swiped both our shoes and confides to me that he has an ace up his sleeve: he intends to purchase another pair of shoes tomorrow out of the band's money. I am still not convinced about him, though. I am unsure whether he genuinely believes it was Barney, or whether he just wants me to think that he does and is trying to trip me into confessing. Or perhaps he is just trying to deflect suspicion away from himself, having swiped mine. *If* he has hidden my shoes. Hooky was quite busy around the time the shoes went missing, but that could be convenient for him. Could it be *Hooky*?

Barney and I are still alone in HA and the others are in the Control Room. As it happens, we would have had time to re-film the bicycle pump trick several times.

'Whoever's got them,' I say, 'time's almost up. We'll be cold-footing it back tonight.' But it is a late session.

2:30am

Mike and Mark's taxi is waiting. Rob seats himself on the couch in HA and adamantly refuses to budge until his shoes are returned. No one except Barney knows I've taken them, but he doesn't know where I've put them, so I am safe. I need to ensure my own shoes are returned. It is the only leverage I've got. A stalemate has resulted. It's a kind of game – a kind of political brinkmanship – I normally hate playing, but I'm beginning to see that here it is par for the course.

Rob skins up.

So they can get home, the engineers search for Rob's plimsolls . . . and find them where I have badly hidden them, near the billiard table. It is what I feared – that someone not directly involved in the mischief would discover them – and I kick myself for not hiding them more carefully. My position is now back to what it was earlier in the day.

At the last moment, New Order make an exerted show of searching around for my shoes. Hooky tells me (rather pointedly, I think) to search inside the numerous empty cabinets. But I am not prepared to search and by so doing concede that my shoes weren't taken by any of them, when patently they were. Looking slightly put out by my inactivity, but grinning, and still shouting at me to help them look, my boots are shortly discovered – by Hooky.

I now suspect Hooky, Barney and Rob, in that order – the reverse of before. But it does not look like I am going to discover the culprit. It was all three equally, I decide, but Rob slightly less equally I now conclude. Which is now a little unfair on him, because of the film Barney and I made.

Back at the flat, it *does* play. The film cuts from Rob charging at Barney straight to an erupting sphincter. As planned, unless I'm kidding myself, it does seem like Rob's. Barney has zoomed in on it, and it looks like a hideous, sightless, trunk-less thing roaring out into the world. It gets twelve action replays before our rib-cages fall apart and we tire of it.

Friday, 12 November 1982

As work takes its toll, the nights get later . . . but the mornings get later, too, so there is really no saving. Today we lie in until 11:00am.

While we are listening to Rob's choice of breakfast music – tracks by the recently re-formed Clock DVA – the apartment manager drops by to say New Order's tenancy ended last night. Rob negotiates a further week. They may leave next Wednesday, he thinks.

He and Hooky discuss the band's single. It will probably be differently mixed versions of two tracks from the album, one of which may be 'Blue Monday'. Rob favours 12" and 7" formats, but Hooky isn't prepared to kowtow to the industry, so they agree on just a 12".

There is now no chance of getting an outtake single released in time for Christmas. Yesterday, they overdubbed four bass and two keyboards, a good work total considering the equipment failures.

I leave for Derry & Toms (as I still prefer to call the Kensington department store) to meet Mike Moorcock and Linda Steele for lunch. We are meeting in the restaurant at the Rooftop Gardens, which have become part of the literary mythology of London due to featuring in Mike's 1971 anti-Vietnam Jerry Cornelius war novel, *A Cure for Cancer* – in which Jerry arrives at the gardens by chopper and stylishly machineguns the patrons. The gardens are a favourite haunt of Mike's and he returns to eat there when the mood takes him.

Today the gardens are windswept, littered with leaves and dripped on by a grey sky. Mike and Linda ring to say they will be late and I'm left among the flamingos and peacocks trying vainly to nurse a sidecar.

But I have to order another drink, as Mike and Linda are now over an hour late.

Whilst everyone else is eating lunch I am alone in the reception area, watching the sun break through the clouds, illuminating the few gold-and-grey leaves that are still attached to a horse chestnut tree. The wind catches the leaves so that they stream horizontally, flashing like a quick-moving shoal of fish.

They have invited me for lunch, but I also have the vague notion of a possible meeting between Mike and New Order. Hawkwind, a band Mike often performs with, are touring and will play tonight at the Hammersmith Odeon. As Mike is likely to appear on stage I am hopeful of getting Steve and maybe Hooky to come along and meet him.

The band have had brushes with Hawkwind throughout their careers. Joy Division played on the same bill with Hawkwind and Public Image at Futurama, the world's first SF festival, in 1979. New Order supported Hawkwind at Glastonbury in 1981.

I have let Steve know that Mike and Linda may be going and he responded that possibly he and others will go if they have time.

But Mike and Linda are flustered when they arrive – made late by Linda's wilful hairdresser who has delayed her with his fashionable cut – and they are still unpacking after their move to London. Will they be turning up for Hawkwind, I ask? Mike is unenthusiastic. He would like to meet New Order, but if he attends the concert it will mean he will probably have to appear on stage and he's just not feeling like it.

After lunch, we stroll about the gardens, which for a rooftop are extensive. Parts are like a walled garden stocked with full-grown trees and shrubbery, flowerbeds and lawns, ferns and ornamental urns.

We leave by taxi – I for my tube, they for the Hyde Park Ascot where they are staying until the flat is ready. It is now the rush hour and on the Underground at Paddington my sense of existing in a contrary realm to the workaday is reinforced as I find myself in the opposite flow-stream to the commuters who, while I am trying to get in to the city, are trying to get out.

It is a relief to find myself once again on the narrow row leading to Brit Row – the street has assumed almost talismanic properties, signalling familiarity and certainty – and re-enter HA, where an early black-and-white film of the Animals playing 'House of the Rising Sun' is playing to an empty room. Half of New Order appear to be absent. Only Barney and Steve are at work with Mike in the Control Room. Rob and the others, I discover, have gone to Kelly's to pick up the repaired synths.

After they return I learn that the driver from Britannia Row has been sacked for a long list of driving offences and accidents, and a new driver found out of necessity. The best – or rather the worst – incident happened on the way back from a Rolling Stones gig during the summer when the driver in question had been following the path made by a speeding emergency ambulance through the congested streets. He'd mounted pavements and knocked over a policeman attempting to halt him.

Barney is laying vocals on 'Your Silent Face', composed by Barney himself yesterday. But he is stopped partway through by Mike, who declares he is flat. 'It should be more harmonic,' Mike suggests. Barney is talking, when he should be singing.

'That's the trouble with music,' Barney's voice comes over the Control Room's speakers from the live studio. Through the glass he looks ruffled, one of the earpieces of his headphones hanging off the side of his head.

Another wet joint from Steve . . . Sadly, he cannot make it to the Hawkwind concert tonight either, though he has been looking forward to talking with Mike M. He is just too pushed.

The Rod Argent manual for the drum machine has arrived, he says.

Yazoo are now on. They are on Channel 4's *The Tube*. Terry is reading Hunter S. Thompson.

Barney tries the song all ways – singing, talking, whistling. He discounts talking altogether because 'I sound like a twat'. Singing makes the song sound too much 'like the Beatles'. Whistling is too much like the inside of a 'barber's parlour'. In the end they decide to move onto the next song, 'Leave Me Alone', written yesterday by Steve . . . but Steve discovers he has lost the lyrics. He must have dropped them on the way to the off-licence earlier.

Hooky, Terry and I collect pizzas and stop off at the pub. Terry regales me with his adventures on the road. However wild his stories, they are essentially about how good he's been at getting the gear to gigs on time in working order. Hooky playfully interjects, relating times when things didn't go *quite* according to plan, despite Terry's best efforts.

'Well, when it hasn't happened as it should, it's not been my fault!' Terry declares flatly.

After eating, all except Gillian, including Rob, gather together in the Control Room to work out lyrics for 'Your Silent Face' . . . and new ones for 'Leave Me Alone'.

Gillian has gone back to programming the equipment near the billiard table ready for their tour. She has already finished the drum machine and is on to the Emulator and synths, inputting sequences from some of the completed backing tracks.

Terry brings tea and coffee to the scribes, but he hasn't taken Barney's order, and asks what 'Boy George' wants, to laughter all round. Barney looks up astonished. Terry bashfully puts the blame on Gillian. He claims she told him she had seen a picture of Boy George in the *NME* that reminded her of Barney. Rob pipes up that he saw a picture of Boy George in the *Melody Maker* that reminded him of Gillian (who is out of earshot). For a band who have produced such genuinely tragic and doomy songs they are piss-takers supreme.

While his space has been taken over, for a rare moment Mike has been able to join 'the other side', and has flopped down in the games room.

There is no time left to compose linear lyrics, so lines and words are pulled out of books and magazines almost at random (Gogol, Scott Fitzgerald, Phillips' *Humument*), even from old Joy Division and New Order lyrics. 'But no *Kipps*,' I comment to Barney in frustration. 'Where's that book I got you?' They spin new lines off the words and phrases they pull out, and link them, until they 'fit'.

'They always tell us we write shitty lyrics so we might as well do it like shit!' Barney comments sardonically. He reads out one of the composites: 'Leave Me Alone'. 'Actually, it's half-way good.'

'Uncle Bill [William Burroughs] will be proud,' I tell him.

After three weeks in the studio it is starting to feel like we're on a conveyor belt. The smooth flow of time is breaking up.

'It reminds me of being in New York,' Rob says. 'Disorientation from being tired.'

Tiredness builds up like a dam.

Barney takes a dab of speed. He says to Rob that the vocals will be completely laid down by 8:00pm tomorrow night. We say nothing.

He picks up a bottle of Audax analgesic eardrops from the table, lies down with his head on the arm of the couch, his injured left ear pointing upwards, and sticks the dropper inside. Rob puts some in his own ear.

Steve suggests a line of coke.

Then, back to composition. Rich, exotic and suggestive phrases emerge. But they are discarded in favour of simple, plain lines.

From my head to my toe
From my feet to my nose

Adlibbing, free-associating absurdities, obscenities, piss-takes, even farts.

We decide the general malaise must be because the dope is too weak. We roll one joint after another. It is 2:33am and Barney sings 'Leave Me Alone'. He lays the vocal in sections, led through it by Mike. While he is singing, Rob and Steve throw Maltesers at each other.

I return to HA with Mark (Elvis Costello didn't need him, so now he's ours for the weekend) to talk with Gillian, who has been working in solitude for about four hours. It is Mark's birthday, and tomorrow he will get his first experience with a new digital master-tape machine the studio have ordered. Gillian and I listen politely, secretly just wishing he'd flash his fags.

Steve's coke is the pick-me-up we've all needed and shows just how wrong you can be to follow your common sense and not your instincts.

There are two vocals and just a few Emulator overdubs to lay down – 'Crawl, crawl. I hate them,' Caligula's cry from the 1979 film, is one of these and it goes on 'Murder'.

'We've done some shite today,' Rob says, on the way back to the flat. 'These mugs will lap anything up if they take this.' No one can be bothered to respond. We ride on in silence.

'Well, what are we doing about tomorrow, Hooky?' he demands. Hooky tries to collect his thoughts, thinking he means work, and starts to speak. But Rob interrupts him: 'I mean, about the *dope*? I mean, if it really is no good?'

'Its quality is a foregone conclusion,' I comment wryly.

At the flat, Steve, Barney and I can't sleep, despite being tired and stay up talking until about 6:00am. The final bits of recording will be done tomorrow. We run through the *Caligula* tape. Barney suggests they should do the mixing at low volume, then play back at high. Mixing at high volume can result in top-sound being lost. They have worked harder and longer on this album than any other. It would be madness to lose their efforts in the mix, he says. With tiredness, earache and deafness to contend with he too is concerned about the wisdom of touring without recovery time.

The mixing of their last album, Steve contends, was done in the way Barney is suggesting, but it didn't really give them an advantage. He smiles sardonically. The fact of the matter is there is no more time. They will have to work under pressure, but they've proved before that they can do that. He declares the album will be a record of the moment – if it is a good moment, it will be a good record.

'Murder' sounds a bit too bland and needs something drastic doing to it, Barney thinks, but Steve disagrees. In the run-through of the film they reach the final orgy scene and the words roared out by Caligula, for sampling tomorrow.

Talk shifts to *Movement*, written immediately after Ian when they were learning new roles, before they'd found themselves. Some of the tracks Barney says he is less than happy with.

Steve and I are left alone to speculate once again how the world will end. Science has replaced politics as the Number One Instrument of Control. Together with evolution, it is bunk. Communication (the hope of mankind) might not be all it's cracked-up to be because of the impermeability of human skin. Conformity will kill the race. Atoms are intelligent.

English skinhead football supporters clad in Union Jacks storm the pitch in Perth, Australia.

Saturday, 13 November 1982

We watch the Nolans on *The Saturday Show*, the ITV morning-time children's programme that has just replaced *Tiswas*. This puts Hooky in mind of a venue they did in Manchester about a year ago when they were appearing with the Nolans. They were both using 10cc's road crew – New Order's then usual arrangement – and the Nolans were on for a week. The dressing-room conditions were appalling, with only a black curtain hung for privacy. While the women were changing, the road crew discovered they could watch them through the curtain, and did. They went on watching them for the full week.

Gillian is wearing all black – a one-piece black suit, her fishnets and heels. Barney now can't hear anything at all in his ear and is prodding it with cotton wool buds. *Spectre*, *Caligula* and *2001:A Space Odyssey* are packed away.

Even the levels of weak dope are now perilously low, Rob announces solemnly.

I am dropped off at Jim's for toasted sandwiches – five bacon, three egg-and-bacon, two sausage and one egg.

It is now 1:00pm – another late start. Mark Johnson has arrived, dressed casually on his day off from Proteus bank duties and is rolling a joint, whilst Barney lies on the couch massaging his ears. Steve is setting up the video. Gillian starts work on her sequencing, a laborious manual task.

Hooky is also all in black and I ask whether they are in mourning for the recording session. He wears a black 'Johnny's Speed & Chrome – Buena Park, California' T-shirt, black bikers' boots and black jeans. He has stuck a colour shot of Boy George on the dartboard – after Terry's re-naming of Barney – and is taking careful repeated aims.

In the *Sun* newspaper are large photographs of two tragic victims of maternal neglect and aggression – three-year-old Russell Smith, smiling in a seaside photo, stabbed in the throat and cut to death with a razor by his mother, and two-year-old Lucie 'Little Angel' Gates, burned to death in her home after an electric fire fell on her while mum was at the pub. John Ford's *Grapes of Wrath* is on the telly.

The tape of *2001:A Space Odyssey* is found to be missing from Steve's bag and, as Mark (Johnson) has a copy of the album, he races home across London to get it. He is less uptight today – more relaxed – perhaps because of the dope, and New Order are more friendly with him.

Malcolm McDowell's sexually devouring scream from *Caligula* – destined for 'Murder' – has been looped and is repeating itself. Instead of using the Emulator, which they have decided would cause the sound to degenerate too much, they are feeding it through a Sequential Circuits Pro-One monophonic synth – a junior version of the Prophet, which takes less time to set up and gives a better quality of distortion.

The scream is run experimentally along parts of 'Murder'. 'Crawl! Crawl! Crawl! I HATE them!' Spoken with such tormented angst and re-contextualised like this it seems to be directed at all humanity.

Minu, back in London, rings. One of the Prunes' vocalists has fallen ill and the tour has been cancelled, so she may call to see us.

'Requiem', from *2001*, the vinyl album brought in by Mark, is played. It is the part in the film where the strange monolith appears, guiding the astronauts towards Jupiter and infinity. Captured, it is added to 'Murder', its ascending strings transforming Caligula's cry into a primal scream of hurt vengeance. It sounds like the tantrum of a planetary species on the threshold of space, the scream driven upwards by the savage mesh of guitar and drums. Or perhaps it sounds like a blinded warrior?

A copy of Dee Brown's *Bury My Heart at Wounded Knee: An Indian History of the American West* has appeared on one of the couches in the games room:

> Scarcely were the refugees settled behind the security of the 'permanent Indian frontier' when soldiers began marching westward through the Indian country. The white men of the United States – who talked so much of peace but rarely seemed to practice it – were marching to war with the white men who had conquered the Indians of Mexico. When the war with Mexico ended in 1847, the United States took possession of a vast expanse of territory reaching from Texas to California. All of it was west of the 'permanent Indian frontier'.

More *Caligula* is taken – the part where Tiberius, before he dies, screams to his citizens: 'More conviction!' The sample is placed just after the sound of a whip-crack.

Malcolm Whitehead of Ikon, Factory's film wing, is visiting from Manchester tomorrow afternoon and wants to know if he can bring anything. He is given a shopping list: Herzog's *Fitzcarraldo*, Kubrick's *Barry Lyndon* (for pastoral effects), *The Long Good Friday* and something with a 1944 sea battle for Barney.

Michael Moorcock rings for speed and I offer to get some. He says he didn't manage to get any for his guest appearance with Hawkwind yesterday at the Hammersmith Odeon. While performing 'Sonic Attack' he fell asleep on stage. Serves him right then, I think, for going after all and never saying a word to me! We are to meet at King's Cross.

To my surprise, whilst I have been away, Genesis P-Orridge has hired a studio upstairs, where Psychic TV are making a video. The story has got out about my wanting to see a copy of *Planet R101*, and Genesis has graciously been in touch with Rob today to let him know that he has a spare copy. Apparently, he has acted as

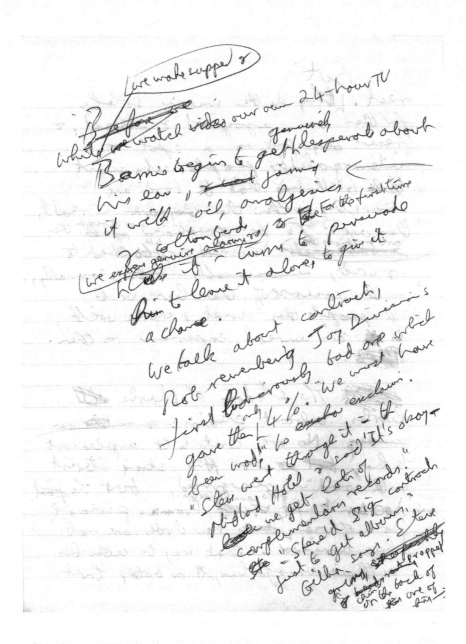

From the fourth notebook. Bernard has damaged his ear by prodding it and the situation is worsening. We take it in turns to try to persuade him just to leave it alone, but he won't. Rob tells me the details of Joy Division's first 'ludicrously bad' contract. It gave them only 4 percent. According to Rob, Stephen was the one who okayed it, enticed by the promise of 'loads of complimentary records'. Gillian comments that she's not surprised.

midwife for the book, placing it with *RE-Search*, the magazine I saw lying about on Wednesday. The run has sold out except for a few copies.

As ill luck will have it the balance of the Stockholm Monsters' rehearsal rent has not yet arrived and I have no money to buy my copy of the book off Genesis. But Rob rides to the rescue, loaning me the fiver I need, and I soon have the book in my hands. I experience a surge of pleasure, for the book has managed to end up with the best publishers on the planet. Champions of Ballard and Burroughs, *RE-Search* have cool contemporary production values and a wide cult readership. But my pleasure is short-lived. Flicking through the book I discover my involvement as commissioner is not credited. Terry has made out he is sole originator. Sadly, I conclude, the omission must be intentional.

Not wishing to spoil Genesis's generosity I do not let my thoughts out. Very grateful to him, but feeling whumped, I leave for Kings Cross. Down in the tubes, on the London Underground, are posters for *Amor*, Julio Iglesias' new album. A picture of the singer's face is propped on a table, resting horizontally along the lower edge of the poster, one arm across his mouth and chin. Only his eyes, the top of his nose and his head are visible, staring out at passers-by. Something about this reminds me of Adam Ant and I wonder whether the marketing department of the record company has taken a tip from the ant warrior.

The tube train is jammed solid with standing travellers, except for the smoking carriages. When I get off, even these have filled up, with soccer fans for the Leeds versus Arsenal game, and the tube platform is black with police. I am shepherded along, part of the mob, all the way to the mainline station and the taxi rank where I have arranged to meet Mike. I take the small packet out of my pocket and press it to him, grateful not to have been mistaken for a football fan by the police *and* done for possession.

Linda has stayed behind to watch the tennis, but the brightly-coloured lights in the darkness outside the station remind me of the time, both speeding off our heads, she and I did the Blackpool Pleasure Beach together – the Revolution, the Ark, the Wild Mouse, the Roller Coaster. When I came off the Ark a shock from my heart travelled so strongly through me that it almost threw me to the ground.

The weather has gone chill and the station is still electric with police, lights and confused motion, the concourse littered with debris. We push our way through the throng and, as soon as we are able, fall into a café where we have egg-and-chips and three coffees each. While kids try to hit us for money and steal everything visible on our table, we jokingly chat about euthanasia for non-workers. We discuss the functional use of street drugs and how the establishment has little understanding of their importance to industry and to wealth creation. Talk then turns to Linda, how happy they are together. Now she has arrived his life will straighten out, he feels.

But his children are finding it difficult. He doesn't get to see them so often now, and misses their company.

When I return the band are eating their one proper meal of the day in HA and Peter Saville and his work colleague Brett Wickens have arrived. They have dropped by from Peter's London studio to say hello. [Recalling the occasion to me thirty-three years later, Peter described entering a 'recreational area' and at some point noticing a piece of paper abandoned on the table bearing lines of writing. It struck him as odd that a different hand composed each line. That had made him look at the paper more closely and he could still remember the words: 'No hearing . . . / No breathing . . . /No movement . . . /No colours.' What had particularly taken his attention was the fact that at the foot of these attempts at lyrics for 'Your Silent Face' someone else – Hooky? – had added the facetious rejoinder: 'No lyrics!' This poignant visual evidence of the struggle New Order were having writing lyrics without Ian struck Peter almost instantly on his brief visit to the studio.]

The band have dubbed the laughter of the 'upside-down girl' from *Spectre* on to 'Murder' and are debating whether to leave it on. Hooky says it sounds like the laughing man outside the fun house at Blackpool. Someone else suggests it could be replaced with the tearful voice of the old man from the Will Hay film: 'It's no use. It's no use. They wouldn't listen to me. They wouldn't listen to me. I'm just a poor little old fella.' They decide to fade out with that.

Steve tells me that whilst I was out Barney, who is still having reservations about the song, wanted to see if the 'whip crack' sound could be improved by recording their own. They had both tried to make a whip, a drumstick, some cable and a lot of gaffer tape to join them together, but the cable was the wrong weight and texture. The resulting sound was pathetic, he said. After several abortive attempts by all of them at whip wielding, the idea ended in helpless laughter.

Gillian is programming. It is 8:06pm – past the time Barney promised Rob that he'd have the lyrics laid down. Hooky is preparing to lay down the last bass on 'Murder'.

Barney and Mark (tape engineer) are chatting. Barney is saying how he would like to create music in the studio without any fore-planning at all, to see what they could come up with. That would be *interesting*, he says.

He has taken to wearing a white lab coat about the studio and disappears in to HA to make a full round of teas and coffees. His white-coated figure reminds me of my old days technician-ing in chemistry labs. He says to me, in his drawl, handing me my cup: 'Bet you've never had a cup of tea made by a man in a laboratory overall before.' But I tell him: 'I've probably had hundreds.'

Later, Mike tells me it is his lab coat. It was his uniform, he says, when he worked on the KitKat production line at Rowntree's in York in the winter of 1976–77. I tell him that one of my jobs used to be in the quality-control labs at Halls Mentholyptus Sweets in Radcliffe, Manchester. I'd go on the production line wearing my white lab coat to takes samples, return to the laboratory, analyse them to make sure they had the right levels of menthol and eucalyptus oil in them, then phone back my results to the line managers. If the samples were 'out', then whoever was in charge on the line would make the necessary adjustments. And here was Barney, we laugh, thinking he was the bee's knees, teaching his grandfathers to suck eggs!

Psychic TV are doing a video for Riverside Studios. Barney and I go up to the top floor to see them, but they aren't in. We stare through the rehearsal room window into darkness. Barney rests his head against the glass for several moments. He described to me how he had gone up earlier and seen them rehearsing with a skull on a stick.

'They may have to be careful,' he says.

I'm thinking he means that this left a harmful effect on them in some way, but he means the room.

'There was something about it,' he says. 'Something in there.'

On the way back downstairs he tells me New Order may perform on Psychic TV's cable channel.

I'm afraid.
I'm afraid, Dave.
My mind is going.
I can feel it.
I can feel it.
My mind is going.
There is no question about it.

Hal's words to the pilot of the Jupiter ship are drifting out through the open door of the Control Room as we return.

9:30pm
It is probably my last day and I decide to forgo the keeping of my diary for a few hours and just relax into the moment . . .

12:45pm
Have been toying with the idea of doing a Hawkwind book, and have worked out a rough proposal for Virgin Books.

Minu finds me in the office. She slides playfully along the wall, waiting quietly for me to look up and notice her. I am happy to see her. She is followed by Hooky, who moderates the bright office lighting to a subdued red. Beaming radiantly, he announces that they have finished.

I ask him whether he feels relief. He says that it's not really like that – not clear-cut. When they start mixing they'll probably play around again with the sound and get new ideas. He seats himself behind the desk across from us like a rock'n'roll mogul.

More large pot plants have appeared in the room, a yucca, a weeping fig and a large aloe vera. A trailing philodendron pours down from a glass-fronted shelf unit. The rubber plant looks suitably mute in the new company. The bamboo window blind is pulled down, giving the room a snug feeling. But Minu is tired. She has not slept properly for six days, arriving in London this morning from Scandinavia after travelling for fourteen hours. She has come straight from working on the Prunes' accounts and paid them off. The tour has cost her personally (once again), but she doesn't mind. Money is only important when it is needed, she comments. She is never in one place for more than a few weeks and cannot use banks.

Hooky chats with her about the Australian tour. They think they are using Iron Maiden's PA and John Cooper Clarke is supporting them. Conversation moves to the Stockholms. She says she has heard 'Happy Ever After', the new single, several times in Europe.

Barney enters in his lab coat and pours himself a Pernod-and-orange from the fridge. He still cannot hear anything in his right ear. He is remarkably unconcerned that they have finished. In fact, apart from Hooky, New Order seem as indifferent now as they did when they started. The slight anxiety about leaving sufficient time before the flight has evaporated. Rob, Steve and Gillian are in HA, watching *The Avengers*, periodically rolling joints and rising to take dope and skins to me when it is my turn.

Minu asks Barney about the Sex Pistols – did they influence the band? He says they were the first recent band to directly inspire the ordinary kid on the street who wanted to play. The example showed that *any* kid with talent could do it. Kids didn't need big record companies, they didn't need to have experience, just so long as they had talent and were prepared to work. 'Anyone can do anything,' he had said to me on one of our cab journeys. We were going down Regent Street, lit up with lights.

Terry drops himself in one of the swivel seats and relates tales of long drives across Europe. On one of them, the time he had to drive nine hundred miles to the port on his way to England without sleep or properly eating for many days, and without money he could spend. At the start of his journey he had converted money into a convenient currency, anticipating a slap-up meal later in the afternoon, two hundred miles from the port, in good time for the boat. When he felt that he had done good time, he decided to pull over and eat, but when he came off the *autobahn* he realised he'd overshot fifty miles into the wrong country. The banks were closed, so he couldn't convert his money, and was forced to drive fifty miles back the way he had come before he could eat.

Minu is smoking. Each time we meet she says she is giving it up. She is feeling ill through tiredness, but happy in her mind. She does not usually use drugs, but I urge her to take a line of coke that Steve has just brought in. It will take away the physical discomfort, I tell her. After half an hour she says she can't feel any effects, but I ask whether she is still feeling ill. She says no.

The others drift out to listen again to what they have done and we are left on our own. I realise now what her 'illness' is.

Petros booked the Prunes with New Order for the Greek gig, which is how she met the band. She has only known them about a month. Melbourne, where New Order will play next, is the hometown of her band the Birthday Party.

'If you have fallen in love with someone,' I say, 'what are you going to do?'

Becoming suddenly more alert she says that she has decided not to see New Order in Melbourne. She has now also determined not to see them at Danceteria – when she will be in New York at the same time – or again, unless their paths cross unavoidably. She hopes I will be able to tell them when they get back from America.

We follow the others and sit with Hooky in HA. It is about 1:45am and television programmes have come to an end.

Hooky has finally swung the big axe on Mark Johnson, who'd overstayed his welcome as early as 10:00pm – perhaps having grown more confident since the afternoon when they had allowed him to help them. His one-track focus and constant questioning was made worse after he brought along David Lees, a researcher on his book, uninvited by the band.

Rob's procedure with such people – it is a speciality – is to suss them, then play with them. So someone could be making a complete arse of themselves, treading on the band's toes and they wouldn't be aware of it. But they have all grown tired of amusing themselves at other people's expense in this way, and as no one else seemed to want to tell Mark to go, Hooky took it onto his own back to do so.

'The dirty work nearly always falls to me,' Hooky tells me jovially. Fondly, he relates how he had to get rid of Mark once before, at a sound-check. Before gigs, these had become a kind of free performance for fans and hangers-on to network, but some of them used the opportunity to tape and photograph the band – taking, not giving – and the band had eventually gotten fed up. Hooky told a group of them, including Mark, that he didn't want to see them at the next gig. They could still get into the venue, but he didn't want them at the sound-check. When the band arrived at their next gig they found a somewhat smaller queue waiting to get in, the few regarded by the band as friends. But among these, Mark had included himself and Hooky lost his temper.

We talk about the motivations of fans and hangers-on. The band have fans they are pleased to see. The rest they feel neutral about. They do their music for their own enjoyment and interest as much as others, and resent being put on the spot and interrogated like machines to be turned on and off, or ideologues with a grand purpose and reason for everything.

The shadow of Mark lurks about the studio. His interest is recognised. No one wants to be unkind to him again.

Back at the flat, whilst we make supper, Barney gets desperate about his ear, jamming it with oil, analgesics and cotton buds until, queasily, we have to tell him to lay off and just give it a chance.

We talk about contracts, Rob remembering Joy Division's first ludicrously bad one, which gave them only 4 per cent.

'We must have been mad,' he exclaims. 'Steve went through it in the Midland Hotel and said, "It's OK, we get loads of complimentary records."'

'Steve'd sign contracts just to get albums,' Gillian confirms.

Steve grins, chin propped on the back of one of his hands, blowing smoke.

Sunday, 14 November 1982

It's Rob's turn for the alarm and he wakes us with tea at 2:00pm. Hooky emerges from the backroom wearing his black gear. We watch a well-made Japanese soap on Channel 4. Steve is next in the bathroom, then Gillian. Lastly, Barney, who first stands in the middle of the room, head inclined and finger twisting madly inside his ear as though he is trying to eject a demon.

We finally emerge at 4:00pm. It is already quite dark outside and wet, the starry sky of last night replaced with cloud. Malc is due at the studio to talk properly to Rob after his abrupt decision to quit Factory.

Mixing starts tomorrow, Monday, 15 November, and will continue until Thursday or Friday, when a party is being thrown somewhere in London by 'Kickboy Face', Claude Bessy. They will get a few days rest in Manchester, then fly to Melbourne for their first gig on the 25.

Claude came to the Haç from New York, straight from co-editing *Slash* magazine, a Stateside platform for UK punk bands. His party is in two parts: 'Part 1' is tonight, 'Part 2' is next week.

But I have to pull myself away. I blag another fiver off Rob, telling him to take it back out of the Stockholms' money, and say my goodbyes. Hooky, the perfect chauffer for me throughout, drops me off at Euston at 6:00pm, to be sure of me getting a train tonight.

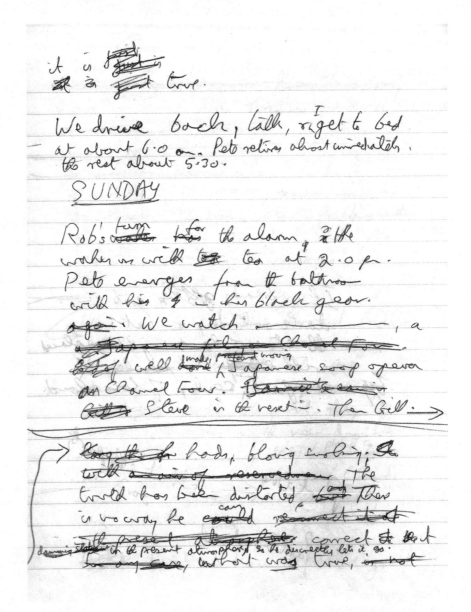

it is ~~fast is~~
~~it is~~ ~~fast~~ true.

We drive back, talk, _I_ get to bed
at about 6.0 a.m. Pete retires almost immediately,
the rest about 5.30.

SUNDAY

Rob's ~~turn~~ ~~water~~ ~~too~~ the alarm, & the
worker us will ~~tea~~ tea at 2.0 p.
Pete emerges from the bathroom
with his & in his black gear
~~again~~. We watch ────────────, a
~~a Japanese film on Channel Four~~.
~~baby~~ well made, ~~slow moving~~ a Japanese soap opera
on Channel Four. ~~Then~~
~~Then~~ Steve in the rest. Then Bill →

→ ~~long the~~ for heads, blowing smoking.
with ~~a air of recording~~ The
world has been distorted, ~~but~~ then
is no way he ~~could~~ _can_ ~~reconnect it at~~
~~this present atmosphere~~ correct ~~it but~~
~~in the present atmosphere~~, so he discreetly lets it go.
~~in any case~~, without any true, or not

From the fourth notebook. Recording is finished. We wake up at New Order's rented apartment in Kensington. It is my last day with the band and Hooky is preparing to drive me to the station.

Suitcased, typewritered and briefcased I stand on the escalators leading to the train hall above. The concourse is never free of people, day or night. I feel disorientation stirring about beneath the speed, glad that it can't surface, and sit in a freezing Glasgow train. My copy of the *Observer* tells me that President Reagan, battling to stop the Soviets building their gas pipeline, has lifted the sanctions he imposed on a European firm supplying exports of technology to the USSR.

The only ticket I have is a cheap saver return from London to Lancaster, the other half of the ticket Michael Moorcock got for me two weeks ago. [Lancaster is the closest rail station to Ingleton, from where I helped him and Linda move house]. I am not allowed to use the ticket for Manchester, even though Manchester is less rail miles than Lancaster, so will have to get off at Crewe and change onto an Altrincham line from there.

A Glaswegian soldier returning from leave, my neighbour across the table, has had £10 ripped off him by a 'mate'.

'Will you see him again?' I ask politely.

'He won't see himself – in the mirror,' he replies levelly.

I feel for the mate.

As the cocooning effect of the speed and the last tokes of Rob's dope begin to wear off, reality starts to catch up with me also and the loss of an ending to my book hits home.

The cry of 'bailiff' begins to circle around in my head like some lazy bird of prey, riding on the wind thermals, looking for carrion.

I have no doubt that there *is* a bailiff – but could his arrival be happy unhappy convenience? Surely, an 'arrangement to pay' would take just a few hours at most. I would then be free to take the next train back to Britannia Row.

But I feel that what is really being said to me is, 'Your time gallivanting about with New Order is up'. I will not be returning this time, I decide ruefully.

Mournfully, I watch as the brightly lit empty platforms of Litchfield Valley station flash past outside the train window.

My Diary ends. But as the train sped through the night my thoughts continued to jump about all over the place. Coming down from the speed, I felt alternatively depressed and excited, missing the relaxed camaraderie of the band as well as the creative high of such an intense experimental musical environment; feeling uncertain about the book I had planned, yet excited by the fact that, despite having to forego the crucial mixing stage, a rubicon has been crossed – not just for the band, but for me personally.

By contrast, the boundary I had stepped across was the threshold of a recording studio for the first time. Apart from anything else, this was to give me a new and unexpected involvement with one of the members of New Order. But before I come to that I will attempt to reconstruct what I missed.

Rob Gretton (centre) presides over the band on 1 November 1985. From left to right: drummer Stephen Morris, bassist Peter Hook, singer Bernard Sumner and keyboard player Gillian Gilbert – looking exactly as I remember them at Brit Row.

'DUB IT UP!'

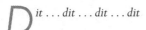

D it . . . dit . . . dit . . . dit

'Blue Monday' opens with a semiquaver bass-drum riff. A daring production decision, yet one that surprisingly works. On the eighth bar, a wah-like synth joins in, playing a quaver melody. Backed up with a 16ths delay line, it slowly fades in. A few bars of this and the entire track bursts into life.

Primarily based around a quaver and semiquaver rhythm and a I–V–III cadence, it catches your body, forcing the most unenthusiastic of dancers to move at least one bone. Then comes the killer: not content with using a kick drum as the main hook line, this band use a dotted-quaver pulse as a drum-break. It throws you off-kilter, yet somehow manages to keep you waiting for the next onslaught of music. A giant walks the earth.

Stripped down to just drums and synth bass, the band's real bass guitar enters, following the familiar cadence set out from the start. Tom-toms are also given their recognisable airing.

Immediately following another drum-break (snare this time in 16ths), a kind of orchestrated mix of synthesisers and ethereal sounds are heard, making what was initially a solid dance track turn slightly majestic.

The lead vocal is joined by a sequenced 16th synth playing triads, whilst the bass guitar plays its mandatory melody. These three elements jostle for prime position and in doing so create a sort of identifiable trinity of sound.

The track now weaves in and out of various incarnations picked from its initial chord and melody structures. A jet aircraft roars across the digital roof of our collective heads, but does not fail to keep the momentum going. Even the drum-breaks seem to have an appeal of their own. The outro is defined by the orchestral-like sounds and exits in a sea of arms-up pomposity. Perfect.

'Blue Monday' is four performers at the height of their craft, dancing, spinning, floating, stomping, prowling in a tight interlocking unit of forms; the parts, each one a virtuoso performance, interdependent but supremely free, never once 'colliding'. It is a glorious moment in time – triumphant, explosive and, above all, happy. Perhaps it is a celebration to release Ian's spirit, to set it bursting out of grey seventies and early eighties Britain, to become a joyous anthem throughout the world.

Despite its length and original purpose – intended as a 'play-out' track for live gigs – 'Blue Monday' was the recording session's obvious 12" single. It was the song that was playing when I first walked through the doors at Brit Row and the track that the band went back to time and again during my first week (even if it wasn't the first one they started work on), recording it onto the 2" wide spool of 24-track tape revolving on the enormous freestanding recorder operated by Michael from his control desk.

As practical matters dictated and ideas came, the tracks recorded at Brit Row were developed in a seemingly haphazard process during almost four weeks of recording, but from my diary I was able to discern a kind of sequence in which work had commenced, with 'Blue Monday' close to the top:

'5 8 6'
'The Village'
'Ultraviolence'
'Blue Monday'
'KW1' (renamed 'Your Silent Face')
'The Village'
'We All Stand'
'Only the Lonely' (renamed 'Ecstasy')
'Age Of Consent'
'Leave Me Alone'
'Murder'

Conversely, 'Blue Monday' was the last song to be mixed post-recording. The schedule for mixing is as follows:

15 November 1982	'Murder' (left off album)
	'Leave Me Alone'
16 November 1982	'Only the Lonely' (renamed 'Ecstasy')
	'We All Stand'
17 November 1982	'We All Stand' (continued)
	'The Village'
	'KW1' (renamed 'Your Silent Face')

18 November 1982	'Age Of Consent'
	'5 8 6'
4 January 1983	'Ultraviolence'
5 January 1983	'Ultraviolence' (continued)
	'Blue Monday'
6 January 1983	'Blue Monday' (continued)
	'The Beach'

(Mixing list and dates provided by Michael Johnson after consulting tape-box labels for the backup stereo analogue master tape.)

There was good reason for working on the song last, for it meant there was marginally more time (plus necessary creative distance) to devote to their most challenging and ambitious track whilst adhering to their very tight schedule.

Frustrated at having to leave the studio so suddenly, I had always assumed that mixing would take place in one go. But I was surprised to learn from Michael Johnson that it had been split into two sessions: the first taking place before the tour and starting the day after I left the studio; the second in January, over six weeks later. Overrunning of the recording sessions had pushed it too close to their Australian tour. They also wanted to take time over Christmas to wind down. For that reason, the two New Year gigs at Danceteria had been cancelled, which must have been disappointing, as it was one of the New York clubs that had inspired the new music and they were impatient to try it out before the kind of discerning crowd it was meant for.

Could I have documented the mixing in its entirety, therefore, even if I had wanted to? I *had* wanted to, but – probably not. Taking two further leaves of absence from my work in Manchester might have been pushing it. Knowing all this, I was slightly less bothered at having missed out, though all these years later I still felt rankled by it! Even so, I needed to complete my story and for this I sought the help of Michael and Stephen Morris. Much to my surprise, they were able to provide a wealth of technical detail – and some personal touches too – to help me build up a necessary picture, some thirty-three years after the event.

In the eyes of someone from the world of books – as I am – mixing is the musical equivalent of an author editing and re-editing a work after it has been set down in writing; the final 'shaping' that most accurately reflects the writer's intentions before the work reaches the public. From the musician's standpoint, it is the process that conjures into a pristine soundscape the various elements of the recorded music.

This decisive part of the recording process took place in Brit Row (it could have been in a different studio altogether), in the Control Room – the small space I can still conjure in my mind's eye into which everyone had to squash at key moments, the confinement alleviated only by the view through the big glass window to the Live Studio, where most of the drums, guitars and vocals were recorded. Michael also confirmed that everyone was present (another basic fact that had to be established), including Rob.

The band made a leisurely start on this process, which may have been just as well. After I left them on Sunday, they'd maybe met Malcolm as planned and gone on to celebrate (though apparently not to Claude Bessy's party, if it ever took place).

It was leisurely because, for the first few hours of each mix, Michael had the song in bits and – as the band couldn't tell what was happening – he encouraged them to do other things. Apart from the ever-present Hooky who preferred to stay in his favourite seat to the left of the mixer, reading and telling the odd anecdote while Michael worked, the other members were in and out, shopping, watching videos, playing snooker, returning when the songs were set up.

At different times Bernard and Hooky took the lead mixing, Bernard having the most input, followed by Hooky.

The same procedure was followed with all the tracks. It conjured a scene very similar to the one I'd been part of during recording, with everyone attentive but relaxed. Yet the difference, I imagined, was the looming presence of the upcoming tour, for now nothing else stood between them and it. After mixing, they would have virtually no time to get distance on the new material – the worst situation to be in, Bernard had told me a week earlier, where the music 'all starts to sound like rubber'. They would also be performing 'Blue Monday' live for the first time. They would be taking studio equipment on to the stage, which would be one of the most daring musical experiments of the era by a popular band.

Having by then gone into recording myself, I discovered that each of the studios I came to know had a different attraction, and therefore a different reason to go to them – the particular skills and interests of the house engineer, or the quality and kind of equipment or even (for live recording) the architecture of the building. Vocals might be recorded at one, backings at another and mixing yet somewhere else.

By comparison, Brit Row's qualities were comprehensive and understated, its sound reproduction equipment, which had the full range of frequencies, ideal for producing dance music. Despite its high-quality equipment it was not at all showy like some. Housed in an older industrial building it also possessed interesting acoustical spaces like the Games Room (which the band re-christened the Hanging About room) where a reliable club-sound could be achieved.

It had a basement room known as 'the pit', tiled for use as an echo chamber. Hooky claimed that the band got the sound for the bass drum on 'Blue Monday' in the pit (as per Ian Harrison's sleeve notes for *Power, Corruption & Lies*, London

Records 2008) though, when we spoke about it, Michael didn't recall the studio having such a room until a couple of years later, by which time New Order were mixing *Low-Life*. Hence, he told me, the 'Perfect Pit' track on the 'Perfect Kiss' 12". If 'the pit' existed during the time I was with New Order, I was unaware of it. Anyhow, as Michael recalls below, the Games Room was where the bass drum for 'Blue Monday' was treated.

One of the best things I found about Brit Row was that it felt hermetic, self-contained and cut off from the outside world. It altered my perception of time. I become more 'in the moment', as though I was in time or had become time, riding with it rather than racing ahead and feeling anxious because disconnected (as I usually was), or falling behind and allowing events to happen in an uncontrolled way. This sense of being in the 'now' for such a protracted period played a big part in the immediacy of my diary. I don't think I could have achieved this at any other place or time but then.

The Control Room – with its single bench-seat, where all the work was done – was packed with the best equipment. The studio came as well, of course, with Michael, with his receptive engineering style, ready suggestions and previous history with the band. Of a similar age to New Order, he made important musical contributions, and matched them with his musical interests and aptitude for innovation, if not perhaps with his sobriety. In an email to me, Stephen recounted that:

> Compared to us, while we were getting out of it, Michael stayed responsibly sober. In kind of the same way that George Martin, I imagine, was with the Beatles. He seemed to belong to that old-school tradition; well-spoken, not quite posh, polite and *very* professional, meticulously keeping track of what was going on in the session. I seem to remember him mostly sitting on the right-hand side of the desk working the auto locator for the 24-track, shuttling the tape backwards and forwards, finding the right spot for a drop-in or an edit. He had neat hair, dressed smart-casual, somehow exuding an air that suggested a military (navy?) or public-school background. I think we used to tease him about this by asking if he was related to Prince Andrew on the quiet. We got on with Mike very well. I think he understood us and we shared a similar sense of humour.

During the mixing of 'The Beach' (the dub version of 'Blue Monday', on the flipside of the original 12" as a tribute to Lee 'Scratch' Perry and King Tubby), dub-style repeating echoes were added to the track. At these moments the lush distinctive tones of dub would permeate the studio, to the approval of Stephen and Rob. Rob was a huge fan from his days DJ-ing at the Manchester club Rafters where he first met Joy Division (as Warsaw). After this, Michael told me that, at every opportunity, Rob would urge him to 'Dub it up!' This recollection was a powerful one and suddenly I was transported right there with them, seeing Rob looking up from his desk in his office next to the rubber plant and strolling out into HA, a big smile on his face, probably trying to pull Gillian to her feet to dance, but having to make do with Terry instead.

'You alright, Terry?'
'You alright, Gillian?'
'You alright, Mike?'
'You alright, Barney?'
'You alright, Hooky?'
'You alright, Steve?'
'Dub it up!'

The addition of effects was the only new recording that took place. Greater ambience was given to the dry, basic drum-machine kick drum heard on 'Blue Monday' by pumping it through a big speaker placed in the games room and capturing the sound with microphones. A 'digital delay' was used to lend a feeling of movement – with three outputs, one set to a 1/4-note delay, another to a 3/16-note delay and the third set to a 5/16-note delay. The pulsed synth parts of 'Blue Monday' were often sent to this piece of equipment and the outputs mixed back in with the original synth sound. The song's choral sound was sent to a 27-band graphic equaliser with alternate bands set to extreme boost or cut – Bernard's idea, Michael told me, to add extra harmonics lacking in the low-resolution samples produced by the Emulator.

Other than this, the arrangements – written in Salford and then built up with the addition of synth, guitar, bass, drum overdubs and vocals at Brit Row – were the same, post-mixing, as I remember them on leaving the studio.

According to Michael, 'Blue Monday' was 'challenging' at mixing stage. Like nearly all studios in 1982, Brit Row was analogue, that is to say, not digital. Without even a computer for remembering fader positions, songs had to be done in one pass. Long technical tracks were especially difficult. Many of the engineers I've encountered prefer this older, more hands-on way of mixing because they claim it gives them a better feeling for the music. Having had direct experience of this technique I can imagine what went into the mixing of 'Blue Monday'.

A few pioneering artists were leading the way for a change in the market. Ry Cooder's *Bop till You Drop* (1979), Hawkwind's *Levitation* (1980), Donald Fagen's *The Nightfly* (recorded 1981–82) and Peter Gabriel's *Peter Gabriel 4* (1982) were all fully digital albums. But the process was slow. Most studios were reluctant to replace their equipment without good reason – especially desks, the costly centrepieces of their businesses.

Brit Row was fully analogue. It had a perfectly good MC1 400 40-channel desk that its engineers were used to operating. But by using video recording technology, it is possible to store analogue recordings digitally and thus achieve a digital mix. This is what New Order decided they wanted to do, as expressed by Stephen in an email to me:

> To be pedantic, we mixed down to digital – analogue multi-track recorders being largely nonexistent at the time. There were a couple of 4-tracks, I believe, but I imagine they would have been both hideously expensive and unreliable. Why did we decide to mix down to digital? Well, digital was the coming thing – it *had* to be better! I think we did actually mix down to both analogue and digital, but the bright shiny Sony seemed to sound better. In truth it just sounded different. In what back then seemed a good way. Now, of course, it seems a bad way and those mega-expensive digital 2-track convertors (Sony 1610) are most often found being used as doorstops, if they are used for anything at all. Then, of course, it was cutting-edge heaven and for that reason . . .

The Sony 1610 system machine was hired in accordingly, consisting of a box that converted the analogue input first to digital, then to a signal that could be recorded on videocassette. There was no available digital tape-machine, so Sony U-matic broadcast-standard videocassettes were used.

The Brit Row desk had forty faders, a daunting array that often needed more than one hand to operate, which was the reason 'Blue Monday' would prove interesting. Helped by one or other of the members of New Order, Michael had to remember the positions and 'play' the fader-levers in real time, while the mix was recorded onto the stereo master. At this stage, analogue consoles became musical instruments in their own right, giving engineers the chance to perform.

After a mix had been got going, the band returned to listen and to offer suggestions or criticism, and Michael spent time making amendments. Positions were marked on the desk for different parts of the song. Michael took control of the lead-vocal fader and one or two members of the band took control of other critical faders. As the music was playing from the 2-inch master (on the 24-track machine), the faders were moved manually in real time, increasing or decreasing the volume of the different parts of the song. When the 'right' mix was achieved some faders were left as they were, but as recording took place many still had to be moved to adjust the instrument's level for each part of the song. In the case of a lead vocal or guitar solo, the fader was often moved for each phrase or word. With the song playing through the desk like this, it was recorded. Not all the mixes worked, or were felt to be the best that could be achieved, and some had to be done again. The best attempt became the master.

As well as recording the mix digitally, Michael simultaneously recorded it on 1/2-inch stereo analogue tape as a backup, in case the digital technology let them down. But the system behaved itself and the backup analogue tapes were never needed.

Mixing completed, before pressing of the vinyl could take place, several other stages were undergone. First, the songs had to be 'sequenced' into the desired running order for the album and single and the length of gaps between the tracks determined.

I wrote to Michael to ask how the digitised songs were edited after New Order had opted for digital mixing. With songs mixed to 1/4-inch analogue tape, as in the analogue studios I had worked in, sequencing would have been achieved by physically cutting and re-joining the tape, entailing a control room full of long pieces of tape, hanging wherever space permitted and waiting to be re-joined in the desired order. But video editing – as chosen by New Order – called for a very different method. Michael told me it could only be accomplished by hiring extra video machines as well as a hardware-editing controller. For some reason the band were unable to hire-in this equipment and so the stereo masters were taken to an outside facility.

The day after mixing was completed, on 6 January 1983, Michael and the band therefore found themselves at the London studios of Advision, Fitzrovia, where the editing was done.

The sequenced digital master tapes next went to a 'cutter', who made the songs into acetates or lacquers – the proto-disc used to make the metal moulds or stampers at the pressing plant from which the vinyl copies would be pressed. Cutting was another real-time operation requiring the skills of a specialist engineer who had to manually allow for the changes in sound that affected how wide the space for the groove needed to be on each rotation. For the 'Blue Monday' 12", wider groove spacing was made, allowing for louder levels to be cut, giving a wider dynamic range and better sound quality overall (but a shorter play time compared to an LP). After completing each disc the engineer signed his work by scratching on the lead-out groove, where it was usual to scratch or stamp identifying codes to distinguish each lacquer.

At Savoy, nearly all our 12" singles were pressed from masters cut by George Peckham at Porky's Mastering Ltd, Shaftsbury Avenue. In his heyday, Led Zeppelin had especially benefitted from George's ear, and we went to him because he was reputed to produce the loudest and best cuts for rock music. His tag on the run-out groove was 'A Porky Prime Cut'.

New Order took the lacquers for *Power, Corruption & Lies* and 'Blue Monday' to Strawberry Mastering Studios, in Victoria, a short drive across the West End from Advision. Strawberry's northern recording studios, based in Stockport, were where *Movement* had been recorded.

Michael and the band arrived at Strawberry late on the night of 7 January. A young engineer who, Michael recalls, was named 'something like Ravi' cut the songs – by now all on a single master 1610 U-matic cassette. When 'Ravi' came to cut 'Blue Monday' he brought up the fader late at the start, which is why the first kick-drum beat is missing on the 12" vinyl version. In true Factory fashion the error was left uncorrected and chance was allowed to rule. The run-out grooves had the hand-etched identifiers OUT VOTED and FAC73 1A.

It was now just a simple matter of taking the lacquers to the pressing plant. Or was it?

The 12" single and album were pressed at MVS (Record Pressing) Ltd, Islington. By this time, Factory Records had a stake in MVS and this was the record presser they were mostly using. But when 'Blue Monday' was due to be pressed, Factory was suffering one of its periodic cash-flow impasses. Bluntly put, there was no money to press the single. While the money was raised from somewhere, the production process, which had gone relatively smoothly until now, temporarily ground to a halt. This was something of which I also had direct experience! As at Factory, creditors were constantly squeezing Savoy Books to the detriment of our production schedule.

Tony Wilson once described how VAT bailiffs had pursued him to Rob's house, and how he and Rob had then been forced to ignominiously hide inside (a 'disappearing' trick at which David and I were past masters). In the same interview (reproduced in James Nice's book, *Shadowplayers: The Rise and Fall of Factory Records*), he said that before 'Blue Monday' could be pressed, the necessary plastic had to be ordered. But the plastic manufacturer was refusing to release the plastic to MVS until they received a cheque from Factory for £40,000. At the same moment, the brewery that supplied beer for the Haçienda also demanded a cheque for a similar amount before they would provide the beverages. It's obvious which bill had to be settled first. 'Blue Monday' was put on hold.

What I Would Have Heard Coming Off the Mixing Desk

For these musical descriptions of 'Blue Monday' (above) and the album (below), I sought the help of musical arranger Stephen Boyce-Buckley.

New Order claim not to have written anything directly about Ian: 'We've never put our feelings into one song, but they've emerged . . . in phrases and lines here and there. You can see them when you look back,' explained Hooky, in an interview with *The Face*'s Paul Rambali in July 1983. It might be my overwrought imagination, but when I 'method-acted' my way into the Control Room while these songs were being mixed, they felt like his celebratory epitaph.

'Age of Consent'

This track was mixed on 18 November – the Thursday after I departed London by train – before New Order's departure to Oz. It was destined to become the opening song of the album. Stephen Morris thinks the title may have been taken from the 1969 Michael Powell film about an ageing artist and his underage muse (as he revealed in an email to me).

Both driving and triumphant, and mournful, this song begins with a bass-guitar riff, played in a higher octave so that it almost sounds like a low-tuned, six-stringed electric guitar. There is what seems like an edit, but it is a full bar that may have been played as an inversion. This leads nicely into the rhythm – a classic four-to-the-floor sixteenth, dance-influenced riff. What follows is a guitar playing broken chords that sweeps seamlessly in from nowhere, evolves into a memorable riff and then sits delicately on top of the underpinning rhythm.

Amidst all of this is a droning synthesiser bass, reinforcing a production that is fast becoming steadier in its metre yet slightly hypnotic.

At thirty seconds the vocal enters – not overloud – with a calming effect on the sound overall. Very much like the bass guitar at the start, it switches gear in the second verse and soars into the next octave up, with the music still retaining its magnetic property. Once this verse has finished, we're introduced to a new element: a synth-string that plays yet another main hook line. This is quite upfront and is layered with some reverb or echo but eventually gives way to the bass-guitar riff.

Despite the song possessing several instrumental melodies, they all manage to retain their own space, and their syncopated eighth-note rhythms seem to glide fluently over the semi-manic drumbeat.

What follows a little later is a frantic guitar, played in sixteenth-beat bursts. Quite different from the rest of the track, it doesn't offend but rather adds to the building tension.

A vocal, in the style of a reprise, makes an appearance towards the end, with several previous motifs battling for key positions amid a volume rising sustained held note bass tone.

'We All Stand'

Mixed over the 16 and 17 November, this is questioning and dreamy, in an uncertain kind of way. It may be reality or a nightmare – ironic, perhaps. Maybe we don't all stand?

An eighth-beat hi-hat, a lilting but syncopated rim-shot snare engulfed in reverb, calm yet busy, and a lone kick-drum pulse on the downbeat are the rhythmic elements that drive this song. Every so often an agitated tom beat plays a semiquaver-based pattern.

The bass guitar, complete with a double-tracked effect, plays another hypnotic melody that intertwines with the two guitars that meander in and out of the track. One plays a quaver-based riff, whilst the other plays arpeggiated chords. The vocal is emotionally delivered as it follows a four-note uncomplicated journey.

A bass guitar with studio effects, playing a blues-based, flattened fifth melody structure, carries the solo section fluently, with a piano playing simple but effective triad-based chords.

This cacophony slowly drags you into its murky wall of sound. The instruments continue, repeating their riffs, licks and rhythms to the end of the song, with the tom-rolls gradually getting louder and more frequent.

'The Village'

'The Village' got its name from the 1967 British television series *The Prisoner*, starring Patrick McGoohan. It refers to the residence of 'Number Six', the central McGoohan character. Mixed alongside 'We All Stand' the track is happy, playful, perhaps ironic and – with its echoes of Joy Division – rejoicing.

Tight-pulsed, it is carried by the prominent bass synth, playing sequenced quavers, until two-thirds of the way through when it changes pace and there are sudden splurges of semiquavers. A synth also plays semiquavers, which seem to rhythmically underpin sections of the song that require a lift. Then the omnipresent bass-guitar riff makes its entrance, playing another quaver-based trance-like melody.

At various points of the song an acoustic or clean Fender electric guitar plays a post-disco rhythm that starts on beat two and ends on beat three, reminiscent of the Lipps Inc. track, 'Funkytown'.

Also at this point, a tough percussive sound enters that counterbalances the guitar. Its sequence is one of urgency, totally complementing the other sixteenth-based rhythms around which the track revolves.

As with 'We All Stand', we get to hear all the elements as the track progresses to the end. What is quite evident is that, yet again, despite the potential for cacophony – with so many additive and subtractive components – the song and vocals remain crystal clear and uncluttered.

'5 8 6'

Mixed following 'Age of Consent'. Stephen Morris told me via email that the title's conception was 'pretty boring, really. It was down to the number of riffs in the order of the song when we were writing it – "How does it go again?"

'"Five of the first one; eight of the second; six of the third." The order and the riffs changed, but the name stuck.'

What sounds like a cheeky deconstruction of 'Blue Monday' (it is in fact the earlier of the two songs in ancestry), '5 8 6' starts at a very slow fifty-four beats per minute, similar to a requiem mass. The introduction is presented with a two-bar syncopated drum rhythm in quavers, before being joined by a meandering bass synth playing quite a melodic riff that reaches into the lower octaves. The synth has been played, as opposed to sequenced, as there are a few moments where it isn't quite in sync with the drums.

The bass-guitar riff enters, playing a game of musical ping-pong with the other elements, which creates a kind of fugue-type feel, adding fluidity to an otherwise awkward pulse before ceasing. The track is then engulfed in pink noise and a backwards synth that leads into an up-tempo semiquaver beat at around 126 beats per minute.

The synth bass transforms into a more settled quaver octave pattern, with the real bass assisting in creating a musical illusion that entwines the two; giving the track an infectious dance feel.

On one side of the stereo image is a plucked synth sound, playing a tight semiquaver pattern in a higher octave, paying homage to the guitar riffs of late 1970s US dance records.

The middle breakdown sees the track being stripped and having its rhythmic components play a simpler quaver on the beat pattern, before the full instrumentation returns, but with additional semiquaver drums and a sparkling synth that gives the impression that it's been sequenced, when in fact there's a sixteenth delay added; with some feedback applied, in reference to Kraftwerk or Giorgio Moroder.

The ending winds back to the beginning as the song unexpectedly slows down. Stopping. Dead.

'Your Silent Face'

Mixed after 'The Village', the overall feel of this insistently Germanic track (it started out life under the moniker of 'KW1' – Kraftwerk 1 – and still gets called that to this day) is mournful, wistful, but with an affirmative synth that hints at a new awakening.

It has a more conventional opening, featuring a delay-enhanced semiquaver synthesiser pulse with a decorative character alongside a programmed drum machine. Proudly rolling over a steady 4/4 eighth rhythm at 118 beats per minute, it exudes an air of delight.

Following the eight-bar intro comes a spacious synth melody that is both catchy and ever so slightly pompous. There's also a bass synth that underpins the I–VI–I plagal cadence.

After sixteen bars of this memorable phrase, a melodica, referencing New Order's previous album *Movement*, is unveiled, daubed in reverb and playing a haunting melody.

A four-bar re-introduction is inserted before the vocal makes its entrance and doesn't fail to build.

At 1:40, guitars become audible, but are far more sedate than on previous tracks and seem to echo the restrained sentiment of the surrounding music. The bass guitar plays a simple but beautiful melody that, if orchestrated, would be undertaken by the cellos and double basses, allowing the ensuing arpeggiated picking, which the guitar plays, to be executed by the remaining violas and violins.

From hereon, the song plays out in various musical inversions and mixtures of thematic and instrument combinations; all of them providing quite a controlled cacophony of a symphonic nature. As it proceeds towards its inevitable finale, additional white noise is introduced, along with what seems to be an increasing gain on the effects and some percussive drums.

The studio fade is quick and not too precise, leaving you with the urge to listen to it all over again.

'Ultraviolence'

Another ironical track at odds with the droogs' taste for 'ultra-violence' in *A Clockwork Orange*, the novel by Mancunian author Anthony Burgess.

Mixed over 4 and 5 January 1983, at the start of the second mixing session 'Ultraviolence' is complex, topsy-turvy and humorous, with a four-to-the-floor dance rhythm and a two-bar repetitive bass-synth riff based on a I–VI–V–VI minor cadence. The trademark toms enter almost immediately and are further bolstered by a hand-played counter-rhythm syndrum (electronic synthesised percussion). There is a slight cacophony with the addition of a guitar, playing another counter-melody parodying the bass.

When the vocal eventually enters and the music settles down to a more sedate collection of instruments, the bass makes its entrance and continues its dedicated role as a melody counterpoint; playing a musical game of tennis with the vocal as it winds its way through an uncomplicated yet slightly tortured journey. Both vocal and bass are similar in notation as the introductory synth bass; therefore they provide a strong melodic and identifiable anchor point.

The song works its way through various structural incarnations, with the main rhythm and riff line unfaltering. About halfway through, the vocal begins its final descent, leaving the way open for a near production annihilation. With all instruments vying for centre stage, the song fades out.

'Ecstasy'

Mixed on the 16 November 1982 after 'Leave Me Alone', a journeying instrumental with little sun (or ecstasy for that matter – the title and the drug that New Order came across on their 1981 American tour), it moves across a dark techno landscape. Within this track, the two heads of Joy Division and New Order mesh. Bug-eyed voices, angry outbursts, upsurges of meanness and hints of doomy Joy Division contrast with the optimistic, determined pounding and trekking of the percussion.

It starts with an ominous sound like thunder or an approaching tsunami wall of sea. A bass-synth melody enters, with a few sound effects strategically placed in the stereo picture. This rasping saw-toothed sound plays a quaver-based pattern for eight bars and is joined on the seventh with a snare-drum riff. The whole drum kit (playing a punk-like staggered quaver rhythm) swings into action on the next downbeat, its overall sound making this track also very fresh and crisp.

Once again, the guitars are used as a sequenced synth pattern would otherwise be, providing yet another clever interplaying rhythm that winds its way through this intro; which, like the other tracks, is very difficult to define in terms of a set number of bars.

The vocoder vocal is steeped in reverb and set back in the mix, adding an interesting texture and an air of mystery. Once all the elements have been introduced, they merge with one another. Some take centre stage whilst others are merely used as a backdrop, creating a very complicated counterpoint style that can sometimes be difficult to follow.

'Leave Me Alone'

Mixed on the first day after 'Murder', 'Leave Me Alone' draws its title from its lyrics and is a broken-hearted paean to Joy Division. Attempting to reconstruct the experience of hearing it fresh from the mixing desk, I am overcome. With mournful damped percussion and a broken heartbeat, the song is beyond bitterness or joy to my ears. Sad, small creatures – entities, ghosts, souls – clamour in the air, refusing to go away.

By contrast with this atmosphere, the relentless drumbeat makes the track feel very solid and paradoxically danceable. A quaver pattern on the hi-hat drives the 138-beats-per-minute metre backing. It has no synth-bass intro. Instead, a real bass plays another four-bar riff, eventually to be joined by guitars using counter-melodies and eighth patterns.

Further into the song is a pedalled bass guitar playing semibreves. This makes possible the audibility of the higher bass melody, which is now playing in parts, a two-note chord and intertwines almost seamlessly with the vocal echoes and aforementioned guitar licks.

The sense of sadness and melancholy is due somewhat to the dominant melody line that's acting as part-vocal support, part-texture, forming a classic major seventh, then sixth, perfect fifth and finally major third over two bars. (This one-note movement can be heard in many soul and blues tracks of the sixties and seventies.) Following on from the vocal, the characteristic format of New Order's song structure develops – combinations of instruments interweaving with one another in mock-fugue.

Peter Hook (left) and Stephen Morris at the Haçienda, Manchester, *circa* 1985.

'WE WERE LIKE THE GUINEA PIGS'

Uncommonly for a piece of art that was so far ahead of its time, 'Blue Monday' captured the public mood widely. This was as much to do with the dichotomous nature of the band – encompassing the two apparent 'extremes' of Joy Division and New Order – as it was with overlapping technologies.

The duality was closely mirrored in its times, from the indie angst of the recession years to the 'new rock'n'roll' of the more feel-good dance era. Other innovatory bands like Cabaret Voltaire and A Certain Ratio helped to pioneer the transition, but New Order were different in the way they interpolated themselves musically after Ian's death and the manner in which they wrote and produced their music. Similar to other indie bands and DJs experimenting with dance styles, they brought a techno-electro edge, but they also gave the music a big-sound excitement that the rock-inclined crowd, who would never otherwise have been drawn to the genre in a million years, fell for. This would, of course, lead to 'baggy', the Happy Mondays and 'Madchester'.

One of the causes and conditions of Factory's innovatory label was its DIY, anti-establishment credo. This philosophy of 'art for art's sake' was shared to varying extents by everyone involved with Factory – and Savoy as well. New Order, like we did, embraced this ethic entirely. After deciding they would continue as a band after Ian's death, they made the decision that, whatever they did, they would *not* play Joy Division. This restriction forced them to evolve musically.

Fortunately, they'd a range of influences to draw upon. They had a predilection for black and reggae music (Rob was a particularly enthusiastic fan) – musical forms that often utilised experimental 'science fiction' effects – and were already predisposed to like electronic music, introduced to them by Ian through his liking of Kraftwerk. While playing their first American gigs in September 1980, they saw firsthand in clubs how the black, Hispanic and gay dance crowd were using electronic music. Loving its cool, they were suddenly able to envision their own future. It happened just as it had four years before at the Lesser Free Trade Hall, when they'd watched the Sex Pistols perform and realised they could form a band. They would get an electronic guitar-based sound with drum machine and live kit. But first, they would have to figure out where and how they'd acquire the equipment needed to create the stylised sound they were dreaming of. As Bernard explained via the *NME* in a January 2015 post entitled, 'How We Wrote "Blue Monday"':

> I remember just being turned on by the latest technology that was becoming available, and I'd built this sequencer from an electronics kit. We programmed everything in step-time using binary-code digital readouts. It was . . . complicated. We could drive a synthesiser through it, but we couldn't hook it up to anything. Steve had bought a drum machine, but we couldn't get the sequencer to talk to it. Through Martin Hannett, we'd gotten to know this scientist called Martin Usher, so I took the sequencer and drum machine to him, and he designed a circuit that could make them speak to each other. The day that we wrote it was the day that we brought the circuit in, hooked it all up and pressed 'GO' on the drum machine, then the synthesiser started chattering away, and somehow it all worked. Rob thought it was witchcraft. He really did! That sounds weird now in the age of the internet, but he really thought it worked by magic.

'The bass line for "Blue Monday" was a Moog Source sequenced with a Powertran homemade sequencer that Bernard had built himself,' the producer-programmer Roger Lyons noted, in 'Recreating New Order's "Blue Monday" Live' in *Sound on Sound* online magazine.

Describing the change after the months of uncertainty and confusion about their future, a bemused Hooky (appearing in the 2015 BBC documentary, *Sounds of a City: Power, Corruption & Lies*) recalled: 'We were like the guinea pigs of all this new equipment.'

Demarcation came in December 1981, with the release of New Order's third single, 'Everything's Gone Green'. It was their fist step into electronic dance music, using an Oberheim synth, a drum machine and a live kit. In a metaphorical sense, everything literally did go green, for this release marked the end of their musical relationship with Martin Hannett and therefore with Joy Division. Their producer until now, Martin either couldn't or wouldn't see the significance of the new sound they were pioneering from America and found himself unable to do what they wanted. They had to mix the song themselves. From now on, they would also produce themselves.

Further visits to US clubs during their November 1981 tour reinforced the conviction that they were taking the right course. They returned home more fired-up than ever. Their new album would draw together everything they had learned so far about the equipment they had amassed and the new music they had heard.

The start of 'Blue Monday' features a distinctive beat that Bernard randomly overheard at a gig (as revealed in his 2014 memoir, *Chapter and Verse*) when a sound mixer messed about with a delay and 'something extra' got added to a drumbeat. Bernard heard the affected beat again on a Donna Summer song and decided to try incorporating it in a New Order track.

Gillian recalled in an interview with Dave Simpson of the *Guardian* on 11 Feb 2013:

> We tried to play something like Donna Summer's 'Our Love' [1979] and came up with that instantly recognisable thud. It was my job to program the entire song from beginning to end, which had to be done manually, by inputting every note. I had the sequence all written down on loads of A4 paper sellotaped together the length of the recording studio, like a huge knitting pattern. But I accidentally left a note out, which skewed the melody.

Three other songs were key to 'Blue Monday': the 1978 Sylvester disco song, 'You Make Me Feel (Mighty Real)', acted as a guide for the bass line; Kraftwerk's 'Uranium', from the 1975 album *Radio-Activity*, became the model for the keyboard 'pad' sound at the start and end of the track; and the much more recent early-1982 Italian electro track 'Dirty Talk', by Klein & M.B.O., was the template for the beat.

Cross-fertilisations of music between America and the UK had been taking place since the original American R&B and rock'n'roll of the forties and fifties, mainly through disenfranchised working-class kids. Based on an American sound heavily influenced by European electronica, 'Blue Monday' would itself be 'taken back' by American techno DJs like Kevin Saunderson.

At the end of the seventies New York disco DJs found they could use electronic sounds to link the three-minute songs that were standard at the time, giving DJ sets the illusion of continuity. Long, machine-like Kraftwerk tracks fitted perfectly into this format.

In the early eighties Chicago DJs like Frankie Knuckles were mixing European electronic music with disco, creating a kind of house, while Afrika Bambaataa and Arthur Baker in New York were developing electro, combining the work of Kraftwerk with Roland TR-808 beats.

The beat New Order suddenly found in their Salford shed-cum-laboratory was definably house, though house music was still three years in the future and, in the UK, dance music was half a decade away. In *Sounds of a City*, Tony Wilson describes 'Blue Monday' as being 'a very early dance music experiment'.

While New Order were writing 'Blue Monday', the song's final ingredient was being broken in the UK by DJ Greg Wilson in his clubs Legend in Manchester and Wigan Pier, where 'Dirty Talk' had already become huge with black audiences.

In May 1982, black Mancunian Hewan Clarke became the first resident DJ at the newly opened Haçienda. Greg Wilson knew Clarke as a jazz specialist who'd appeared on many of the same bills as himself – for numerous all-dayers. Writing for the *SoundCloud* website, Greg remembers that the club's clientele consisted mainly of students and indie kids back then. Clarke, obviously clued-in to what was happening in the black clubs, picked up on the success of 'Dirty Talk' and began playing it himself. In conversation with Greg Wilson for *Electrofunkroots* website, in August 2004, Hewan told how:

> I remember getting 'Dirty Talk' and wow! This is an amazing track, especially that clapping bit halfway through. I remember the first time I played it in the Haçienda it totally cleared the floor. But I believed in it, you know what I'm saying? I kept on playing it, kept on playing it and that's how it grew and then it became absolutely massive and there's an interesting story that came out of that because at one point, members of New Order came to the DJ box and asked what that track was and asked if they could borrow it and I gave them a copy and they disappeared with it and then I got it back and then a couple of weeks later, they gave me a white-label copy of 'Blue Monday' which had been fashioned off the beats.

Stephen Morris remembers things slightly differently. In an email, he told me, 'we borrowed Hewan's disc because ours didn't have the right version on it.' In other words, they already knew the song.

As much as the technology and the 'found' sounds that were being harvested, the essential 'ingredient' of the daring sound and commercial success of 'Blue Monday' was its guiding ethos, the free-spirited 'can do' of the Factory label. It is the result of what happens when company managers who are artists themselves give original artists – aiming for the limits of what it is possible to express – the reins. Without the determined efforts of this atypical, eccentric, non-industry label, there would have been no 'Blue Monday'.

If Joy Division had followed the route taken by many other bands and signed to a commercial label early on, their creative energies could well have been dissipated in trying to fit the industry mould. What kind of music would four lads from Salford and Macclesfield have gone on to play, if they had been bothered?

Tony Wilson's intention with Factory, he told author Mick Middles in *From Joy Division to New Order*, was to fulfil a strong urge to transform his ideas into reality, inspired by the Manchester music scene. Though rough sums were done – and had to be done – making money was never what Factory was mainly about.

The Factory project was to be a coming together of creatives and its manifestation was probably one of the last times youthful waywardness could win out over conformity and get something going; when, with spectacular hubris, you could put a dream first and the money to pay for it second – and expect to carry it off. Experiment, follow your own rules and, most importantly, play by your own rules, not those of the industry. Why play the industry game when you know you are giving the world something original, new and wholly unexpected – which conformity would render less?

New Order's decision to leave singles off their albums (they felt attention should be focused on the work itself rather than the sales and marketing machinery of the record industry); Factory's determination to distance itself from the conventions of the industry; the choice of both the label and the band to embrace happenstance (leaving off the first kick-drum beat on the 12" vinyl version of 'Blue Monday'; Gillian fading in the opening melody at the wrong moment so it is out of sync with the beat); Factory's determination to get the *right* sleeve design for the single, even though the high production costs allegedly lost money on every copy of 'Blue Monday' sold; the uncompromising length of the single, even though it meant that initially it received no airplay; their insistence on playing 'Blue Monday' live on *Top of the Pops*, on a television format that rarely did this; Factory and Rob's decision not to promote the single, working on the assumption that quality music sells itself; and – not least – New Order's denial of audience expectations by refusing to do encores. The very existence of 'Blue Monday' is down to this, initially having been devised to be left playing at the end of performances (the reason for its then atypical length, at seven minutes-plus).

Though designer Peter Saville disputes his sleeve was 'problematic'. In a February 2013 article for the *Guardian*, he told how:

Tony loved to say the sleeve was so expensive they lost 5p per copy. But it's unlikely; Factory never talked budgets. Nobody ever said to me: 'This is a costly sleeve'. No one sent me a copy, either; I had to go to a record shop. The record sold so quickly that the version I bought had a black sleeve but no holes. The printers hadn't been able to keep up with demand, so had banged out a cheaper version. I don't know how many thousands were sold that way, or whether Factory were charged the full price for something they didn't get, which would be very Factory. But I'm pleased it's a legendary cover for what turned out to be a classic track: the principal moment of conversion between progressive rock and dance. Similarly, colour codes have become widespread in graphic design.

Writing for *The Face* in July 1983 – just nine months after the Brit Row recordings

– Paul Rambali caught the band's punk ethic in an interview. Rambali sought them out at their Salford rehearsal room, where they shared the following insights into their process:

> 'Producing ourselves we get more satisfaction,' adds Sumner [. . .] 'We always know how we want [the songs] to sound. The way we write a song is usually to start off by improvising in the rehearsal room. Then we take it out live. Sometimes you haven't got any lyrics so you just make up some garbage. Then you listen to the live tapes, write some more words, and go back and rehearse some more. By the time we record it we pretty well know how it should be.'
>
> 'We spend an awful lot of time together in here,' muses Hook. 'But we're lazy. We sit around here until we're so bored that we have an idea.'
>
> Typically, they see no need for any outside views on their career or their music.
>
> 'You don't really get people who are in a position to give you advice,' says Hook.
>
> 'A career is forward planning,' asserts Stephen Morris. 'There isn't any forward planning. We don't do what we think will be successful. We do what we want to do.'

In his 2010 biography of Tony Wilson, *You're Entitled to an Opinion*, David Nolan makes the interesting observation that the Factory figurehead, whose other career was at Granada Television, was an 'analogue man'. By this he meant that Tony was defined by the television transmitter at Winter Hill, Lancashire. Until 2009, the transmitter broadcast an analogue signal to a region of England – which became known as the 'North West' – defined by the reach of the signal. The area was Tony's fiefdom as TV presenter and music entrepreneur.

'Analogue' might be the defining characteristic of punk, which – to date – is the West's last recognisable youth movement of rebellion. Although the acid house summer of 1988 was heralded as being the Second Summer of Love (after the hippies' first Summer of Love in 1967), the dance generation was escapist in nature rather than ideological; hedonistic rather than rebellious. Dance, with its ability to swallow all musical styles, was and remains a product of the digital age.

Perhaps there have been no further rebellions because digital has had the effect of fragmenting the music world into smaller, more self-contained scenes. It has also brought simultaneity to what previously seemed time-stretched. Social media brings instant awareness to everyone and everything. The rate of technological development adds to this impression. Radical art of any kind that owes its uniqueness to some kind of technological innovation is quickly superseded.

Although the official release of 'Blue Monday' had been delayed until March, the lacquers were ready for pressing much sooner. A small number of 'white label' promotional records (discs, usually supplied in a plain white inner sleeve, without printing or packaging except for a white centre label on which the song title is stamp-printed or handwritten) had been circulating since mid-January. These promos had been rushed to club DJs, who had then done their work with them.

Hewan duly dropped his white-label copy at the Haçienda on 16 January 1983. Hidden from view in his cramped DJ box – which was below floor-level – he became the first DJ ever to play the track there. The booth had a slit-like one-way window from which DJs were able to view the feet of dancers; therefore it was impossible to reliably gauge the atmosphere on the dance floor.

Playing 'Blue Monday' for the first time in public, perhaps anywhere in the world, was a musical moment. Members of the Haçienda staff and a few clubbers, who realised what was happening, applauded. But to most present on the night, the moment was underwhelming. No one sprang to their feet or made their way to the dance floor. Not the first time it was played, anyway.

'This was early 1983 and the dance floor was for the most part thinly populated,' Stephen Morris confirmed in an email to me, adding dryly, 'along with the rest of the club.' He added: 'Blue Monday must have gone down alright though – no one complained.'

'I do not think [the reception of "Blue Monday" at the Haçienda] would have been high on our list of priorities at the time,' Hooky told me, when I posed the same question to him via email. 'Rob might have been excited, but I remember nothing. I do not remember anything about the white label being played at the Haç, by Hewan or anyone. If I remember rightly it was the DJs who were excited about it much more than the punters. It was the DJs that made it a hit after the summer.'

There was no visible DJ to complain to. Greg Wilson, who played the Haç's funk night the following year, claimed that the regulars wanted Bauhaus and Siouxsie and the Banshees. He said there was a lot of resentment at the New York electro style he was dropping.

The early Haçienda crowd were veterans of Factory Nights at the Russell Club, also called the PSV Club, in the Hulme district of Manchester. There, Tony and Alan Erasmus had attempted to rekindle the spirit of the Electric Circus where Warsaw had given their first performances, but with one difference: the music. Factory Nights at the Russell Club were meant to be post-punk art-synth-industrial themed. But for commercial reasons, they had to remain heavily on the punk tip. When the Haç opened two years later, it was mainly this same crowd who came through the doors. No one told them that this time round, the music policy really would be different. As Hewan Clarke told Greg Wilson in 2004 (published on *Electrofunkroots* website):

On the opening night you had Mohicans there and goths . . . and here I am playing Sharon Redd 'Can You Handle It?' I freaked them out and it freaked me out, 'cos of their reaction. There was no way they were gonna move to it and they couldn't even find me in my little hidden-away box to complain about it! And so for me, as the DJ, that did my head in sometimes. I'd go out and buy poppy stuff like Stray Cats and I'd mix them in and it worked really well. I'd like mix the odd track in every now and again just to coax them on to the floor . . . I had to fill the dance floor. I had to come up with ways of doing it. It was an amazing learning experience for me really . . . Whenever I'm playing a funk track and there's a break I'd play like . . . I used to play a lot of Kraftwerk. I'd get their imaginations and after a while they got used to my style and I got to know what they liked. I was able to use it that way and introduce them to new stuff.

The Haçienda's *raison d'être* was to bring New York to Manchester, right down to the vibe, the style and the size of club. In typical contrary Factory fashion, the Haçienda was built not to cater for a scene, but to create one. (Exactly as David and I were trying to do on the other side of town with Savoy.) After Ian's death, there was to be no turning back to the old post-punk indie sound for anyone connected with Factory.

New York's Danceteria, promoted by Ruth Polsky (RIP), who was also New Order's booking agent, had three storeys of dance floors and stages, and catered for dance and rock. The Haçienda set out initially to copy this. Rock was welcomed, but only as live performance, and not on club nights, which were to be dance only.

The Manc clubbers who turned up had to be educated away from their comfort zones. And to be fair, the futuristic goths and Mohicans at the Haçienda were curious about the new music of New Order even if they didn't at first readily dance to it.

Another problem facing the DJs was that the clientele was tiny by comparison with the capacity of the club. Designed for a purpose that hadn't yet been realised, the building was spread over two floors. In addition it had a long, spacious balcony. It was built to house, altogether, two thousand revellers. The main bar was on the ground floor across the dance floor, on the end wall. In the basement was the Gay Traitor bar – an ironical reference to Soviet spy Anthony Blunt – which was more of a cocktail affair, with soft seating. (After the club eventually took off in the late eighties, an unused part of the basement was opened, to make a huge new dance area.) In the middle of the club on the ground floor was a café, partially sealed off from the main dance floor. In semi-darkness, set well back along one side of the dance floor, were about half a dozen alcoves with seating, later the domain of drug gangs attracted to the club. More seating could be found upstairs on the balcony, where the DJ box would later be moved.

Compared with most Manchester clubs, the Haçienda was *huge*. It took a good few minutes to walk from one end, downstairs, to the other end, upstairs. If forty or fifty, or even a hundred or two hundred people turned up – which in those early days was a good figure – there were sufficient places to sit or drink for the club to feel almost deserted. The floor would fill briefly after a popular track was played, but often it felt like a large wedding venue before most of the guests had risen from their postprandial seats.

'Blue Monday' eventually filled the floor and, very slowly, the Haç got going. First to draw crowds were the live nights, when bigger bands began to be booked, many of these through the contacts of club video jockey Claude Bessy. New Order also played the club regularly, serving as 'de facto fundraisers for the club' (Hooky's description in *The Haçienda: How Not to Run a Club*). I also remember packed performances by Einstürzende Neubauten, Violent Femmes and the Cramps. In May 1984, the Cramps played there twice, and packed the club out on both occasions.

One of the gigs was filmed by my sister Linda Dutton, then part of Ikon Video (Factory's video wing). It was standard practice for Ikon to document the bands, but on this occasion the other members of the crew remained aloof, and so Linda grabbed a camera and filmed it for herself. Years later, we eventually released the footage in the form of *The Cramps at the Haçienda* (Savoy Music, 2015).

But club nights at the Haç remained sparse for a further three years until DJs Mike Pickering and Dave Haslam were recruited – and later Graham Parks. Ecstasy arrived and suddenly the people did too.

I have strong positive memories of both eras of the club, but *24 Hour Party People* (book and film) make scarcely a mention of the early years. Factory seemed to want to write it out of existence, to say 'nothing happened then'.

Yet, even in its early days, as a kind of arts laboratory, the Haç was simply amazing. It was years ahead of its time – certainly in Manchester where there had been nothing like it before. As well as the regular appearances of international rock acts, New York luminaries like William Burroughs and John Giorno performed there, Madonna gave her first UK performance, the Manchester comedian Bernard Manning opened its doors, New Order played there regularly, Hewan Clarke DJ'd there, you could drink there, you could eat there, you could hear poetry there, you could watch films there. 'Blue Monday' was first played there . . .

From New Order's point of view, the indifference about that era is understandable, because of the amount of money being haemorrhaged from their record sales when no one had properly sat them down to make them aware of the cost of the project. (In fact *no one* was actually aware of the costs; the whole thing having no basis in commercial reality.) But when you take into account that the club was a dream –

an ideological experiment, a brilliant child – how can you discount your brilliant child's early years simply because it couldn't walk or talk properly? No parent would do that, would they?

Nothing happening? Give me a break . . .

Ten days after Hewan Clarke dropped the 'Blue Monday' white label and still two months before the delayed official release, New Order performed the track live at the Haçienda on 26 January. It was their first gig after returning home from their Australian tour. Even with malfunctioning equipment, the richness and complexity of the track meant that performing it was always an intensely exciting experience. With the complicating factor of the club's eccentric acoustics, its performance there evoked feelings of grandeur and awe, like watching a huge ship moving unsteadily down the slipway.

By now, New Order had performed it several times live on-stage; the first was at the Palais Theatre, Melbourne – their first Australian date, after they had broken off mixing.

Bernard had been testing the equipment at Heaven and was very dubious about the wisdom of taking it on the road. 'Playing live added an element of chaos,' he explained in an interview with *Mojo*'s Andrew Male in September 2015. 'We never used tapes. Rob always insisted, "You're not using fucking tapes". But Rob didn't have to go on the fucking stage.'

As for Hooky, he was pessimistic but upbeat about New Order's stage presence. Speaking with *Interview* magazine's Leila Brillson in 2013, he revealed it still struck him as 'insanity' to take the music round the world, the way that New Order did. Performing it on-stage, they often had to abandon carefully laid plans and improvise, because some piece of equipment had failed. '[But] it was part of our punk ethic. Even when the tech was considered to be good, we used to have three set-ups running on-stage so that when one went down – and it wasn't *if* one went down, it was *when* – we could switch to the other. It was a very exciting time: there weren't many bands that actually ran it live.'

Stephen and Gillian concurred. In an email to me, Stephen, in typically dry vein commented that:

Even in the controlled atmosphere of the studio, the gear we were using was temperamental to say the least. I doubted that shipping it to the other side of the world would improve this tendency. There was also the fact that we would be going straight from the studio to Australia without actually working out how to play 'Blue Monday' or 'Your Silent Face' live. Bernard claimed that 'Blue Monday' would be impossible to play live – so that *was* a worry. So, soon as we got to Oz, we went straight into a little rehearsal space and worked out if the gear was still working or not and then how to play the new stuff. I think it worked out pretty well considering.

It was another future they were moving painfully toward: the future of computers. As Stephen never tired of maintaining, computers 'will take over' . . . but not just yet.

The Oz tour was the start of a process of trial and error performance that lasted for the next few years and almost two hundred performances before the need to become more consistent at live concerts gradually predominated. Stephen added that:

> When we first did 'Blue Monday' live in Australia, we used the same gear we used to record it – DMX drum machine, Prophet sequencer, Moog Source et cetera. In the mid- to late eighties we updated our setup and switched to Yamaha drum machines and sequencers, and Voyetra 8 synths, still using samples on the Emulator. Later still, we moved over to Akai samplers, and sampled the drum machines and synths sounds into them. It was a similar set up throughout the nineties (sequencers playing samples and/or synths) . . . more or less.
>
> In 2001, we switched to Akai hard-disk recorders (basically a digital multi-track recorder) which meant we didn't have to use sequencers anymore.

One of the more interesting developments was the commissioning in 2001 of Roger Lyons – a producer, engineer, programmer and synthesist – to help them regulate the performance of 'Blue Monday' and other difficult numbers once and for all. They decided, while they were about it, on a major revitalisation of their back catalogue. The chosen tracks included some of the new *Get Ready* album material and an assortment of songs dating right back to the band's original incarnation as Joy Division.

Roger had been one part of Lionrock, along with MC Buzz B and Justin Robertson, and when I was clubbing – first at the No. 1 Club on Central Street (Tim Lennox, LuvDup), then at the Haçienda at Flesh Nights (Tim Lennox again) and the Friday Bugged Out sessions at Sankey's Soap or Jack'n'Jill's Burst nights at the Phoenix and the Park – Lionrock was the kind of music I listened out for. Their tunes were distinctive and clever, and had a deep tech-house groove.

Lyons was most keen to get to grips with 'Blue Monday', as he had never been happy with its live sound, heavily dependent as it was on samples, vocoding effects and multi-layered keyboard parts. He first sorted out the parts of the original multi-tracks, listened carefully to the bits the band wanted to play live and then determined how the recorded bits would sympathetically fit together with the live parts in the performances. When it came to 'Blue Monday', however, he faced an unexpected problem. The original recording could not be found. As Lyons revealed online via *Sound on Sound* magazine:

> For some reason, there was no multi-track for 'Blue Monday' in the vaults of London Records! [After the collapse of Factory in 1992, New Order signed to London Records, and the masters for their back catalogue were transferred there.]
>
> After a bit of detective work, I found out that Quincy Jones [Jones' Qwest Label had been New Order US label] still had a Sony 48-track digital reel of 'Blue Monday' from when he'd copied all the parts for a remix in 1988. He'd just bounced the twenty-four analogue tracks onto his 48-tracker so that he could put his bits on the remaining twenty-four tracks, so I got a copy of that.

Stephen Morris also confirmed to me via email that:

> So Roger went back to the analogue multi-track from Brit Row, transferred that to the Akai hard-disk recorder, did a bit of editing and improving of sounds till we had an amalgam of the version we always played live and elements of the original 12" single – this time being played by a digital recorder instead of sequencers triggering samples. If you see what I mean. I suppose Roger could be credited with 'reprogramming' the song for live performance.

On the cusp of two eras (post-punk and dance) and two technologies (analogue and digital), with the paradoxical nature of innovatory genius – years ahead of its time, yet utterly in and of the moment – 'Blue Monday' had arrived out of nowhere. Now it had achieved the status of respectable classic. But it still sounds fresh and futuristic – like science fiction from the North.

SUITE 16

In the nineties, when I was clubbing, I occasionally caught sight of Rob amongst the crowds in Manchester nightspots. But he wasn't dancing. He was overweight, standing motionless amongst the throngs, a sad and solitary figure. To my shock he looked most unwell and almost unrecognisable from the man I had come to know in the studio thirteen years earlier. Dance music, in which he had played such a key part, had become an unstoppable force. Staring out from amid the dancing crowds, if he could see them at all, he put me in mind of the ageing King Arthur at the end of Henry Treece's novel *The Great Captains*, trying to fathom how it had happened. Stripped of his power, Arthur's role in bringing about extraordinary change has been forgotten. Did he really help bring it about?

Towards the end of Rob's life I was relieved to see that he had slimmed down and seemingly gotten himself back together. We occasionally bumped into each other at lunchtimes in Atlas, the Manchester café bar on Deansgate, where he looked much healthier and happier. Only a short year or two later, I learned he had died of a heart attack. He died on 15 May 1999, at the age of forty-six.

As for the members of New Order, in the years after I left Britannia Row I can recall seeing Bernard and Stephen at the Bauer and Millet car showroom where the band were being filmed for Channel 4; I have no memory of meeting Gillian . . . but more than a couple of Hooky, whose path unexpectedly intertwined with mine again in the first few years after I left Brit Row.

Hooky and I had bumped into one another a few times, once watching the fireworks in Manchester's China Town New Year celebrations not long after the new millennium, and again (around the time of New Order's 2001 album, *Get Ready*) inside a desktop publishing centre in Withington, the south Manchester village to where Savoy Books had recently downsized. The reprographic shop occupied a tiny detached brick building at the corner of Palatine and Wilmslow Roads (it later became a barber's shop), and Hooky had come in to collect some publicity material.

A few years later, when I wanted him to read an early draft of the manuscript for my book about New Order at Brit Row, we met again, this time at a favourite

Hooky eatery, the Little Yang Sing, in Manchester's Chinatown. By this point, I'd already dug out my old diary, typed it up, added an introduction and managed to get an agent for it. Before taking things any further, I wanted the band's approval.

Hooky and close friend Carl 'Twinny' Bellingham had just finished eating when I dropped by. Hooky and Twinny went back a long way, first as drinking buddies then as clubbers at the Electric Circus. After that, Twinny had become New Order's roadie. Promising to read my manuscript, Hooky took it away with him, emailing me a couple of weeks later to give me the thumbs up. 'It's brought back a *lot* of memories,' he wrote, commendably adding that it was 'friendly' – high praise, that!

Around the same time (2011), I sent the manuscript to Stephen and Gillian. Stephen emailed to say how he'd enjoyed reading it, adding: 'I had completely forgotten the name of one of the videos – *Spectre* – so thanks for clearing that up! It's been bugging me for years.' I also sent this early draft to Bernard, through Rebecca Boulton of Prime Management, New Order's management company. Rebecca told me that Bernard doesn't generally like reading about the band and had decided not to read my book – but she kindly made a couple of crucial suggestions herself, pertaining to the Diary section.

I met Hooky again most recently in May 2012 at the party he organised to mark the thirtieth anniversary of the opening of the Haçienda. The club night was held in the basement car park of the new 'Haç' apartments that have been built over the club's original site. Except for the name, there is not much similarity with the old building, but the basement – with its concrete floor – had eerie similarities. Its footprint was roughly the same size as the old Haç dance floor and it seemed to be in exactly the same place. The familiar stripy black-and-yellow hazard paint had been carefully daubed on the support pillars and around the dance area, adding to the impression. Once the night got going I was easily able to imagine myself dancing at Hot, the club's weekly rave night, or Flesh, Paul Cons' and Lucy Scher's monthly gay and transgender night.

Hooky was there to greet everyone as we went in and was the perfect on-stage host for the evening. When my celebratory E started hitting (the first drug of any kind I had taken in twelve years – a special occasion!) I went straight onto the floor, where the clubbers – about a thousand of them – were friendly, smiley and up for it... though all a little bit older than we used to be. The acoustics were shite, as ever – but even in the old days you never went to the Haç for its acoustics – and I managed to give myself some temporary ear damage dancing too close to the right-hand speaker stack.

There were sets by Graeme Park, Dave Haslam, Peter Hook, Jon Dasilva and 808 State. The one sad thing for me was that there was no Tim Lennox, who migrated to the Haç's Flesh night from his legendary night at the No. 1 (a Liverpool-run Manchester gay club, later to become One Central Street). Tim was a tech-house and gay music pioneer in Manchester. I still have mix tapes that I bought from him at the end of nights at the No. 1 and Paradise Garage, another Manchester club where he worked the decks. (Paradise was housed in the old – and last – Factory Records' office, on Charles Street, Manchester; in 2010 the building became home to Hooky's Factory nights).

My most significant encounter with Hooky happened much earlier, however, in 1985, a few years after the Brit Row recordings. New Order's third album, *Low-Life*, was about to be released. It happened after David and I decided to start producing records, and Hooky opened a recording studio – a case of great minds coming together . . .

How did a book publishing company come to make records? The answer is simple. Music has always been very important to us. We had long wanted to do records as well as books, but we kept putting it off until a variety of things made us take the plunge. One of these factors was watching New Order at Britannia Row (an unintended side effect, as I hadn't gone there for that reason). Another, most crucial one was meeting fallen sixties pop star P.J. Proby – or Jim as we came to know him. As explained elsewhere, David and I came to know Jim by intending to write his life story. But after a few months of pursuing him with a tape-recorder we saw that what he needed most of all was a record deal. That magical voice of his was going to waste. For a pair of ivory-tower pedagogues, we knew that producing a record star of his stature would be no easy task. But we decided to get our egos dirty and give it a go. Hooky, meanwhile, buying into a recording studio was another big deciding factor for us. We now knew someone we trusted to help get us started.

The studio was Suite 16. Located in Rochdale, at 16 Kenion Street, off Drake Street, one of the town's main thoroughfares leading down from the railway station. Previously it had been Cargo Studios. Under the stewardship of John Brierley, ex-recording engineer for John Peel, it had been one of the North's main punk recording studios, where Joy Division recorded 'Digital', 'Glass' and 'Atmosphere', so there was pedigree in it for Hooky. Stephen had famously once been asked by Martin Hannett to take his drum kit onto the roof, to little usable effect except as an anecdote – the band had driven away leaving him stranded!

Hooky's partner, Chris Hewitt, was a big part of the myth that grew up around Cargo. Chris was once the main organiser of the legendary Deeply Vale free festivals, which I remember attending. These were held outside Bury, Greater Manchester, in a valley that has amazing natural acoustics owing to its winding canyon-like geology. Straight after forming Factory Records in 1978, Tony Wilson compered there, introducing the Fall and the Durutti Column. The annual festival ran for four years from 1976 to '79, uniting the punk and the free festival scene, but the event became too populous and was closed down by a panic-stricken council.

On the day we arrived, in February, the studio was still in the process of revamping and only the first floor of Suite 16 was ready for occupancy (we got a rebate – another incentive). The place smelled of paint and fresh wood, and downstairs Hooky was busy doing the joinery, perched atop a painter's ladder in jeans and cowboy boots, from where he exchanged pleasantries. We were his first clients, he announced cheerfully, waving a carpenter's saw. This made P. J. Proby his first recording star and much was made of this in the studio's early publicity.

Suite 16's blonde spiky-haired engineer was Chris Jones, who had been headhunted from Strawberry Studios fresh from engineering Terry Hall's *Colourfield* album. Still in his early twenties, 'C. J.' as he was called, was one of the first of many engineers to help us produce our songs. He had a winning smile and an up-for-it attitude. He also had – or seemed to have – a cool head. Just as well, considering the anarchy we were about to bring to him for the next few years. For a while, 'C. J.' and 'P. J.' (P. J. Proby) were to become legendary in the studio.

Jim, like Ian Curtis had been, was shamanic. He had (and still has) a pitch-perfect operatic voice with a heroic command and range, and was an original and compelling showman with a dangerously contradictory camp theatricality. In the sixties, his audiences of mainly teenage girls were captivated. His aim was to live the rock'n'roll lifestyle with cultural and intellectual pretensions. Brought to England from Texas in 1963 by television impresario Jack Good for Good's show, *Around the Beatles*, the power of his charisma and performance easily offset the immense talents of his show hosts. He scored instant stardom and set about maintaining it with a string of hits. One of his specialities was 'destroying' hallowed anthems, by using his voice to bend the notes of the songs in mock seriousness. The Proby versions of 'Somewhere' and 'Maria', Stephen Sondheim ballads from *West Side Story*, are classics of subversive pomp.

He soon went too far. On the 1965 Cilla Black tour, he split his trousers on-stage. The rents went across his knees and up the inside of his thighs and in the staid atmosphere of the times – before the Rolling Stones were photographed pissing against a petrol station wall – this was sufficient to bring about the outright bans that resulted in his downfall.

But several years down the line, a remarkable thing happened. A rebel of the next generation copied this sartorial rupture and turned what had been Proby's act into a global fashion. Iggy Pop acknowledged his debt to Proby, but decided he would rip his jeans *before* he went on stage.

Our work at Suite 16 ultimately led to us cutting three versions of 'Blue Monday', which I will describe in due course. None of these were cut with P. J. Proby. But one of the songs Jim did for us at Suite 16 was Joy Division's 'Love Will Tear Us Apart'. We found ourselves in their old studio about to demolish it. This wasn't planned.

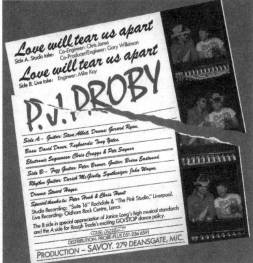

Above: P.J. Proby's cover of 'Love Will Tear Us Apart,' issued on 7" and 12" vinyl by Savoy Records in 1985 and mainly recorded at Suite 16, Hooky's new studio. We were his first clients and Proby was his first superstar. Left: Reverse cover of 'Love Will Tear Us Apart' showing stills of Proby and Hooky playing the fool behind the studio's recording desk. They were being filmed for *Granada Reports*, ITV Television. Design: Chameleon/Britton.

It's how it happened. We wanted to produce records. We had found an artist, we were natural piss-takers ourselves and now we had a studio. It was simple. But as it happened, I don't think we demolished the song at all.

When news got out that P.J. Proby was recording at Hooky's new studio, local broadcaster-presenter Bob Dickinson brought a Granada Television film crew to interview them. The interview took place on 7 March 1985. Bob had just started work as a researcher at Granada's Quay Street studios in Manchester where new recruits were required to cut their teeth on *Granada Reports*, the station's daily local news programme. Apart from giving them a chance to work alongside presenters like Tony Wilson, Judy Finnigan and Bob Greaves – all talented journalists as well as local celebrities – they rapidly learned practical skills like directing a news item with a film crew, writing a script and editing an item – all for same-day transmission. In an email to me, Bob recalled how:

I was eager to make as much of an impression as I could, so when a friend – the documentary film director Peter Carr – told me he'd heard the infamous American pop star, P.J. Proby, was not only living locally but about to record in Rochdale, a cover of a Joy Division number, I was desperate to get the story approved for production at one of their morning editorial meetings, with me being responsible for getting it on air. Personally, P.J. Proby was something of a legend from my sixties childhood. I'd watched him on *Ready Steady Go!*, *Top of the Pops* and other TV shows, belting out his hits in that slightly operatic, but also strongly rockabilly-punk style, while moving his body in ways that were unmistakably sexual, although my youthful mind reassured itself he was just fooling around.

Fortunately my programme editor, Sue Woodward, was equally enthusiastic and told me to make contact with the producers of the project, Michael and David, of Savoy Books, and get over to Rochdale with a camera crew right away. The news in the north-west of England had been dominated for the past year by the miners' strike and Proby's new project, a cover of Joy Division's 'Love Will Tear Us Apart', seemed incredibly appropriate. The trouble was he hadn't recorded it yet, so I had no music to use in the film I was about to make, other than a choice of his hits from the 1960s.

Arriving at 10:00am at Suite 16 studios, we were greeted by Peter Hook, whom I'd met once before, when I interviewed Joy Division for a local magazine, *New Manchester Review*, in 1980.

Peter remembered me, which helped. I don't remember, though, the exact course of events that followed immediately, as camera equipment was brought in, lighting set up, and introductions made between me, Savoy Books and the

Granada crew. I don't remember, for instance, what Peter Hook may have said on record about the whole nature of the project: a new version of a number he'd helped to create, one of the most extraordinary and important pieces of music to emerge from post-punk Manchester. How could it better the original? What was the crazy thinking behind doing this? I am not sure if he, Michael or David, knew what would happen. I certainly didn't.

P.J. Proby was different, however. My memories of any introductory remarks ('Hello', 'pleased to meet you', et cetera) are hazy. He seemed to have been present all the time, stalking the space. I only recall that his presence made me nervous. Importantly, he had a girl with him, and she was very young, a teenager. Apparently she came from Leeds and had run away with him. His charisma was undeniable. Both he and the girl were dressed in best country & western threads; denim, leather, more denim, and Stetson hats. And both were swigging away – and had been for some time – from cans of Carlsberg Special Brew. Later, I understood Proby – nervous about being tracked down by the girl's parents – was also carrying a loaded handgun.

Whatever the circumstances, it has to be pointed out that at the time, no matter how uncomfortable it made me feel, I thought this situation with a 'famous rock star' was actually, strangely normal, and to be expected. I'd met so many paranoid, drugged-out, drunken, mad egotists in the music scene of the late seventies and early eighties that I thought this situation, despite being awkward because of the TV camera, was full of potential.

For a start, the guy was making a record. It was a creative moment. We were privileged to intervene in his process, and maybe he could actually re-invent himself by doing it. But as the moments elapsed, I began to doubt this. Proby was Proby and couldn't/wouldn't/shouldn't be re-invented; and in fact, that was the point of Savoy working with him. I realised this, although I didn't end up articulating it in the subsequent television report, the length and style of which allowed little space for semi-subtle considerations on cultural shifts and creative behaviour. So we filmed an awkward, crazed interview, compressing Jim Proby's complex career into a few guffaws and grunts and remarks, plus his thoughts about Doing This New Project.

If I hadn't had to get back to Manchester by lunchtime to start editing and for the film crew to be re-assigned, I'd have stayed all day, and watched what happened as the hours unfolded. Unfortunately this was not a documentary film-shoot. Before we entered the studio, I had asked the cameraman to record a wide, establishing shot of the studio buildings looking out over the Rochdale landscape of rooftops and chimneys, in the style of *Coronation Street*'s opening credits. Back in the editing room, I used that shot to combine with Proby's

1964 hit, 'Somewhere', the record's opening orchestral notes running under the landscape visuals and Jim's voice coming in, 'There's a place for us . . .' And then, in close-up, in Rochdale, he appeared, along with his teenage runaway girl accomplice.

The item – and it was just one short item within a thirty-minute, 1980s' regional news programme – was transmitted that evening. Everyone seemed to love it. Sue Woodward laughed and laughed. But she and they probably didn't, or couldn't understand – or even think about – why on earth Proby was covering Joy Division's 'Love Will Tear Us Apart', largely because there was, at that moment, no available evidence of what it might sound like.

A few years later, maybe in 1990 or 1991, a colleague of mine at Granada, Sarah March, made a documentary about P.J. Proby at Suite 16, and we tried to find my earlier *Granada Reports* item, for possible archive film to use within it. But it could not be located in Granada's archives. It had disappeared. It had probably been wiped and I have never been able to locate amateur video recordings of it (I didn't own a video recorder at the time, either). It's a lost piece of evidence, the details of which have faded a good deal in my memory: of the time one of pop's wildest offenders from the formative period of the late fifties and sixties made later, splattering contact with Manchester's most important group of the post-Second World War period. It was otherworldly. This thought interests me to this day.

Still alive at the time of this being written, P.J. Proby was in his time beyond control, while Ian Curtis, who performed in a way that appeared beyond control, died young, providing the material for Proby to take and gnaw on and chew over. Savoy's was not even remotely a commercial project, but certain energies that were very much around in Manchester at the time made it an appropriate, even an inevitable one. I would love to talk to Proby about it again, even now.

Bob's feature, which appears to have been wiped by Granada, was aired that same day. All that probably remains of the interview is our record sleeve with its photographs of Hooky and P.J. playing the fool, seated behind the mixing desk swapping P.J.'s straw Trilby around.

The single was recorded at Suite 16, but mixed at Liverpool's Pink Studios (Hambi Haralambous's studio, of Hambi and the Dance). Gary Wilkinson, a young engineer who made a big impression on David and I, engineered it. Hambi had just pulled rank on Gary about some matter or other and Gary's anger went into the mix we did. The song is powered by a series of sparse orchestral stabs that contrast perfectly with Proby's crooning in the second part of the song. It was released in 1985, cautiously played and liked ('yes, I think I like that . . .') by John

Peel. Paul Temple writing in the *Melody Maker* called it 'a full-blown Hitchcockian masterpiece' and a 'portrait of sexual paranoia'. *Creem* made it 'Single of the Month' in an enthusiastic page-long review by Ken Barnes.

A year later, our venture into the world of music led to us doing a version of 'Blue Monday'. Once again, something we tried to subvert turned out to have its own quality. David had noticed 'Blue Monday' fitted perfectly with Springsteen's 'Cadillac Ranch' and wanted to try mashing the two together to see what resulted. If we got the sound we were looking for it would be released under the Lord Horror *nom de guerre*. To help us achieve this, we needed another singer with a big voice and we brought in Liverpool rocker Bobby Thompson (ex-Kingsize Taylor and the Dominoes). The idea worked and became our first Lord Horror recording – also mixed by Gary Wilkinson.

Not unsurprisingly, the song was pronounced a 'pile of shite' by Hooky . . . but hey, Hooky, perhaps that's because we mixed it at Pink again instead of Suite 16? Elsewhere, it was well received, DJs at the Ritz in Manchester regularly mixing it with the New Order original and William Leith, reviewing it for the *NME*, finding the sleeve art deranged but the track itself 'musically, rather tasteful'. Paula and Genesis P-Orridge for *CUT* magazine declared that it was about time someone got round to taking 'the piss out of New Order in such a humorous and constructive way'.

'Blue Monday' must have gotten to us, for it led to a serious obsession (so much for piss-taking) and two further versions twenty-six years later in 2012, cut for us by the legendary chanteuse and *Carry On Screaming* actress, Fenella Fielding, whose distinctively husky voice made us late fifties schoolboys her instant fans. (Among other notable roles, Fenella is the 'Tannoy' voice in sixties television series, *The Prisoner*, the overdubbed voice of Anita Pallenberg's character in *Barbarella* and the 'blue voice' in every dope-smoker's favourite episode of *The Magic Roundabout*, 'Dougal and the Blue Cat').

Both these new 'Blue Monday' tracks appeared on an album Fenella made for us in 2012. By getting her to sing 'Blue Monday', 'the chaps' as she called us were experimenting with a mix of two cultural eras and generations. In the fifties and sixties, Fenella had been a star of the 'review'. She had her own show, during which – in the traditional 'review' way – she would perform a range of songs and monologues on-stage to live accompaniments. It was a form of entertainment that, by the early sixties, had disappeared. But it reflected the kind of music in which she was still steeped. Had 'Blue Monday' been around in her day, it was the kind of song, with its almost spoken delivery, that would have ideally suited her act. So, on the one hand, we had Fenella, a living repertoire of a fascinating musical period, and on the other, a groundbreaking classic contemporary dance track. We wanted to see what could be made of this. Fenella, of course, is also a woman and 'Blue Monday' is a gender-neutral song, adding an added element of frisson.

By this time we had moved to another Rochdale studio, Lisa Stansfield's Gracieland, managed by Martin Rhodes, where our recording wing finally stayed put after years of moving about. For many years we have been entrusting our musical destiny to the capable hands of Gracieland's resident engineer, Stephen Boyce-Buckley, who does our arrangements and co-produces our songs. (He also helped me with my musical descriptions of the Britannia Row recordings for this book.) Stephen is well liked and respected on the Manchester music scene, and able to call on a seemingly endless stream of musicians and singers, some of whom appeared on our album with Fenella. This has brought to us the considerable talents of Denise Johnson and Rowetta (duetting!), Andrew Price, Melanie Williams and the late Barrington Stewart. Stephen's production magnum opus (not one of ours) is the Kenni Wenna album *Real Lite*, for which he brought together his entire talent pool.

The longer of the two 'Blue Monday' versions on Fenella's album has more of a rock-influenced groove. We segued it with a cover of Eddie Cochran's 'What'd I Say', played on the guitar and sung for us by Darrel Higham, and produced with a dynamite punch for us by Peter Saynor. (Another trusty 'musical factotum' of Savoy's, Pete was part of the Altrincham music cadre where my story started and a one-time neighbour of my mother's in Charter Road).

The shorter version of 'Blue Monday' was produced for us by Stephen Buckley, and is markedly different. When we first got Fenella to sing New Order's song we purposefully kept her unaware of the band's tragic history. We wanted her to capture 'Blue Monday's' neutral emotionless tone. After she delivered her vocal (perfectly – in a different session she also read from J.G. Ballard's novel *Crash*, for us, in the same neutral voice), I decided to explain to her about Ian's death and the latent feeling that might lie behind the song's distanced lyrical tone. I intended simply to let her know the history. But we didn't anticipate her reaction. She was very moved, almost agitated, and immediately asked if she could re-do her vocal. On this second occasion, although she still sung it with some of the reserve 'Blue Monday' demands, she delivered unexpected emotion and empathy, and an edge of something darker that I thought perhaps might be anger. Perhaps it had hit at some personal experience of her own? When we heard what she had given us, we decided to make two versions, and made this one the opening track on her album, *Fenella Fielding: The Savoy Sessions*. It is Fenella's own version, sensitively accompanied by Stephen Buckley's arrangement. It is also – something I hadn't realised then – a tribute of my own to Ian.

SCIENCE FICTION

Joy Division's music playing in the room above my bedroom at my mother's Altrincham rooming house in 1979 had been the sound of the future leaking in. During the long summer when Malcolm Whitehead was making his film, I was not just trying to get some sleep for work the next day. The music, with its strident energy and pessimistic edge, really did seem like a future paradoxical paean of doom (though in its darkness there was an equally strong positive force, trying to emerge). Under the spell of William Burroughs and Captain Beefheart, I was struggling to write a story of swords and sorcery set in the deserts of a nuclear war. The harsh, furious sounds evoking images of discordance from above me – state collapse, social dismantling, Ballardian cityscapes – intermingled with the images I was attempting to set down.

No one knew whether civilisation might collapse or, as the seventies turned and the eighties wore on, whether a new fascism might emerge in the UK. There was a television series called *The Guardians*. What if Her Majesty's government refused to leave power? The possibilities were undeniably dystopian . . .

In a sense, Joy Division's music pounding down into my bedroom was returning to the same world from whence it sprang – back when Stephen and Adam, later joined by Ian, discovered Savoy's chain of bookstores. Snatches of 'New Dawn Fades', 'Transmission', 'She's Lost Control' and 'Leaders of Men' playing repeatedly, night after night, became for me aural codas for a parallel reality.

After Ian's death, New Order's music did not lose these science-fiction connotations: the music simply flipped from being dystopian to celebratory – *joie de vivre* with an electro edge. The affirmative energy of Joy Division, there all along, found a way of bursting out of the gloom.

When the 'Blue Monday' lyrics were being collaged together, some of the imagery came from boats (Bernard is a sailor and, oddly, the Haçienda was a former yacht showroom), but its name is borrowed from an American sci-fi novel. In a February 2013 interview with the *Guardian*, Gillian revealed that: 'People have interpreted the title of "Blue Monday" all sorts of ways. It actually came from a book Stephen was reading, Kurt Vonnegut's *Breakfast of Champions*. One of its illustrations reads, "Goodbye Blue Monday". It's a reference to the invention of the washing machine, which improved housewives' lives.'

Goodbye Blue Monday is the alternative title of *Breakfast of Champions*, and the novel was on sale in our bookshops where Stephen may have found his copy. (The punk DIY ethic was as open to possibility as the fiction of ideas; one tended to power the other.) The 'Goodbye Blue Monday' illustration inside Vonnegut's book is of a flying bomb that looks a lot like Fat Man, one of the two atomic devices detonated by American forces over Japan, which brought World War Two to an end. Scrawled on the bomb's casement are the words 'Goodbye Blue Monday'. The slogan was actually coined in the 1930s by a company that was trying to develop an automatic washing machine. But the washing machine, as Gillian said, failed and the company sold some of the technology they'd developed for washing machine technology to the American government, which used it for bomb detonation mechanisms. (Some of this information comes courtesy of the MacRumors website.)

Why did the washing machine fail? Vonnegut's novel mocks *laissez-faire* capitalism for its amorality, but doesn't stop there. Going deeper, it hits at the underlying American attitudes that brought development of the machine, by one company at least, to a halt. Monday was the day of the week when American domestics did the household washing. Although the machines of progress improved housewives' lives, they freed black and white women alike. Most domestics were black. Modernity, as exemplified by such egalitarian automata, threatened the kind of Americans who felt the American Civil War had cheated them out of their slave-owning lifestyles. That was the reason. The automatic washer almost went the way of the everlasting light bulb.

Meaning in New Order's work is characteristically ambiguous, perhaps because they are not natural writers and have not tried to form a single cohesive narrative, preferring to pull in ideas – and words – from around them. But the thought and erudition they bring to this writing process – whether borrowing from musical, technological, filmic or literary sources – are varied and eclectic. They are every bit as effective as Joy Division's more traditional linear approach. The difference is that the ideas are applied more lightly, more playfully – less analogue and more digital, perhaps.

For me, the ironical satire implicit in the title of 'Blue Monday', the method of the song's construction and the punk inspiration that lies behind it (the whole Factory experiment), puts both it and *Power, Corruption & Lies* in the company of seminal literary works inspired by the sixties' post-modern science fiction authored by Moorcock and Ballard, in the same company as books like William Gibson's *Neuromancer* (1984) or Alan Moore's *Watchmen* (1986/87), which appeared within a few years of the Britannia Row recordings.

In interview with the *New Statesman* in July 2015, Moorcock said we live in a 'Philip K. Dick world'. By this I think he means that our world today is the expression of 'soft' science-fiction writers like Dick, rather than hard science prophets like Isaac Asimov, Arthur C. Clarke or Robert A. Heinlein. Traditionally, SF is about outer-space, weird life forms and the distant future, whereas the focus of new-wave authors like Dick (and Vonnegut) is the world as it is now.

The 'future' is constantly being generated from the past by the decisions we make (or don't make) in the present moment. Because much that happens to us in life is unpredictable, so our decisions are often based on randomness, and the decisions we make at these unexpected moments are often the most important. Ian's unexpected death froze for all time the band's early body of work rooted in its perceived darkness and despair, clearly distinguishing it from other music of the time; but because of New Order's and Rob's response, it caused an entirely new body of equivalent work to rise. Their rapid grasp of a new dynamic and their conscious decision not to emulate Joy Division, brought about the musical development they were seeking.

My friend, the late psychologist John H. Clark, was fond of telling me that, 'death is the final edit'. He said this sagely and triumphantly and sometimes, I imagine, very sadly as he suffered from depression. And in fact his own death from a brain tumour wasn't far away. It cut short his career. John was the author of *A Map of Mental States* (1983), a geometrical model of a human mental life. He taught at Manchester University and his death in 1992 was linked to radiation left over from one hundred-year-old experiments by Ernest Rutherford, the father of modern nuclear physics. John's office, which he occupied for two decades, was Room 2.62, directly below Rutherford's old one. His colleague, the psychologist Dr Hugh Wagner, who occupied the actual Rutherford room, also died early from cancer. Two further deaths from cancer were subsequently linked to the building.

But John's death didn't make his insight wrong. Indeed, it is actually an astute observation. His favourite art 'size' was minimal. Less is more. He enjoyed Oriental art because of its economy of expression and genuinely believed that the fewest words or brushstrokes said the most profound things. What I think he meant by his proclamation is that death can be *the* prime arbiter in an artist's life. It is a very effective simplifier, either physically, by stopping further work being produced, or critically by bringing the focus onto an artist's best work.

James Dean, Percy Bysshe Shelley and Amy Winehouse were caught by the editor young. Had they gone on to live long lives, would their legacy have been quite so impactful? Some artists continue producing milestones into old age. Others need as long as possible to make even the smallest impact. Still others may shine brightest young. The band Joy Division-New Order had a double-barrelled start, one barrel firing after the other.

It's possible they couldn't have continued as Joy Division. As Joy Division they were part of the more reflective post-punk music – Ultravox (with Midge Ure), Depeche Mode, OMD, synth-pop act the Human League (all the League, incidentally, big Philip K. Dick, Michael Moorcock and J.G. Ballard fans – singer Phil Oakey visually influenced by Moorcock's Jerry Cornelius character), Spandau Ballet, Clock DVA, mainstream singers like Elton John, Devo in their dying industrial Cleveland . . .

The Sex Pistols' 'no future' declaration had picked up on the latent mood of disenfranchised Britain. For some it really did seem like the end of history, and these exponents of punk's new wave responded in different ways. A signifying strand of the new post-punk music looked backward, yearning for a different future, a non-future, the future of the recent past – the cultural epoch of modernism that in reality had ended in the 1950s. Songs were imbued with the imagery of autobahns, mysterious assignations on deserted concrete esplanades, European railway journeys, communist utopias, the Soviet Bloc, a fascination with totalitarianism and corresponding post-Nazi longings for a lost Europe. Polish author, Agata Pyzik expressed it perfectly in the 'Ashes and Brocade' chapter of her book, *Poor but Sexy: Culture Clashes in Europe East and West*, where she gives an evocative description of this musical era, and also hypothesises that the West's attraction to Berlin at this time was the result of the respective visitor-countries' blandness, their depoliticisation.

David Bowie, who first embraced fascism as an antidote to the recession years of the seventies, was brought back to his senses just in time with *Scary Monsters*. Catching the same mood were films like *Christiane F*. It was the future of an alternate universe, a noir, new-wave SF, because the real world of the eighties – or so it seemed – was gripped in social stasis, frozen in a time where the most outrageous thing you could do was to swap gender, dress extravagantly and escape into inner-space and drugs.

No more real heroes, Pyzik noted. From now on the most desirable thing was to be fabricated. What was genuine, authentic, was boring.

This strand of the music, before dance, was relatively short-lived and as Thatcherism prevailed and society moved on, it had nowhere else to go. Had tragedy not struck, Joy Division might have been trapped at this historic but short-lived musical moment. Although their music – weighted by the psychological darkness of their singer, furious and aggrieved, frightened and frightening – was a genuine reflection of the feelings of a generation stalled in the dour North and arguably in a category of its own, and although they were gaining in following and critical acclaim, the group might well have remained stuck in this cul-de-sac and never have escaped their status as a cult band. For Bernard, their music as Joy Division was about 'the death of optimism, of youth', as per Jon Savage's liner notes for 1997's *Heart and Soul* box set.

In its unique fusion of opposites – Mancunian dour and the sunniness of New York – the sound New Order eventually produced, epitomised by 'Blue Monday', took them to a new level, without losing any of the ground that they had gained. It represented an optimism that was a decisive move away from the dystopian SF noir of the pre-Berlin Wall years to the kind of science fiction that, for me, they epitomise now. Additionally, although the Brit Row tracks were imbued with Joy Division, they are mature reflections from a position of strength, not tragedy. It worked.

Joy Division and New Order are one band. Ian's catastrophic death highlighted their early work. But his torch has shone both ways. The band have reached a kind of maturity that they may never otherwise have attained. Such a loss as they suffered, as well as bestowing legendary status, could very likely finish a band. Instead, it gave New Order what many artists try hard to achieve and fail: a convincing mainstream mythology.

With 'Blue Monday' finally tamed by Roger Lyons, I went to see New Order headline at Jodrell Bank Music and Science Festival in July 2013. It was the first time I had seen them play since Hooky's departure. New Order played next to the giant radio telescope. Stage and telescope were literally yards from each other. The eye logically expected there to be common intent, but of course there was none. Mounted on huge buggies that moved around a circular rail, the Lovell Dish turned slowly to face different areas of the sky, observing phenomena diametrically distinct from the concerns of, and invisible to, the relaxed post-Haçienda crowds with their children. Its movement was almost imperceptible and, with our attentions divided, awareness of it was lost for long periods of time. The dish might be pointed away from the stage, distantly preoccupied, but when we noticed it again we would find it had silently turned towards us, shockingly close, like some huge sensor prying or expectant. Anthropocentrically, we had to remind ourselves that it was interested not in us but some distant pulsar that happened to lie roughly in our directions.

As the afternoon wore on and bands succeeded each other – the Whip, Public Service Broadcasting, Johnny Marr who co-headlined – as darkness fell and New Order took to the stage, the deep dish did briefly seem to cease its work and acknowledge the social gathering by its side, tilting purposefully towards the stage where it remained for a fitting length of time, acting as a projection screen for a spectacular display of lasers bouncing backwards and forwards in its concave depths, the incomprehensibility between man and machine being briefly banished in a friendly gesture by New Order fan Professor Tim O'Brien, Associate Director of Jodrell Bank Observatory, and his colleagues. My fellow concertgoer, brother-in-law and musicologist Bob Grafton, later mused fancifully:

Ostensibly looking outward for aliens, the dish is itself an alien presence looming over the proceedings all afternoon. It is arguable that the real aliens lie beneath it – within hailing distance. The generation fed on a soma of instant digital gratification has congregated in its shadow to see New Order, their only previous knowledge of science a hotchpotch of outlandish theories gathered from Marvel comics and sci-fi movies. It is gratifying to see New Order (belatedly themselves perhaps) trying to bridge the gap between their acolytes and the few true scientists who are still working this afternoon in their preciously allocated timeslots, serving the 24/7 demands of the beast. Their poignant radio-Tannoy communications with the crowd, only serve to emphasise the distance between their own dedication and the apparent hedonism of their audience.

The presence of the telescope and the still-youthful crowds made me think again of *RebelWithout a Cause*. In this film, director Nicholas Ray's use of the observatory as a symbolic portal to the infinite universe lent significance to the behaviour of the juvenile delinquents who – like the hominids in the later *2001: A Space Odyssey*, fighting for territory – seemed to signal a fatal flaw in mankind: the tribal unavoidability of war. Ray's portrayal is shocking in itself. Yet the untimely death of James Dean, the film's young star, before *Rebel* was even released made it even more so. How different an occasion was this gig at Jodrell Bank, celebrating the band's post-Joy Division trajectory, where a tragic death had given birth to a positive, creative force. Blinking in the laser-light, I emerged from this reverie feeling I had reached some profound understanding.

Watching New Order at Jodrell Bank I was also reminded, not for the first time, of Pink Floyd. There are obvious parallels between the two acts, of course: the loss of their troubled young singer, their subsequent change of musical direction and huge mainstream success. This was the first thought that struck me when I entered the Brit Row studio, and it became particularly strong when I heard the music they had written. The impression did not leave me the whole time I was there. In each song, their earlier, darker sound was discernible, shaped by Ian's lyricism and personality, and their narrower earlier concerns. But it had now become the robust foundation of a new sound, underpinning music that was wide-ranging and inclusive, just like Pink Floyd's newer material. After the Brit Row recordings, Rob Gretton admitted as much. 'From now on, it's going to be like the Pink Floyd,' he assured Paul Rambali in an interview with *The Face* in July 1983. And there had been the humdrum fact that New Order were cutting their new records at the Floyd's recording studio.

But listening to New Order that afternoon, a most glaring similarity to add to my list, I suddenly realised, was the absence of Hooky. Hadn't founding Floyd member bassist Roger Waters also left the band and not performed with them again for eighteen years? Hooky has not played with New Order since 2007. When the current line-up started playing together in 2011, Hooky wasn't part of it. His absence at Jodrell Bank, his replacement and the band's new line-up, brought an eerie feeling of déjà vu. Ostensibly, I had come to the science festival to conduct research for my book about 'Blue Monday'. I quickly saw there was another reason. Part of me had come here wanting to reconnect and I could not help thinking back to the Brit Row sessions where I first properly came to know the band, when they were all still friends together, living – as friends do – with their differences and joined by a common goal.

Now they had separated in two, each taking a piece of their once conjoined past with them. But on that crowded sunny afternoon at Jodrell Bank, the New Order sound, in which Hooky had played such a significant part, was ineradicably there. The professional additions of Bad Lieutenant members Phil Cunningham and Tom Chapman confirmed, with the solid core of Bernard, Stephen and Gillian, New Order's durability.

Hooky, for his part, is touring with a new band named the Light – a playful development, but it is the 'light' New Order brought to Joy Division as well as the 'new light' Hooky claims his personal appreciation has brought to the band's back catalogue (the Light have been known to play *Unknown Pleasures* and *Closer* in their entirety at live shows), in particular the contributions of Martin Hannett to their recorded sound, about which, at Brit Row, I felt he had been pragmatic. There, he had been accepting of Hannett's smoother more cerebral sound because Hannett had been part of the Factory equation . . . when in truth Hooky's heart went the other way and he had preferred their earlier recorded sound.

The Light centres more on Joy Division than New Order, and Hooky has fashioned himself as the gatekeeper of their old material, while Bernard prefers not to look that way. Nevertheless the spirit of both of Hooky's old bands is detectable in his new one, a quiet dignity infusing his take on the sound. When ex-Happy Mondays' singer Rowetta joined the group for its *Unknown Pleasures* tour, you could 'hear' the history playing around her subtle vocal line.

There is not enough light in the world anyway . . .

At the time of the Jodrell Bank gig, the UK was still emerging from recession. Looking round at the crowds with their children, and the Ibiza-like antics of some of the partygoers it was hard to think that anything was amiss. Yet there was irony in the fact that *Power, Corruption & Lies* and 'Blue Monday' were created in the grip of the last global recession before this one . . . the severity of which had clipped Joy Division, whose music reflected the privations of the decade and a generation settling-in for worse to come. The resulting jobless figures were intensified by the

Thatcher administration's radical restructuring of UK industry. This harsh medicine was administered concomitantly with the recession. In 1982 unemployment soared to 3 million – the highest it had been since the days of the Great Depression of the 1930s. In the first half of the eighties it climbed even higher and young people, unable to find work and accommodation, began sleeping rough on the streets. Dispossessed, homeless youths, with dogs on string, begging for money or food, became a common sight on the UK streets.

Power, Corruption & Lies had the working title of '*How Does it Feel?*' (the opening line of 'Blue Monday'), until New Order realised the name had already been used by UK anarchist punk-rock collective, Crass. The line 'How does it feel?' is more usually construed as referring to emotional loss. But given the ambiguous nature of New Order's random 'cut-up' lyrics, when Bernard 'wrote' the song it could well have been a sneering address about austerity. The Brit Row songs were wrought from regions of deprivation, written by performers who knew the social effects of austerity all too well. Constantly left playing, the television in the recording studio broadcast these scenes into the random mix of influences. The album's eventual title – as arbitrary as any of their lyrics – might confirm this. In the words of designer Peter Saville, it declares how 'power, corruption and lies infiltrate our lives'.

The lyrics of 'Blue Monday' have no logical meaning. New Order may as well have pulled them out of the Dada poet's Tristan Tzara's hat; like all the best rock'n'roll lyrics, they are irrational. 'Blue Monday' is the product of a collaborative mind. It is a *feeling*. Read into this what you will.

And perhaps it is coincidence that 3 million copies of 'Blue Monday' sold in 1983? If it is too great a stretch of plausibility to link sales with those who were put out of work, then it is at least poetical correlation. But there is little doubt that after the formation of Factory Records, the fortunes of Manchester began very slowly to rise out of recession. According to the 2011 census the city region with which New Order is identified has experienced the highest population growth outside London. The total population of Greater Manchester is expected to grow to just under 3 million by 2031. (That figure again.) The ripples of Manchester music, like Liverpool's before it, spread out, playing its part in eventually renewing the zeitgeist of the country: science-fiction music to lift the country out of recession.

The cultural tsunami that began when I heard Malcolm playing music above me – and the door that opened for me personally – has now merged into the historical background. Four of the leading figures – Ian Curtis, Tony Wilson, Martin Hannett and Rob Gretton – have passed away. So have more minor players like Claude Bessy, who died in 1999. As have the innovative physical out-workings of Factory Records and the Haçienda.

But the legacy of the time of punk DIY lives on in the small things as well as the big. Once a week, Peter Miles, Barney's primary school mate, visits Tony Wilson's grave in Southern Cemetery on the southern outskirts of Manchester, tidies it and leaves small ornaments – model trains and houses. 'Man of the people' Tony once spent time with him, and Pete has never forgotten it.

And across the road from where the Haçienda once stood is the new development of First Street, containing Home – a centre for the arts that could not have existed had the earlier Factory arts laboratory not paved the way. It is on Tony Wilson Place. Ironically, the new centre has been busy from the moment it opened in 2015. A huge £110m arts venue, the Factory Theatre, named after Tony Wilson's Factory, due for completion in 2019, is to be built on the site of the old Granada Television Studios (Granada followed BBC North to Media City, Salford). It will be largely funded by the government.

The Haçienda must be built.

Inside the rounded four-storey red-bricked building on the corner of Whitworth Street West and Albion Street, which had housed a former yacht showroom and later became a Bollywood cinema, was a humming, super-modern art and dance house. It was something that shouldn't have happened and under normal earthbound rules wouldn't have. It was set in a landscape of industrial dereliction and decay, of abandoned warehouses, behind a canal choked with rubbish, the waterway's towpaths covered in broken glass from the vandalised buildings. At any moment it could have decided to take off and leave. But it didn't. It remained open, fully staffed and waiting.

Michael Butterworth (left) and Claude Bessy in the DJ box at the Haçienda, at a New Year's party hosted by Ikon Video, January 1984.

APPENDIX 1

'BLUE MONDAY': A FACT SHEET

Recorded: 1982

Original release date: 7 March 1983

Key remixes
1988	'Blue Monday 1988', remixed by Quincy Jones and John Potoker
1995	'Blue Monday 1995', remixed by Hardfloor

Highest UK chart positions
1983	#9
1988	#3
1995	#17

Sales: As of 2012, the single is estimated to have sold 1.16 million copies in the UK alone. In the same year, it was ranked #69 on a list of all-time best-selling UK singles. It has sold over 3 million copies worldwide and is still the biggest selling 12" of all time.

Selected cover versions
- US metal band Orgy had an international hit with a cover of 'Blue Monday', released in December 1998. When the cover was played on rock night at Manchester's Ritz nightclub, 'moshers' would take to the sprung dance-floor to perform a synchronised routine in grid formation.
- Norwegian electronic band, Flunk, covered the song in 2002.
- In 2004, a 1988 version of 'Blue Monday' by 808 State, popular at the Haçienda and believed lost, was released by Aphex Twin's Rephlex Records.

Trivia

- At 7:29, the original 1983 version is one of the longest singles ever to chart in the UK.
- It's commonly claimed that this release lost money on every copy sold, due to the high production cost of its ornate, Peter Saville-designed sleeve. In James Nice's 2010 history of Factory Records, *Shadowplayers: The Rise and Fall of Factory Records* (London, Aurum, 2010), Saville claimed that, 'I am so bored with this story. We didn't even know how many of these expensive covers were ever made anyway.'

Fact sheet compiled for me by David Wilkinson, author of *Post-Punk, Politics and Pleasure in Britain* **(London, Palgrave Macmillan, 2016).**

APPENDIX 2

OVERFLOW

For readers wishing to know more about the periphery . . .

Ian Curtis

There were five Joy Division gigs in Manchester during the short space of time I knew Ian. He invited me to two or three of them. The only memory I have of these is a dressing room before a performance. We were drinking bottles of beer that he produced from a 'complimentary' crate. We were chronically shy of each other. Somewhere in the same room were Bernard, Stephen and Hooky.

Part of that time he was still working as a clerk at the DHSS by day. Off-stage he seemed reserved, quite the opposite of the state of Joe Cocker-like frenzy he induced in himself when on it, when his half-reluctant, jerky movements (possibly copied by Morrissey) sometimes became sheer coordinated oddness. Watching him perform was by turns painful, cringingly embarrassing and beautiful, but my overall feeling was one of admiration. He had found a way of expressing inner-conflict that I could relate to myself, and I could see it was not easy for him to do so. Every performance he gave he had to work himself up from cold. There was never the assurance that he would achieve flight.

Our meeting at Bookchain happened not long after the screening of Malcolm's film – where Ian and I first met. It must have been early June 1979, because company records tell me I was away in America from 20 May to 1 June. Between the 18 and 20 May, it's unlikely I'd have had any time to meet him. Also, the album Ian had trouble identifying when he entered the shop, Bowie's *Lodger*, was released on 18 May. The record was still new to him at that time, but it seems inconceivable that it would have remained so for him for long . . .

This being so, when I took him round the corner to the Savoy office afterwards we had a great deal to talk about. On my visit to America, I had met Burroughs for the first and only time – and in October, Ian had plans to meet Burroughs himself, at the Plan K gig in Belgium (Joy Division's first opportunity to perform outside the UK). He was also very curious to understand how book publishing works.

The signed copy of *The Third Mind* I showed him was the 1978 Viking Press hardback edition, which I'd brought back from America with me. I had gone there with David to buy stock for the bookshops and we chanced a meeting with Burroughs, who was then sixty-five years of age. We went with a request to buy the UK paperback rights of his most recent novel, *Cities of the Red Night*. In this venture, we weren't holding our breath . . . but to our surprise, on our return to England, the rights were offered to us.

Pre-armed with our copes of *The Third Mind*, we had met Burroughs in his home at the Bunker, a partially converted YMCA building at 222 Bowery, in the downtown part of the New York. Written by Burroughs in collaboration with his mentor and artist-friend Brion Gysin, *The Third Mind* is a systematiser of the rules and practice of the literary technique of the cut-up. When the works of two or more different authors are inter-cut, the voice of a 'third' agency can be found in the cut-up. It is a process that can equally well be applied to sound or film.

In *Blue Monday: New Order at Britannia Row*, I posit the idea that 'Blue Monday' and *Power, Corruption & Lies* were in part the products of a form of cut-up because of the sometimes random means by which information was gathered and used to generate new songs – in contrast to the approach of Joy Division, which was more 'linear'. To my knowledge, Ian never experimented with the technique, despite knowing about it and being intensely interested; yet New Order, who are not particularly confident as writers, absorbed the process almost unconsciously.

Ian's October meeting with Burroughs was to have a weird outcome – perhaps in the way it has been reported and not in the reality of the exchange itself. Joy Division was on the same bill as Burroughs at the opening of the theatre troupe Plan K's new performance space, in an old sugar factory. After Burroughs' reading, when he was signing copies of his books, Ian introduced himself and tried requesting 'a spare copy' of new manuscript, *The Third Mind*. Burroughs allegedly told him to 'get lost' and refused to continue the conversation. Supposedly, Ian was most upset at this.

Keith Seward, who investigated the truth behind this story on behalf of RealityStudio.org (in a 2008 article entitled, 'William S. Burroughs and Joy Division'), concluded that any hurt inflicted upon Ian is unlikely to have been intentional. By his reasoning, Burroughs would have been flattered by the attentions of so many young artists and musicians come to pay tribute to his work – particularly a handsome young man like Ian.

Cabaret Voltaire's Richard Kirk, who also performed at the event, told Seward he found Burroughs a 'very friendly and a very polite old gentleman'. He couldn't see the story having any foundation.

If Burroughs really said what he is supposed to have said, my feelings are that it must have been intended playfully. 'In character', perhaps, Burroughs delivered in a comical growl, 'Fuck off, kid'.

When quizzed by Alan Hempsall about the incident a few months later, Ian merely claimed that Burroughs had told him that he 'hadn't got a copy'. Whatever exchange took place, it may well have been overheard and repeated without its humorous nuance – or simply invented. Ian's obsession with Burroughs was well known, and that may have made him the butt of a joke. Wherever it came from, the popular version of the story is also highly apocryphal.

In the end, for entirely different reasons, David and I fared little better in our encounter. What we requested – and briefly attained with *Cities of the Red Night* – remained in the realms of a dream, for raids by James Anderton's vice squad became so intense they temporarily shut Savoy down. We had to give back the rights. But we did come away from our meeting with a section of *The Place of Dead Roads*, Burroughs' forthcoming novel, for a new anthology we were putting together. When it finally appeared, *Savoy Dreams: The Secret Life of Savoy Books* (1984), contained this, and also the story I was trying to write in my bedroom beneath Malcolm's room, listening to Joy Division come thundering down whilst he was making his film.

The Bowdon Vale Gigs

These gigs were promoted by local man Bob Jefferson. Malcolm remembered having seen bands play at the youth club there ten years earlier and suggested the idea. Bob ran Streets Ahead record shop on Lloyd Street, Altrincham, where Malc introduced him to Rob Gretton. Rob was broke and wanted to offload copies of a record by the Panik that he had pressed up. The single was called 'It Won't Sell', released by Rainy City Records in 1977.

Bob was an unlikely record-shop owner. Middle-aged and at least six feet tall, he wore a hearing aid that had to be turned up whenever a customer wanted to engage his attention. He was also quite straight in a conventional sense. But he was kind-hearted and patient to the point of suggestibility, and relied on younger customers like Malc and I to tell him what was 'hip'. When he first opened, in the late sixties, I got him to order Captain Beefheart's *Safe as Milk* and Jefferson Airplane's *Crown of Creation* – both of which had recently had their UK releases.

To promote his shop Bob held nights at the Check-In, a small discotheque in the old part of Altrincham town. In November 1978 I attended a Joy Division gig he promoted there. In my notebook for the time I had written:

Copies of *An Ideal for Living*, still available in abundance four months after pressing, are on sale at £1 each as you go through the door. First on at this normally straight disco are several local weirdo bands including the Bidet Boys and Surgical Support, the latter a new-wave outfit from Altrincham who seem to play anything that comes into their heads and are appropriately derided by the small crowd. Then Joy Division play a hard set on the cramped converted disco floor, incongruous beneath flashing disco lights. They have no keyboards. Morris and Gretton are both hostile to them. They are a cliché, they admonish, while admitting privately they won't be able to escape using them for long.

I am guessing the copies of *An Ideal for Living* on sale were the 7" version, released in June 1978, on the band's own label, Enigma Records. The sleeves bore Bernard's image of a member of the Nazi youth banging a marching drum.

Peter Saville

As well as visiting Brit Row with Brett Wickens, Peter recalled meeting with New Order once again at a studio either in Stockport or Macclesfield. In interview with the *Guardian* on 11 February 2013, he told how:

I met them in their studio to show them a postcard of the Henri Fantin-Latour flower painting, *A Basket of Roses*, I was using for the [*Power, Corruption & Lies*] cover. While I was there, they played me 'Blue Monday' and I instinctively understood what they were trying to do. It sounded like something the equipment could play itself.

I picked up an interesting object and asked: 'Wow, what is this?' I'd never seen a floppy disk before. I thought it was great. I said: 'Can I have it?' And Stephen said: 'Not that one!' So I drove back to London listening to a tape of 'Blue Monday' with another floppy disk lying on the passenger seat. By the time I got home, I knew the sleeve would replicate a floppy disk, with three holes cut in it through which you could see the metallic inner sleeve. The only information I had to impart were the words 'New Order', the song titles (including B-side 'The Beach') and the Factory Records catalogue number. I decided to do this with a column of coded colours, to provide some mysterious data, so I sat down with some pencils and used a different colour for each letter . . . When *Power, Corruption & Lies* came out, I put a colour wheel to the back explaining the code.

A story is connected to this. There are two versions. One was related by Peter in BBC Radio 6's *Sounds of a City: Power, Corruption & Lies*, on 12 July 2015. According to this version, Peter contacted the National Gallery to gain permission for using the Henri Fantin-Latour image. He was told it was unavailable due to it being on a 'five-year loan'. When he expressed his frustration to Tony, the latter phoned the gallery to ask who owned the picture. When he was told that the people of Great Britain owned it, he replied: 'Well, actually, the people of Great Britain want it'.

The other version goes like this: *Power, Corruption & Lies* had already sold 3 million copies when an agent from the National Gallery rang Tony to inform him that Factory did not have the rights to use the Henri Fantin-Latour image. Tony asked, exactly who was the rightful owner, then? 'Why Sir,' he was told, 'the British public'.

'Well,' Tony retorted, 'the British public have fucking got them back!'

This second version of events was related to me by Garry, Bernard's childhood neighbour, now manager of Prestige Locksmiths, Withington. The shop is on the high street. One of the last two remaining Savoy shops, it's the occasional meeting point for Manchester music figures Alan Erasmus and Bruce Mitchell, stalwarts of the old Savoy bookshop days, who drop by to exchange jokes with Garry, the 'jokemeister' locksmith who always has a witty anecdote to tell! Garry stressed to me that this version of the Henri Fantin-Latour story originated from Tony himself, when he once called at Tony's flat in Little Peter Street to mend a lock.

Michael Johnson

After *Power, Corruption & Lies* and 'Blue Monday' were finished, Michael went on to engineer New Order's third studio album, *Low-Life*, at Jam Studios, London. The album was recorded there, but they returned to Brit Row to mix it. By the time I met him, Michael was Factory Records' engineer of choice. He engineered for many Factory bands including A Certain Ration, the Durutti Column, the Stockholm Monsters, even Joy Division (as assistant engineer on *Closer*). Altogether he engineered a total of thirteen New Order discs: four albums and nine singles.

When New Order asked Michael to engineer *Low-Life*, he took the opportunity to go freelance. He remained independent for the next ten years, until Factory went bust. With money still owed to him, he was forced to find a day job. Eventually, a deal was offered to him by Fallen Industries Rehearsal and Recording Studios, where he set up his own studio. He told me how: 'I'd always wanted to build a studio, but I could never make the finances add up. When the opportunity arose to equip and take over an existing studio premises near my home in the Wirral, near Liverpool, I started Tankfield Studio.'

Tankfield was set up in the Fallen complex and the arrangement worked out so well that Michael eventually became their head producer and recording engineer. When I asked him how *Power, Corruption & Lies* and 'Blue Monday' ranked in the sessions he had done, he told me in an email that: 'It's right up there with the best. It was my first album as fully fledged engineer and it was a big success. I got on well with the band and we enjoyed working together. It got my engineering career off to a flying start.'

In the mid-nineties, after Michael moved on, Brit Row decamped to Fulham, London. Their old space in the small business estate down one side of Britannia Row became the training studio for the London School of Sound.

Claude Bessy, 'Kickboy Face'

A regular visitor to Bookchain was the French writer and Slash Records founder, Claude Bessy. Claude's pioneering scratch video for the Haçienda's two huge screens on either side of the stage helped build the club's reputation. In the early days, his contacts in the music world enabled the club to book some of the best American and European bands, drawing in the crowds before dance truly exploded. Management, who were trying to break the newest dance sounds from America, were obviously not wholly approving of this, but they had to pay their bills somehow . . .

As the club's official video jockey, Claude was constantly in need of images and used Savoy as a resource. He often arrived just as the shop was about to close, looking very panicked before that evening's performance at the club. There was a constant tension in these transactions because Claude never seemed to have any money and we never knew whether to charge him or donate the material (considering the worthy nature of the cause). Some of it we loaned . . . and occasionally got back. But overall we probably ended up donating about half the comics, magazines and videos that he used.

Aware of Factory's totally unwarranted image as Nazi sympathisers, Claude's sense of humour led him to splice together scratch footage of Third Reich ceremonials and rallies. When these were subsequently broadcast in the club they helped bring about the *Private Eye* attack on the company in May 1983, a rehash of charges levelled at Factory in 1979 by the *NME* that centred on well-worn anxieties over the names chosen by Joy Division and New Order, and the album sleeve for A Certain Ratio's *To Each*, featuring Wehrmacht officers. After the *Private Eye* 'exposé', the *Jewish Telegraph* ran a critical editorial, upsetting Tony who had many Jewish friends (as recounted in James Nice's *Shadowplayers: The Rise and Fall of Factory Records*).

The rumoured two-part 'Claude Bessy party' in London mentioned in my diary at the end of the Brit Row recording session – 'Part 1' planned for the end of the recording session and 'Part 2' after the first mixing session before New Order left for Australia – seems to have vanished from history. I could find no one who remembered it. With Claude's contacts in the world of cult music and visual literature, and with the Haçienda and Heaven both newly opened, and Factory in the ascendant, it would have been *the* party to attend in 1982: a more than fitting celebration of the birth of 'Blue Monday'.

I often wondered how Claude got the moniker of 'Kickboy Face'. A big comics fan I presumed he had adopted it from there. But around 1983 or 1984, Claude's friend Kris Guidio (the Cramps' artist and Savoy's first Lord Horror artist) told me that it came from Claude's druggy days in Los Angeles. (Turn away if you are squeamish; this story features everyday heavy drug use and abuse.) When Kris called on Claude one day, he was nowhere to be found – until Claude's partner, Philomena Winstanley, suggested Kris might check the bathroom. Claude had been in there for quite some time and she was worried. Knowing looks were exchanged (Kris was then a user too). He did take a look, only to discover that Claude had unintentionally overdosed – as evidenced by a needle hanging out of his arm. He was lying unconscious in the bathtub. Phil asked if Kris would help lift him out of the bath, but Kris didn't think he would be able to. While they were deliberating, another friend arrived, more physically able, who agreed to lift Claude out. He managed to do this and carried him to his bed.

At this point, perhaps, the friend should have let Phil take over. But he didn't and began to dry the still-unconscious form of Claude with a towel. In the act of being towelled, Claude came round. Getting the wrong idea, he kicked his big buddy in the face. Fortunately, his friend took no lasting offence, but ever afterwards referred to Claude as Kickboy Face. Claude liked it so much he adopted it.

The Savoy Bookshops

As well as its proximity to the Free Trade Hall, Bookchain was on the rat-run to Granada Television Studios – a five-minute walk away from the shop – where Tony Wilson hosted *So It Goes*. Peter Street, which leads down from the cylindrical white-stoned Central Reference Library with its classical columns in St Peter's Square, also boasted the Gallery, a few doors down from Bookchain, the small black soul club where we once watched Bo Diddley live. Across the road from the shop was Stop Frame Films, where Bernard Sumner worked as a runner delivering film to Granada. After Stop Frame broke up, it re-formed in Chorlton as Cosgrove Hall, where Bernard found himself promoted to animation. Directly opposite Bookchain was a short thoroughfare called Jerusalem Street, which led into Bootle Street, where Fortress Anderton, the city's main police station, was situated. There, 'God's Cop', Chief Constable James Anderton, adversary of Savoy and Factory, presided. The chief had his hair chopped at a barber's next door to Bookchain and had to pass our shop window with its brightly-coloured displays each day on his way to and from work. However often his men raided us, the shop always remained open for business.

In addition to members of Joy Division – and later New Order – customers to Bookchain came from all over the Manchester music scene. Mark E. Smith,

Jon Savage, Howard Devoto, Tony Wilson and C.P. Lee were regulars, attracted to the cult books and comics, the underground and bootleg recordings, at a time when it was impossible to get these commodities – 'curated' to boot elsewhere in Manchester – in such concentration.

Thomas Sheridan, the shop's co-manager at the time, recalls Howard Devoto dropping by with the artist and musician Linder Sterling. 'I think she bought a few girlie mags: in fact, it wouldn't surprise me if the nude female torso from the cover of Buzzcocks' 'Orgasm Addict' single, with an iron for a head, came from one of those. She did a collage magazine, *The Secret Public*, which contained several nudes that could have come from the same mags.'

Mark E. Smith looked for books on H.P. Lovecraft and Arthur Machen. Often, knowledge was exchanged and discussions broke out about writers and artists. C.P. Lee was still dropping by our shops in 1996, when the IRA bomb shut down Basement Books, our shop on Fennel Street in the Corn Exchange, signalling the eventual end of our bookshops in 1999. Performer, writer, broadcaster and by then course-leader in film studies at Salford University – shopping for research materials for his teaching position – Chris is a force in Manchester, as influential in his way as Tony Wilson. There is even a chance he may have contributed to the genesis of 'Blue Monday' with his single 'Gerry and the Holograms', released in 1979 – in author Clinton Heylin's words 'an obscure Mancunian slice of electronica – which was actually a send-up of the music by arch satirist C.P. Lee, of Alberto y Lost Trios Paranoias, and his friend John Scott' (as per 'Smash & Grab', the *Guardian*, 3 July 2015).

A Residents-inspired piss-take of synthesiser bands like the Human League, 'Gerry and the Holograms' caught the attention of Frank Zappa who declared it to be 'the hottest thing to come out of Manchester in at least fifteen minutes'. 'Blue Monday's' resemblance to it seems more retrospective than real. Nevertheless it is a strange oddity . . . Heylin's review continues amusingly: 'New Order all knew Lee, but decided the joke was on him. They were never sued.'

The Albertos could be a hard act to follow. At Manchester's Free Trade Hall in 1978, with a blistering performance of tracks from their *Snuff Rock* EP (Stiff Records), they upstaged Devo. I went to watch Devo, but left feeling I'd witnessed a double bill. In fact, I believe, the Albertos may have been the unbilled headliners.

Being on the run to Granada, visitors to Bookchain came also from further afield. Anyone who had business at the studios was liable to drop by. Ian Dury and Iggy Pop both came on different occasions and were invited to sign the shop's 'Star Wall'. The wall remained unpainted, bearing their signatures and others, until the demolition men came. Cast members of *Coronation Street* were regular visitors. The music producer and DJ Andrew Weatherall found us there. So did the comedian Max Wall and the young comics' fan Lenny Henry.

About the time Stephen and Adam hung out with us at House on the Borderland, on the other side of town the foppish hustler printer and publisher John Muir was tenanting the shop basement. John later opened White Light Press on Upper Brook Street, further out towards the university, and began Babylon Books. Under which imprint he produced a stream of titles on Bowie, Iggy Pop, Zappa, Blondie and more, until eventually striking gold with Duran Duran, an instant bestseller. But he became famous for publishing (with permission) Morrissey's book, *James Dean is Not Dead* and later (without permission) a book of Morrissey's correspondence with him, on which the singer put an immediate injunction. The few remaining copies of this latter title are now very rare, turning up only occasionally on the internet. When Morrissey started to research Dean, around 1979, he naturally turned to Savoy for pointers. At a meeting in the Savoy office we remember recommending William Bast's *James Dean: A Biography* and David Dalton's *The Mutant King*.

Orbit Books opened in 1974, a couple of years after House on the Borderland and just before Bookchain. Still in the Northern Quarter as now is, it was situated further west, in the Tib Street area, a locale famous for its pet shops and home to an Army and Navy store that seemed to clothe many of our customers. One of the pet shops was owned by a notoriously upfront transvestite and another, just around the corner, was a front for Scottish gangsters, who had their office upstairs. 'Want to buy a £1,000 Rolex, David, Michael? Fifty quid to you.' Orbit Books was in a unit attached to the Wheatsheaf, a transvestite watering hole on Whittle Street, near the old Smithfield fish and vegetable market. Pub, shop and market were marooned by what seemed like bombsites left over from the Blitz. On these crofts tramps huddled around fires made from empty boxes, a ready supply of fuel from the market. The shop had a short-lived sister on Tib Street. Ostensibly selling cheap jewellery this was in fact a front just for our bootlegs (which we also sold at Orbit Books and Bookchain).

In his history of rock bootlegs, (*The Great White Wonders*, Penguin Books, 1994) Clinton Heylin describes how, as a teenager, he made his first purchases at Orbit Books:

Bootleg collectors the world over will remember their initial 'hit' – that first time they stumbled upon a stall or store selling albums you weren't supposed to be able to buy – and the charge that first blast of illicit vinyl gave them. For me it was as a young would-be obsessive that I learned of a shop in the nether-regions of central Manchester, freestanding in the centre of an area modelled on Dresden circa 1945. It was Sunday and the store was closed, but a friend and I bussed into town just to confirm that this really was a purveyor of hot wax. Sure enough, sellotaped to the window were three of their more attractive artefacts.

Heylin returned to the shop to buy. He didn't realise these shops (as well as Bookchain, which he later found) were the retail outlets of Savoy Books. Our bootlegging activities eventually came to an end after raids by BPI agents, as part of their 'Operation Moonbeam'. Like suave gangsters, these London suits pursued us for several months until finally pouncing, hauling us into the London courts. The £8,000 fine, which nearly closed us down entirely, was paid by an unexpected last-minute benefactor, Steve Harley, the organiser of our American book-buying expeditions. Orbit Books ran for over a decade, before closing in the late eighties.

Starplace, at 91 Oldham Street, where we fled after the police raids closed down Savoy Books Ltd, was also in the Northern Quarter. It was a rambling building with a basement, ground floor and two upper storeys. The lease-holding company was based in the Isle of Man, so we felt unusually free to do what we wanted. As well as conducting publishing operations, after hours the large upper floors were let as a rehearsal space to Manchester bands. This meant, for much of the time, the Stockholm Monsters. The Stockholms, from south Manchester, were produced by Hooky, who was in and out of the shop. Shop manager Thomas Sheridan remembers him as being 'a no-nonsense type who you wouldn't want to get on the wrong side of!'

The Stockholms had toured Europe with New Order and debuted on the Factory label with the Hannett-produced 'Fairy Tales' (FAC 41). A video of the Hook-produced 'Soft Babies' had been included on *A Factory Video* (FAC 56).

An endearing – for us – account of them in their Starplace eyrie exists courtesy of Mick Paterson, manager of A Certain Ratio, who interviewed them for *Masterbag* indie 'zine not long before I left for Britannia Row. Paterson wrote:

> The various members of the Stockholm Monsters are scattered around the room amidst piles of books; their rehearsal room doubles as a stockroom for the bookshop below. The books provide an interesting distraction to certain members of the band, who take little or no part in the conversation . . . Lindsay Anderson, the seventeen-year-old trumpet player who played bass on their recent recordings, remains rooted in her David Bowie biography, only lifting her head when teased by the others.

The Bowie biography was not 'stock from the bookshop below'. It was *David Bowie: Profile* by Chris Charlesworth . . . the title we had recently packaged for Proteus Books, who were to become the publishers of Mark Johnson's book about Joy Division, *An Ideal for Living*. We had left copies of the Bowie book lying around for bands to read. The Stockholms persevered as a band for about six years, supporting New Order many times, until finally splitting up just before the Madchester explosion.

Savoy Books

By happy chance I started my publishing career with a small press magazine at roundabout the same time as David started a magazine of his own. After the printer who printed my first issue refused to print my second – they objected to the content – I was introduced to John Muir, David's friend and printer at House on the Borderland. He was no longer based at the bookshop but, a big fan of David's artwork, it wasn't long before he introduced me to him in the hope that I would publish some of it. I did, and that's how Savoy Books started.

The company took its name from the *The Savoy*, a magazine published in the late 1800s by Leonard Smithers. Smithers intended to use *The Savoy* as a platform for the artwork of Aubrey Beardsley, illustrator of Oscar Wilde's *Salome* amongst other works. Following the trial of Oscar Wilde, Beardsley's work had been tainted by association and blacklisted, but the danger didn't deter the fearless Smithers who published Beardsley's scandalously risqué drawings regardless. We rather saw ourselves as publishers of a similarly discerning temperament.

The first Savoy publication was an oversize graphic adaptation of Michael Moorcock's novel *Stormbringer* by James Cawthorn, featuring Elric the Albino. It was co-published by Manchester author Charles Partington, David's long-standing friend and partner in the House on the Borderland bookshop.

Savoy Records

As well as my experience of being in a studio at Brit Row, other influences played their part in David and I taking the joint decision to become music producers. One of the biggest was a series of demo tapes and vinyl discs that had been arriving on our desk from the London-based Open Head press since around 1977. Run by the anarchist poet-playwright Heathcote Williams and *Oz/IT* designer Richard Adams, Open Head was a print-based publisher – yet they were producing music. Such departures by our peers into a new medium had an incendiary effect on us. The arrival on our desks of their record 'Sid Did It' (1979) – a Sex Pistols pastiche released under the moniker of Nazis Against Fascism, with vocals by Ben Brierley and spoken contributions by Marianne Faithfull – and a sexually explicit 'Why D'Ya Do It?' penned by Williams for Faithfull's 1979 album, *Broken English*, acted like our 'Lesser Free Trade Hall moment' when the Sex Pistols performed in the block next door to Bookchain, inspiring Bernard and Hooky and a generation of young Manchester musicians. If Heathcote and Richard could do this, then so could we.

Williams' audaciously clever fictions were both magical and dangerous – some of Open Head's productions were regarded as seditious – and we published them as often as we could. The publications I gave to Ian Curtis to read nearly all contained contributions from Williams, such pieces as 'The Abdication of QE II', an obscene, black-humoured, anti-monarchical fantasy depicting the abdication of the Queen; 'Natty Hallelujah' about a Rastafarian blissed out on joints and cosmic orgasms; 'Security Leak From the Future: Or Things Liberation', concerning the revolutionary uses of Kirlian photography; plus the song lyrics and poems penned for Faithfull.

Open Head's treasonous postcard of Prince Charles fondling the breasts of a smiling naked Princess Diana sold in its thousands throughout the country. Of course we also sold it in our bookshops. A copy ended up in the Haçienda's first DJ box, pasted there as a visual memento, where it remained until the box was moved up onto the club's balcony.

Other Open Head postcards showed Maggie Thatcher stealing from a housewife's shopping bag, or a smiling Maggie giving a V-sign (not for 'Victory'). Heathcote and Richard were eventually warned by plainclothes agents of the Crown and had to desist. But their press continued producing publications of remarkable subversive energy and diversity. David and I weren't anti-monarchy per se, but the insubordinate cleverness and design of these productions – books, magazines, posters, postcards and recordings – was an impressive lesson in how to project an artistic mixed-media ideology. We later used Open Head as a model for the multi-media satirical Lord Horror 'Savoy Wars' and 'Moral Ambiguity' campaigns launched in the mid-eighties, commencing with the Lord Horror cover of 'Blue Monday'.

At the same time as Open Head's music productions, we were being acquainted with the fierce irreverent energy of early club tracks like D.A.F.'s 'Der Mussolini' (1981). Later, in 1984, came Funkmeister's 'War Dance', which sampled wartime radio broadcaster Lord Haw-Haw's voice over a dance beat (from hearing this, David made Haw-Haw the model for Lord Horror). Such numbers had a mad surreality to them. They were mixed into the mainly punk and rock'n'roll playlists at our bookshops.

Savoy and New Order

As we became more embroiled in producing, David and I came to think of pursuing the attempt I had made at Brit Row to introduce Stephen to Michael Moorcock: to see what might result musically from a New Order collaboration. When a young man in 1950s London, Michael had frequented jazz cellars and folk clubs and done some busking. Though he went on to do much experimental performance work with bands like Hawkwind (on such albums as 1975's *Warrior on the Edge of Time*) and Blue Öyster Cult, (on 1979's album, *Mirrors*) and eventually formed his own band, the Deep Fix, it was his folk and jazz roots that interested us most of all. In the way that Transglobal Underground did later, we wanted to mix traditional and electronic forms. But once again, as at Brit Row, I was not even able to bring the two sides together. David and I later experimented with Irish rebel songs like 'Kevin Barry' (Michael claimed to have heard this sung in the folk clubs) and 'Bobby Sands'. We did a recitation of 'That Old Fenian Gun', set to a 'Hooky bass' copied from 'Blue Monday'.

Savoy and Factory

Factory's beginnings lay over the river in Salford, where Tony was born, and Didsbury, South Manchester, home of Alan Erasmus. Savoy's were in Manchester – Collyhurst, Harpurhey where David grew up – and Altrincham, on the southern edge of the city where I misspent my youth. Tony was a Catholic, as were most of Factory. David too was Catholic, though after school he never practiced it. Catholicism was also strong in my own family through my mother and sisters, though I am not Catholic myself.

Savoy operated in a different, parallel substratum of Manchester to Factory. But as with Tony, Alan and Rob, in each other, David and I found licence to do what we wanted. The 'analogue' punk DIY ethic meant that we could see a way of achieving what we wanted regardless of financial limitations, of having no wish to fit into a conventional mould, or having any desire to cut back on costs when prudence demanded, or even to worry about such trifles as whether a product was sustainable in the marketplace. Just as Tony wanted to produce *A Factory Sample* to have a recorded means of playing Joy Division, the Durutti Column, Cabaret Voltaire and John Dowie, we started because we wanted to commission the definitive Elric artist, James Cawthorn, to adapt Michel Moorcock's Elric novel *Stormbringer*.

It was Dada publishing and music production regardless of the consequences. Instead of Savoy's shops providing kudos and day-to-day running expenses for the publishing side of the business, Factory had Tony's local fame and at least £5,000 to play with, inherited from his mother, part of which he used to press up *A Factory Sample*; the balance, together with the proceeds from the sampler EP and trust-fund inheritances, appear to have funded *Unknown Pleasures*.

Factory easily recovered their outlay when *Unknown Pleasures* sold out of its initial pressing of ten thousand. Savoy had financial success with its bookshops, but not with its books. Literature does not always attract a fan-base quite as readily as music. Like Savoy, Factory continued in the same anti-business fashion up until its collapse. Savoy Books Ltd, our first company, went bump in 1981 for £250,000, ten years before Factory. Since then, after regrouping, we continued, but with much smaller print runs and fewer products.

Without this concerted 'non-industry' there would have been no 'Blue Monday' (for Factory) and for Savoy there would have been no *Lord Horror* – the original novel (written by David and myself, and published in 1989), together with its spin-off novels, recordings and graphics, that has become our own eventful apotheosis.

Jim McClellan, reviewing *Lord Horror* in *i-D*, in July 1989, described the book as 'dense, intellectual horror'. David's first novel, with its mix of Grand Guignol, Victoriana, modern-day technology, philosophy and science fiction, is a forerunner of steampunk and the New Weird. Although officially the authorship (very deservedly) is his, it is actually a collaboration by David and I: my contribution to the writing is such that I consider it a co-authored work. About an archetypal killer from the German Reich set loose in the world, it pre-dated *American Psycho* by two years, the other taboo novel of the period and also about a killer. Whereas *American Psycho* has entered the canons of Western literature, to this day *Lord Horror* is 'off-limits' in the West. More serious attention is being given to it in Eastern Europe and Russia, where translations are beginning to appear.

For what is still the best account of Savoy's predicament of finding itself without an audience see Keith Seward's essay, 'Horror Panegyric', published by Savoy in 2008. A Kindle version is available to buy on Amazon and an online version can also be accessed at: supervert.com/essays/horror_panegyric.

David and I have often wryly joked between ourselves that success will arrive when we're no longer around to appreciate it. We console ourselves with the fact that we are still here, whereas Factory went long ago.

Savoy and P.J. Proby

The B-side of Savoy's cover of 'Love Will Tear Us Apart' was a much rougher live version of the song, recorded in the community hall of a school on Ripponden Road, Oldham. By coincidence this was a block away from Pennine Sound Studios where Joy Division recorded their first version of the song and where they had earlier recorded the *An Ideal for Living* EP – the recording Ian Curtis gave to RCA's label promotions manager Derek Brandwood in his Manchester office in Piccadilly Plaza, in an attempt to woo RCA into a record deal whilst the band were still struggling to make an impact.

Both the community hall and Pennine Studios have long gone. The old church in which Pennine was situated has been demolished. The school, where we did our live recording, was burnt down in an arson attack by former pupils, days after we finished work there.

P.J. Proby was, of course, the other main influence on us becoming producers. After deciding to write a book about him, we found him at a public house in Collyhurst, a rough district in North Manchester, where he was about to give a performance. Since being banned from wider public performance in the sixties, he had made a living on the workingman's club and pub circuits, the same small venues where Nico of the Velvet Underground later in her solo career and managed by Factory Records co-founder Alan Wise, sometimes found a welcome. The pub where we tracked Jim down was on Collyhurst Street, a few blocks away from where the Electric Circus had been, where Warsaw/Joy Division had performed as 'Stiff Kittens'– they had been billed under that name without knowing it and turned up thinking another band had taken their slot. As usual, their anger went into their performance; it was because of this intense will to succeed that they eventually did.

We brought with us a wad of money – the day's take from our bookshops. And it would be needed. As we stepped out of the taxi and approached the pub, we were in a territory that was as familiar to David as Bovril and Vimto. Like Bernard's and Hooky's Salford, Collyhurst and the adjacent districts of Harpurhey and Blakely, were rough working-class districts where David had grown up. Whereas B. and H. could hail Shelagh Delaney, author of *A Taste of Honey*, as literary antecedent (Delaney was born in Brougton, where Bernard spent his younger days), David could sport Anthony Burgess, author of *A Clockwork Orange*, who lived on Carisbrook Street where David was born – plus the fact that comedian Bernard Manning lived and performed just around the corner in his Embassy Club and had attended the same Catholic school, Mount Carmel, where David had been an altar boy. He knew the area's serried two-up, two-down back-to-back streets and the hardened faces of its people like the lines on the back of his hand. Manchester's workforce had scraped out an existence for a century-and-a-half there. And it was here that P.J. Proby now felt most comfortable, where he had been for the last sixteen years before our arrival.

He wanted a hundred pounds cash before he would even speak a word to us. But since that meeting, after we decided to jettison the book and record him instead, over a period of eleven years he cut for Savoy nine 12" singles, an album, an EP and two talking books. Many of the vocals for these as well as some of the backings were recorded at Suite 16, where we had such great fun teasing C.J. . . . and later Shan Hira, ex-Stockholm Monsters, whose career kept touching on mine with such serendipity. Shan had now become a co-owner of the studio. Later, he would become its sole owner. Shan sat in on our most notorious sessions, including the Irish rebel songs Proby recorded there and – most infamous of all – 'M97002: Hardcore', a slow rap written by Jim, David, Paul Temple and I, bearing David's Strangeways' prison number. Towards the end of recording, the track ran out of tape. Rather than shorten the song, we simply added another piece of tape. Then the drum machine began misfiring and threw a fit. That sounded good, so we left it in. Paul Oldfield's review – published in *Melody Maker* on 19 September 1987 – read as follows:

Even if you never hear it, another catastrophic shockwave travelled through the body [of] pop. True, this is fanatical obscenity, a record you could probably be prosecuted for owning, even. Hip-hop at its most impacted crosses HM stalactite chords and guitar-abuse solos. Be startled by the disappearance of the beat: it propagates until there is a stentorian thunder, mistracking-stylus mode. It reaches an idiot-hyper-sexuality. Innuendo, rock's usual fig-leaf, is bypassed. So much sexual message is broadcast that 'sex' burns out, is exhausted in an outrage of artlessness and celebration of the sexual drives that pop usually polices or orders. Absurdly apocalyptic, it calls itself 'the last rock'n'roll record made in England', wants to be the last moment, pop's supernova. It spirals into scam, claims to be the collaboration by P.J. Proby and Madonna. I listened to it twice and turned to a pillar of salt.

With its controversial lyrics, doomy sounds and anarchic composition, Rob Chapman writing for *Mojo* described it as being like 'fifteen minutes of the kind of stuff that Frank out of *Blue Velvet* would probably chill out to after an evening on the inhaler'.

'Hardcore' was Savoy's biggest art scam, making the front page of the *London Evening News*. And take note, Hooky, that it was recorded as well as mixed at Suite 16.

Savoy finding and producing Jim Proby in the way that we did brought him critical acclaim, and it eventually led him to doing a collaboration with Marc Almond and *Legend*, a new album written and produced by Almond, and the single 'Yesterday Has Gone', a duet with Almond, both on the EMI label. In 2015 he made a live appearance at the Royal Albert Hall, duetting with Van Morrison, and has since appeared with him again. All thanks, in a roundabout, circumbendibus way, to the 'Blue Monday' sessions at Britannia Row . . .

CHAPTER NOTES

The following chapter notes are designed to give a general view of the sources drawn upon in preparing *The Blue Monday Diaries: In the Studio with New Order*.

BEGINNINGS

'Tim Burgess of the Charlatans on Manchester, music and meditation', Simon Hattenstone, the *Guardian*, July 2015
Bernard Sumner quoted in 'New Order – How We Wrote Blue Monday', Barry Nicolson, *NME* and nme.com, January 2015
Stephen Morris quoted from an email to the author
Thomas Sheridan quoted from an interview with the author

THE DIARY

The Process: A Novel, Brion Gysin, Doubleday, 1969
Bury My Heart at Wounded Knee: An Indian History of the American West, Dee Brown, Holt, Rinehart & Winston, 1970

'DUB IT UP!'

Details of mixing schedule provided by Michael Johnson, drawn from tape-box labels for the backup stereo analogue master tape – via correspondence with author
Quotes from sleeve notes of *Power, Corruption & Lies*, Ian Harrison, London Records, 2008
Stephen Morris quoted from an email to the author
Shadowplayers: The Rise and Fall of Factory Records, James Nice, Aurum Press Ltd, 2011
Peter Hook quoted in 'A Rare Glimpse into a Private World', Paul Rambali, *The Face*, July 1983

'WE WERE LIKE THE GUINEA PIGS'

Bernard Sumner quoted in 'New Order – How We Wrote Blue Monday', Barry Nicolson, *NME* and nme.com, January 2015

Peter Hook quoted in *Sounds of a City: New Order: Power, Corruption & Lies*, BBC Radio 6 Music, 12 July 2015

Bernard Sumner: Chapter and Verse: New Order, Joy Division and Me, Bernard Sumner, Bantam Press, 2014

Gillian Gilbert quoted in 'How We Made: New Order's Gillian Gilbert and Designer Peter Saville on Blue Monday', Dave Simpson, the *Guardian*, 11 February 2013

Tony Wilson quoted in *Sounds of a City: New Order: Power, Corruption & Lies*, BBC Radio 6 Music, 12 July 2015

Greg Wilson quoted by Flexx Records on soundcloud.com

Hewan Clarke quoted in 'Hewan Clarke: A Conversation', Greg Wilson, electrofunkroots.com, August 2004

Stephen Morris quoted from an email to the author

Peter Saville quoted in 'How We Made: New Order's Gillian Gilbert and Designer Peter Saville on Blue Monday', Dave Simpson, the *Guardian*, 11 February 2013

Bernard Sumner, Peter Hook and Stephen Morris quoted in 'A Rare Glimpse into a Private World', Paul Rambali, *The Face*, July 1983

Tony Wilson: You're Entitled to an Opinion, David Nolan, John Blake Publishing Ltd, 2010

Peter Hook quoted from an email to the author

The Haçienda: How Not to Run a Cub, Peter Hook, Simon & Schuster, 2009

The Cramps at the Haçienda, Savoy Music, 2015

Bernard Sumner quoted in 'The Mojo Interview', *Mojo*, Andrew Male, September 2015

Peter Hook quoted in 'After Joy Division and New Order, Peter Hook Steps into the Light', Leila Brillson, *Interview* magazine, 22 September 2011

'Recreating New Order's "Blue Monday" Live', Roger Lyons, soundonsound.com, April 2004

SUITE 16

Bob Dickinson quoted from an email to the author

SCIENCE FICTION

Gillian Gilbert quoted in 'How We Made: New Order's Gillian Gilbert and Designer Peter Saville on Blue Monday', Dave Simpson, the *Guardian*, 11 February 2013

Poor but Sexy: Culture Clashes in Europe East and West, ('Ashes and Brocade' chapter; page 72), Agata Pyzik, Zero Books, 2014

Jon Savage quoted from liner notes of *Heart and Soul*, Joy Division, London Records, 1997

Bob Grafton quoted from an email to the author

Rob Gretton quoted in 'A Rare Glimpse into a Private World', Paul Rambali, *The Face*, July 1983

APPENDIX 2 – OVERFLOW

Richard Kirk quoted in 'William S. Burroughs and Joy Division', Keith Seward, realitystudio.org, 2008

Ian Curtis quoted in 'A Day Out with Joy Division', Alan Hempsall, *Extro* magazine, vol. 2/no. 5, January 1980

Peter Saville quoted in 'How We Made: New Order's Gillian Gilbert and Designer Peter Saville on Blue Monday', Dave Simpson, the *Guardian*, 11 February 2013

Peter Saville quoted in *Sounds of a City: New Order: Power, Corruption & Lies*, BBC Radio 6 Music, 12 July 2015

Michael Johnson quoted from an email to the author

Shadowplayers: The Rise and Fall of Factory Records, James Nice, Aurum Press Ltd, 2011

'The Great Rock'n'Roll Swindle', Clinton Heylin, the *Guardian*, 2 July 1915

The Great White Wonders: A History of Rock Bootlegs, Clinton Heylin, Viking, 1994

Stockholm Monsters review by Mick Paterson, *Masterbag* newssheet, September 1982; reproduced on ltmrecordings.com/stockholm_monsters.html

Review of *Lord Horror* taken from *i-D* magazine, Ian McClellan, July 1989

Horror Panegyric, Keith Seward (aka Supervert), Savoy Books, 2014. Available to read online at supervert.com/essays/horror_panegyric

Review of 'M97002: Hardcore' taken from *Melody Maker*, Paul Oldfield, 19 September 1987

Review of 'M97002: Hardcore' taken from *Mojo*, Rob Chapman, 1987